Where Women
Are Leaders

BAKER & TAYLOR

SEWA Executive Committee

Where Women Are Leaders

THE SEWA MOVEMENT IN INDIA

KALIMA ROSE

Zed Books Ltd
London and New Jersey

Where Women Are Leaders: The SEWA Movement in India was first published in 1992 by Zed Books Ltd, 57 Caledonian Road, London N1 9BU, UK, and 165 First Avenue, Atlantic Highlands, New Jersey 07716, USA.

Copyright © Kalima Rose, 1992

British Library Cataloguing in Publication Data

A catalogue record for this book is available from the British Library

ISBN 1 85649 083 1 Hb   ISBN 1 85649 084 X Pb

Library of Congress Cataloging-in-Publication Data

A catalogue record for this book is available from the US Library of Congress

*I dedicate this book
to my daughter Orissa
who spent the first year and a half of her life at SEWA,
and to the self-employed women,
Kalsang Lhamo and Naheed Aftab,
whose care of her made the writing of this possible.*

Contents

Frontispiece   2

List of Photographs and Illustrations   8

Preface   10

Acknowledgements   12

 1. SEWA: Women in Movement   15
 2. Emergence   36
 3. Independence   58
 4. SEWA's Shakti: Growing Up and Leading Out   83
 5. The Union: Struggles of Solidarity   118
 6. Video SEWA: Focusing on Issues   156
 7. The SEWA Bank: 'This Bank is Like Our Mother's Place'   172
 8. Women's Cooperatives: A Lever for Change   202
 9. Health Services: 'This Body is My Only Asset'   244
10. SEWA Bharat: Reaching Across the Country   257
11. Moving on: Pushing Policy Outward   263

Appendices   276
Appendix I   : SEWA Union Membership, 1989   276
Appendix II : Cooperatives: Kind, Membership, Production   277
Appendix III : Overview of SEWA Bank 1974–1989   280

Glossary of Terms   282

Index   283

List of Photographs and Illustrations

Photographs

Frontispiece: SEWA Executive Committee   2

1. SEWA organizing begins with a survey of workers' conditions. Here, surveying bidi workers in Ahmedabad (see chapter 4). 160
2. Cartpullers were the first trade group to join SEWA. Now they have formed a tripartite board to oversee their payment of wages and benefits. 160
3. Waste paper collectors sorting the day's collection. They need common areas to sort and store what they collect. 161
4. Smiths recycling tins and old roofing material into inexpensive stoves. 162
5. From early on, girls contribute to the family income. They require schools with flexible schedules and creches for their younger siblings so that they can both earn and study, practise traditional skills and learn new skills. Here, girls participate in the incense trade. 162
6. Ela Bhatt (head uncovered) strategizing with vegetable vendor members. 163
7. Laxmi Tetabhai Patni, Vice-President of the Union, appeals to her sister vendors to fight the authorities for their legal rights to vend (chapter 2). 164
8. Ela Bhatt and Shankarlal Banker, trade union leader with Mahatma Gandhi, inaugurate SEWA's newsletter *Anasuya*, 1981. 164

9. Tarabehn Marthak, mobile savings organizer, counting the money from a SEWA television bank on a doorstep. 'The Bank is open !' 165

10. Santokbehn Pritviraj, carpenter and member of Video SEWA team. 165

11. Medina, shopkeeper, left, and Leelabehn Datania, vegetable vendor, centre (chapter 5), learn video sound recording from instructor from Martha Stuart Communications, New York. 166

12. SEWA members celebrate the Supreme Court order recognizing street vending as a Fundamental Right under the Constitution of India. Ela Bhatt (uplifted at centre), with Renana Jhabvala directly to her right. Lalita Krishnaswami is behind. 167

13. Child care for self-employed women is high on SEWA's advocacy list. 30 per cent of self-employed are the sole supporters of their families. Many of these do daily wage labour, carrying their children and cradles with them. This girl is returning from a 44 degree day alongside a road construction crew where her mother works. 167

14. 22 June 1987. The vendors march in protest against police atrocities and in demand of a just licensing policy. 168

15. Samubehn and Ramubehn, Secretary and President of Devdholera's Dairy Cooperative, tell over 1000 SEWA members from 40 villages that they need to be organized for strength, 1989. 169

16. 1000 women at an Ahmedabad district rural sammelan showing their affirmation, January 1989 (see chapter 7). 170

17. Led by Ela Bhatt, SEWA organizers and support staff jumped up from an annual office meeting to march to the Municipal Commissioner's office in protest against vendor harassment, despite a High Court stay on prosecution. 171

18. They stormed the Commissioner's office and used their subtle persuasion to insist he make the necessary phone calls immediately. 171

Illustrations
3.1 The SEWA Tree   82
5.1 From Pressure to Command   155
8.1 Some SEWA Strategies   243

Preface

I arrived in India in 1986, as a journalist and writer who had mainly covered cultural and women's issues in North America. I began tracing the issues that women were organizing around in South Asia, and as anyone who takes up that trail, landed on SEWA's doorway. That first interview with Ela Bhatt, and a small story on the women's dairy cooperative movement blossomed into this book. As readers will note, I was impressed.

While I was there, I witnessed the number of visitors to the organization that came from around the world, but I did not have a context for the breadth of organizations they represented. Women at SEWA were always understated, matter of fact. They did not tout themselves as 'leaders'. At the end of my four year stay in India, however, when I began to cover economic and development issues as they related to women in the broader international context, I encountered a sort of global recognition of SEWA. Women from innumerable organizations worldwide—community organizations, labour organizations, political organizations and institutions—testify to the importance of SEWA's inspiration and leadership in their own regional challenges to shape major economic values and systems.

Now, as editor of a US-based journal for women on the economy, I am a happy (but not surprised) witness to the value of

SEWA's model in communities and countries at all stages of development—women from Africa, the US, Thailand, Mexico, Poland, and others—all places where the rapidly changing economy has left women with a vested interest in developing new and equitable solutions.

I hope this glimpse of their work will lend fuel for that work that women are carrying on in their communities and their countries around the world.

Kalima Rose

Acknowledgements

I want to extend my deepest thanks to Ela Bhatt. She spent countless hours with me, patiently re-explaining ideas, recounting histories, hunting the documentation I required, and reading countless drafts of manuscripts. As readers will gather, she inspired me greatly.

The women I want to acknowledge most are the SEWA women who appear in this book. Though most of them will never be able to read it, they willingly shared their stories with me. Chandabehn Papubhai Jhagaria and Karima Ahmed Hussain Shaikh spent weeks of their time with me in Ahmedabad, introducing me to veteran SEWA members, showing me the sites of all historic events, including me in their religious celebrations, and extending patience and humour toward me and my clumsy language skills. Chandabehn, Karima, Rahima Shaikh, Godavaribehn Padmashali, Lila Datania, and others, sent me home from my four years in India with inspiration to emulate in my own country some of the creative thinking and organizing they have accomplished at SEWA.

Thanks to Savitabehn Patel and Rima Nanavati, who between themselves took me to all the villages where SEWA work is in progress. Sandhya Bhat was a wonderful interpreter and good companion on those long, hot summer days. Mirai Chatterjee, whom I now consider a life-long friend, was a wonderful host to me. I appreciated Renana Jhabvala's insight and analysis of the political workings of SEWA and Gujarat, and the hospitality she extended to me and my family. To all the people who extended me numerous interviews—Dr. Anandalaxmi, Michela Walsh, Rameshbhai Bhatt, Godavaribehn, Rahima, Jayshree Vyas, Renana, Usha Jumani and all others, thank you. To Jennifer Sebstad, who documented SEWA's first decade so meticulously, kudos and appreciation.

The people who have repeatedly, patiently combed this manuscript with me deserve perseverance-recognition. Mihir Bhatt deserves credit for the most interesting anectodes in the history of his mother, and for taking me to task for certain analyses. Sue Schweik, Valerie Miner, Madelon Sprengnether: thank you for trudging through so many drafts, so many titles, so many questions. You were wonderful spirits.

Thanks to the Ford Foundation for grant support for the writing of this book.

And to my husband, Bill Stewart, what can I say? None of this would have been possible if you had not schlepped across Gujarat with me, taken the children away at deadline times, and kept encouraging me when, by any account, you should have been weary of this project. Thanks to you, and to all the supportive partners like you who stand behind the women I have written about herein.

We not only want a piece of the pie,
we also want to choose the flavour,
and know how to make it ourselves.

Ela Bhatt

1

SEWA: Women in Movement

'My hut is an illegal occupation,' explains Saraswati Ramesh-chandra, 'but there is no choice—I do not have money to buy a piece of land. For three years I did not even sleep at night because there was no door to my hut—only a blanket. I was afraid and used to stay awake all night just to keep a watch over my house and my children.'

Saraswati quit school at the age of 13 to earn more income for the family when her father was laid off work in the textile mills. For several years she and her mother supported the entire family on their bidi *(indigenous cigarette) rolling income, until she married and moved to her husband's village. She had problems with his family, and returned alone to Ahmedabad with her three children. She was unwelcome in her parents' house. Because she had left her husband, she was a social stigma to them. As a woman, she had no claim on the family property. With nowhere to go and no assets to her name, she constructed a bamboo hut on a large barren lot in Bapunagar (an eastern suburb of Ahmedabad), and began rolling* bidis *again for the same contractor she had worked for as a child.*

In 1987, the Self Employed Women's Association (SEWA) was

negotiating with all the contractors in Ahmedabad to pay the legal minimum wage of Rs. 13 (about US $1) for 1000 bidis—about one day's work for one woman. Most of them were paying between Rs. 7–8. Saraswati's contractor, Laxmandas, decided to close shop rather than meet his legal obligations, putting her and 95 other women out of work. Saraswati paid her Rs. 5 membership fee to the union with the attitude of 'What is there to lose?' When other bidi workers came and began demonstrating in front of his shop, she became more interested and joined in. The union's lawyer filed a case in court and she entered negotiations through the Labour Commissioner for Laxmandas to pay compensation for closing down.

'At first he refused,' Saraswati said, 'but we all got together and showed him the law. We made him pay each worker a flat sum for the number of years each worked for him. I got Rs. 900. I used that money to put a door on my hut—which ended one anxiety for me.'[1]

I find myself continually impressed not only by what SEWA has accomplished in its 20 years of existence, but also by the magnitude of what it takes on. Based in Ahmedabad, the largest city of India's western state of Gujarat, and working under a name which translates as 'service', SEWA successfully integrates a complex myriad of lives, occupations, and issues into one union. Under SEWA, women have forged a new model of what a trade union can be—a Third World model, which defies conventional conceptions about who unions organize and what they do for their members. Most unions in the world organize workers in one kind of industry, who share one fixed workplace, and concern themselves with problems which revolve only around the work issues of their members. Some unions do take up issues related to women workers, or include a women's wing in the larger body of the union, but there are very few unions in the world which are devoted entirely to a female membership, as SEWA is. SEWA organizes women who work in their homes, in the streets of cities, in the fields and villages of rural India, with no fixed employer, carving their small niches in the economy, day by day, with only their wits to guide them against incredible odds of vulnerability, invisibility, and poverty.

These then are the common denominators around which SEWA has gathered 30,000 members into its fold since its inception in

1972: they are women, they are 'self-employed', and they are poor. From these common bases, diverse individuality in trades, religious and ethnic backgrounds, and living environments are brought together. Where these women are individually extremely vulnerable to the forces of their day-to-day poverty which are compounded by financial exploitation, physical abuse, and general social harassment, they have found that collectively they are able to struggle against these forces and odds to effect change in their lives and work. SEWA's choice of the term 'self-employed' to define this large sector of workers was consciously made to give positive status to people who are often described negatively as informal, unorganized, marginal, or peripheral. How can the self-employed workers who make up 55 per cent of Ahmedabad's workforce and 50 per cent of Calcutta's and Bombay's workforce be considered 'marginal?' Or, how could the majority of rural women who are engaged in the food production of the country be considered 'peripheral?' According to SEWA estimates, women account for at least 60 per cent of the self-employed population. Only 6 per cent of India's census recognized female workforce is in regular employment, 94 per cent of working women are self-employed.[2]

Self-employed is a broad term covering all the workers who are not in a formal employer–employee relationship. It means women who work at home—weavers, potters, garment and quilt stitchers, patchworkers, embroiderers, bidi rollers, incense stick makers, milk producers, spinners, basket and broom weavers, metalworkers, carpenters, shoemakers, painters, sculptors, and toymakers. It includes women who sell or trade their services or labour—agricultural workers, headloaders, hand-cart pullers, waste paper collectors, acrobats, cleaners, and construction workers. And it includes the multitude of hawkers and vendors who carry out trade in the streets and markets from their baskets or cartloads of wares. Both traditional and modern occupations come under SEWA's definition of self-employed, from the bartering of goods to capitalistic piece-rate work.

Women all over India are struggling for survival in a world where the physical resources they have traditionally depended upon for survival are degraded and diminishing in the face of intense population and industrial pressure. Though they are all economically active, they have not acquired the skills necessary to make an adequate living in an industrializing economy, nor are there sufficient jobs for all those in need of them. The hillsides and plains where severe erosion, floods, and drought follow deforestation mirror the faces of families whose deprivation and degradation are plainly written into them.

Not only in Gujarat, where SEWA's work has become firmly rooted, but also all over the country, where its work has begun to make inroads, some common pictures of how women are dealing with their problems emerge. First, women are better fighters than men of the day-to-day poverty which faces them. They exercise incredible ingenuity in making ends meet. It is common for men to remain unemployed for long periods of time when no 'job' can be found. Women, on the other hand, combine many jobs and occupations simultaneously, bringing in small amounts of cash, trading for foodgrains or clothing, exchanging services for access to a small hut, vending small quantities of consumer goods, collecting wood or fruits or recyclable waste from common lands, and using what specialized skills they possess to earn wages. They endow society with their labour, providing cheap services, strong backs, and traditional skills. Wherever they are given the opportunity, women contribute modernized ideas and skills as well. They request very little in exchange for their labour, consuming small fractions of the country's resources in relation to what they produce.

Second, besides being able to piece together the family income out of ingenuity and necessity, women spend almost all of their earnings on the family. Whatever little they do earn, they spend on food, clothing, and their meagre shelter. SEWA women confirm this fact, but countless other women all over India have also attested that if they earn, for example, Rs. 8 a day, they spend all of it on food for the family, whereas their husbands contribute a much smaller part of their earnings to the household—*if* there is a husband, and *if* he has earnings. Up to 30 per cent of poor families are supported solely by women who are self-employed.[3]

The third quality that has emerged is women's concern about the future. They want their children's lives to be better than their own, and make repeated sacrifices in order to ensure this. Not only do they work 12 to 20 hour days to try and effect this change, but they also reveal an exceptional ecological consciousness. While their menfolk often opt for cash income from wood crops, women organizing across the country insist on protecting trees, or planting trees which will provide fuel and fodder and be a long-term resource rather than a cash crop. They increasingly understand the effects of deforestation, droughts, soil erosion, and saline encroachment on both the land and their families' lives as they lose the local resources that they depend upon.

Because of their ability to be flexible, to combine domestic work and income earning activities, and to shift occupational skills as the season or market demands; because they do not need to fit the terms of formal jobs in order to be economically active; and because they have needs which are not fulfilled by the formal sector of society, self-employed women require a very different kind of union than the traditional definitions of unions can meet. Out of their intense needs for fair credit, maternity protection, fair wages for whatever work they are engaged in, skills training, year-round work, and legal help when they are exploited or abused, SEWA came into being.

The organization began on a small scale. When women who pull freight on carts and headload textiles between markets saw what advantages the textile unions were gaining for their members, they approached the Textile Labour Association (TLA), India's largest union of textile workers. They were directed to Ela Bhatt, a lawyer who was then heading the TLA's Women's Wing. They asked her, 'What about us? Can't we get any of these benefits?' At that time, Bhatt had been dealing with labour issues for 14 years through jobs with the TLA and the Labour Ministry of the Gujarat government. Though dealing with organized labour, she was constantly exposed to the realities of the poor working class and the numerous problems of the unorganized workers of India. When these self-employed women first approached her, she was ready to hear their question. She responded with an idea she had been formulating for many years: 'You need to organize yourselves if you want to get some of these benefits.'

About two dozen women came together and pooled a few *paise* and took some decisions to demand that their wages be regularized. Soon used-clothes and vegetable vendors wanted to join them, for protection from police brutality and extortion. Then home-bound women in the Muslim community who stitch textile waste into garments and quilt covers requested some support. Agricultural workers came to these meetings to discuss how they could actually get the minimum wage they were due under law. Carpenters and metal smithing women came seeking access to small loans for working capital. Then the exploitation bidi workers and incense stick makers faced brought them into the fold of the union. Women who had migrated to the city for textile mill jobs, but had faced retrenchment and were reduced to picking recyclable waste from the city's garbage dumps had several ideas of how to alter their circumstances, and came to the union for services and support. Weavers, basket-makers and block printers, all facing displacement of their skills or loss of raw materials or markets, came seeking help to hold onto the only occupations they knew. Women who had been victimized for asking for legal wages in the tobacco processing plants came seeking legal assistance.

In this way SEWA grew, organically, slowly absorbing more and more trades, rooting itself in the reality of poor working women. Each of these trades is usually associated with one or two particular communities, which makes for an unusually varied and vibrant coalition in the organization. The spirit and diversity of SEWA would presently be difficult to come by anywhere else, though this is what its members are working on promoting across India. Tribal, Hindu, Harijan, migrant, and Muslim women; tattooed Vaghari women, women in *purdah*; sinewed, muscular smiths; sun-darkened cartpullers and agricultural labourers; young nimble girl bidi rollers with their mothers and grandmothers, progressively more thin and bent from years of sitting over their rolling work; street-wise and bawdy vendors alongside of women timidly emerging from home-bound communities; all in different dress; speaking different languages and dialects; practising different trades—all are coming together to generate strength. It is quite an amazing convergence to witness.

To sit in the SEWA reception centre on any given day and watch the comings and goings is like being at a market place. Like people coming to deal, a hundred activities and purposes all spill from a compact four-storied building and four converted houses which comprise the bank, the offices of the union, the cooperatives, and the legal, health, and creche services.

This office is generally quiet before 11 a.m. each day, when it officially opens, although all the rural organizers pass through at 8:30 a.m. to meet their colleagues and pick up their respective jeeps to head towards the villages. After 11 a.m., women from all over the city and from the outlying villages begin pouring into the centre. They come to talk about their problems, or to meet other organizers and plan action, or to attend training classes, or simply to meet friends and drink tea, as a break from the constant pressure of work. In the main building, each floor consists of basically one large open room, in which several chairs, desks, tables, and fans accommodate innumerable women in one space. Small screens partially divide the space between the different functions of the organization, but just as with the problems and lives that SEWA deals with, there is a lot of traffic around the boundaries.

At the back of the building is a stone courtyard, onto which the door of the reception opens. Young girls sit here each morning vending strings of jasmine to tie in the hair. On one side they are hemmed by the small house where the teenage daughters of waste cloth quilt stitchers learn fine applique patchwork and the daughters of paper pickers learn electrical wiring. On the opposite side of the courtyard, there is constant traffic between the small house which serves as the legal office and the main building. Through this courtyard and down the lane is the three-storied house which serves as the city offices of the 30 cooperatives which are scattered across the city and four rural districts of the state.

Bamboo workers weave in the open lot next to the bank which faces the main street. The bank receives the majority of traffic on any given day, and is popularly referred to as 'the village well'—the place where women gather to share news and friendship. A queue of women accompanied by their children forms early and keeps moving until closing time. They come to apply for loans or deposit money into their savings accounts. Next to them, a small tea stall is set up under a woven mat, where two women make sweet spicy milk tea for all the people working, visiting, strategizing, depositing and withdrawing money. Block printers work on the roof, overlooking the small shop next door where their products are sold, along with the products of other SEWA artisans. The video production room—where self-employed women produce their own films on the issues which affect their communities—is squeezed next to the meeting room on the third floor where women collect at 11 a.m. to sing their daily prayers, or to discuss issues facing them as a group. They not only discuss problems related to trade groups, but social issues as well, and here they receive training in legal procedures, or running a creche, or English literacy, or some other skill. Above this is the tiniest room of all, which serves as the documentation room, where some of the most progressive studies on self-employed women can be found.

By 5:30 each evening, the activity simmers down and the building slowly becomes deserted. Ela Bhatt's tiny brass handbell, which rings incessantly throughout the day when she is present — to call into her small office the next visitor or the next member who has come to talk or seek advice—finally quietens down. Then all the leaders seek each other out, and sit in one cubby or another, and talk about what has happened that day. Every day at SEWA, crises occur at all levels. Every day, some small or major victory is won in the ongoing struggles of SEWA's members. Setbacks constantly crop up, and new strategies are conceived to overcome them. Out of the overwhelming amount of activity which goes on at once, one senses an underlying ethos of patience. There is not just one goal which is fought for. Women here understand that change is a *process* of struggles. Their experience has equipped them for this—they have struggled all their lives. And while there is still deep frustration about the forces which mire them in poverty, a sense of joy and empowerment also emanates from this place. Now, their daily struggles yield something more than their individual bread. They have a place to come when they are in crises, and they hold a belief based on their experience that they can solve their problems.

Whether small or large in nature, the changes this convergence has generated continue to influence increasingly broader spheres. The day-to-day, grassroots changes centre around trying to improve women's working situations. The tactics vary with each individual trade, but usually begin with confronting the direct exploiter and presenting him with demands for change. For women engaged in piece-rate work, this means asking the contractor for higher wages. For vendors, it means confronting the police officers who beat the women and extract bribes from them on charges of 'encroachment.' For women providing services, it means ensuring fair wages and steady work.

From the beginning of SEWA's work, however, it has been apparent that this direct confrontation could never accomplish all the long-term, structural and social changes needed to seriously change women's lives. Women who earn just enough each day to keep their family going are extremely vulnerable. Missing one day's work can mean a crisis in the family. As in the formal sector trade unions, it is common for women to be victimized when their union confronts the person giving them work. For the self-employed, however, the repercussions are even more acute. Terrified of losing the small sporadic income that they *do* have, or of having violence committed against themselves, self-employed women are initially reluctant to join in making demands on their employers.

Yet SEWA has found that the only way to bring change is to 'organize, organize, and organize some more.' In numbers they have found voice and strength. When they stand in sufficient numbers, their voices *do* shake the balance and change things in their favour—from the tactics of their neighbourhood trader or local landowner, up to the national and international policies. Once they have policy backing, the ground is firmer from which to organize more women and push their demands into broader spheres.

A real problem in organizing the self-employed is that confrontation obviously cannot create *more* work. For agricultural labourers who are unemployed seven months in a year, the union cannot change the seasons. Nor can the union demand that customers buy traditional crafts in a declining market. Out of these vulnerabilities—of not enough work, low skill levels, and victimization of individuals who demand fairer practices—SEWA saw the usefulness of helping women get access to alternatives. Besides agitating *against* conditions, SEWA women have a *positive* vision of the society they are working toward. They perceive that alternative structures could positively create this reality.

If labourers are desperate for work, the farmer can dictate the wages. If they also have their own cattle to milk and skilled craft to generate income, they have the choice about what to accept from the farmer. They also have options which can carry them through if a crisis occurs in one of their occupations, like a drought which dispenses with agricultural labour for one or two years.

SEWA's responsiveness to its members' reality is evident in this approach. Government poverty alleviation schemes across the country support one activity for income generation, leaving the woman financially vulnerable if her buffalo on loan falls sick, or when it is not lactating, or during the off season for her craft. Recognizing that rural women traditionally combine land-based, livestock, and craft activities to provide them with work through all the seasons, SEWA's rural programme is aimed at supporting a multi-occupational base by strengthening women in two or three different trades.

SEWA has organized 30 all-women's cooperatives in rural and urban areas including production, service, and banking cooperatives. Through its concrete experiences in developing these, SEWA has seen that cooperatives can provide a structure for women to control their own assets and to come together on the basis of their work, where they are both the owners and workers. For most women who become members of these cooperatives, this marks the first time in their lives that they have *owned* anything. In a male dominated society, poor women's ownership of assets can become a reality more readily *collectively* than independently. And because cooperatives are small and decentralized, they can develop at each group's own pace and be responsive to individual experiences, letting the women grow into their new roles and realities. Collectively, many small cooperatives can make economically weak women effective in the mainstream. SEWA builds women's cooperatives as modern extensions of the traditional system of self-employment, where people own their own means of production and work for themselves.

All of SEWA's attributes—that it represents the self-employed, that its members are women, that it provides services, that it promotes alternative economic structures—make its definition as a union revolutionary, and give it the strength and leverage to affect change vertically. SEWA is constantly, systematically, simultaneously working on three levels—grassroots, national and international—to bring visibility and change in women's lives.

From women headloaders in one city's cloth market demanding standardization of their wages in 1972, this organization has grown to change the perceptions of women and their work worldwide. This achievement is based on the strength of working from the bottom up, from poor women's experiences to policy change based on their experience. SEWA respects traditional systems of work and their modern manifestations which are largely informal, based on verbal interactions, and decentralized through the lanes, neighbourhoods, markets, villages, and fields of Gujarat. SEWA women build their organization based on these realities, rather than trying to conform to alien industrialized models.

A few examples will illustrate the kinds of intense needs self-employed women have for access to services and resources, and the ways SEWA has responded to these needs. Most of the systems which presently extend these services are in the hands of those who either do not perceive or misunderstand these women and their problems, and they often overlook or exclude the self-employed women most in need of them. SEWA's 20 years of work in developing ways to meet the needs of poor women through their work lives has forged models for women in India, and begun to change the perspectives of western-based international trade unions and labour organizations towards women workers.

SEWA's initial project was credit. Fair credit was a unanimous demand from all the trade groups which came together under SEWA. When families earn the minimum for day-to-day survival, times of emergency or social obligations such as marriages and deaths mean debts. Most lower class self-employed women also take loans for working capital. For whichever purpose they borrow the money, they pay exorbitant interest rates—as high as 10 per cent per day. This indebtedness makes them more susceptible to exploitative wages, as the loans are often extended to them by the traders or landowners for whom they work. SEWA started out by helping its members get loans from nationalized banks, but it quickly became apparent how ill-equipped both the women and these formal institutions were to deal with one another. Most SEWA women could not fill out deposit and withdrawal slips, found formal banking hours inconvenient due to their work schedules, did not understand what queues to stand in, or which banks or branches to make their payments to. The bottom line was that they could not sign their names, and that their names even changed from visit to visit. Sometimes they gave their husbands' name, sometimes their mothers' or fathers' name. All these formalities are irrelevant in their day-to-day worlds within their known communities where verbal dealings are the means of agreement. The banks quickly became exasperated over these discrepancies. Middle class bank employees did not have any experience in dealing with illiterate clients who wanted only small loans, nor with what they termed the 'uncouth' manners of their new clients.

SEWA women realized that what they really needed was their own bank which could fit their needs. This was really SEWA's beginning to innovative solutions for bridging the modern and traditional worlds. To overcome the problem of illiteracy, they would use the women's photographs instead of signatures on their pass-books. The problem of banking hours was overcome by sending bank workers out to the women's neighbourhoods and workplaces, to collect savings and loan instalments. Organizers disregarded professional advice that such a bank for poor, illiterate women would be suicidal. Now, 16 years later, they see that they have better recovery rates and higher profit margins than the most formal institutions, and that their model is being promoted by women's organizations around the world.

Early on in its banking experience, SEWA conducted research to find out why some women were defaulting on loan payments. SEWA found that in many families one family member or another was constantly ill, hampering their ability to work and generate income. SEWA was most alarmed, however, to discover that out of 500 women defaulters who were surveyed, 20 had died and 15 of the 20 deaths were during childbirth. These women were experiencing two major problems: the most immediate cause of their problem was tetanus, due to limited access to proper medical care. In 1975, many SEWA members were still having their umbilical cords cut with a dirty sickle. Their secondary problem was their need for income. If they had no surplus, and no maternity benefit, they could not leave work for childbirth. Many self-employed women have told me about the numerous times they have worked until the labour pains began, and after two or three days, were back in the fields or vegetable markets, or rolling bidis again. This not only endangers the health of the mother, but also of her young child. It pushes her from her already precarious state of poor nutrition and overworked body, into a cycle of poorer health, loss of the baby, a repeated pregnancy to have another child, followed by poorer health. It quickly became clear to SEWA organizers that a self-employed woman needed a way to protect herself from some of the risks of childbirth, to be able to rest after childbirth and recover her strength, and a way to eat and feed her family during this period when she would be away from work.

SEWA strongly believed that society as a whole should assume the responsibility of the nation's children, not solely the poor mother. Unable to find any public support for these women through the government's Life Insurance Corporation, SEWA was compelled to initiate its own maternal protection scheme. When a woman became pregnant, she was registered under the scheme by paying a fee of Rs. 15. Then SEWA linked her to prenatal services appropriate to the area where she lived and worked. At the time of delivery, she was given a stipend of Rs. 100 and a kilo of *ghee* (clarified butter), a high energy food which post-partum women traditionally eat. In addition to linking these women to health services and the cash benefit, SEWA also conducted training courses for midwives in the rural areas where they work, teaching them the need for sterilized tools and sanitary conditions.

Within a very short time, the results of this scheme were evident in the health and survival rates of both the mothers and their children. After several years of expanding this programme, SEWA still believed that the government should be providing this service to women—but *not* as a welfare service. SEWA clearly saw this as an occupational health issue. It lobbied the state to take up a maternity scheme for landless agricultural workers, who make up 75 per cent of the female population. In 1987, Gujarat state—with SEWA's help—began implementing the Maternity Protection Scheme through the Labour Ministry. SEWA meanwhile continues lobbying the central government to launch this programme nation-wide for self-employed women.

These kinds of accomplishments are monumental in the face of slow government bureaucracies and caste distinctions which suppress ideologies that lower caste and poor women can think for and help themselves—*if* they are given access to resources. This is one reason why SEWA recognizes how fragile such gains are on a small scale. Educating people in one district to the needs and methods of such a programme is sufficient only as long as those receiving the training and developing the requisite sympathies are present. If they are transferred to another position, or another district or state, or if the politicians who support the programme leave, the setbacks can be detrimental and frustrating. For these reasons, SEWA is constantly working at each level of society to press for change. The grassroots changes are vital for individual women, but they can only be sustained if they become part of the entire society's consciousness, and if large scale policies support both the programmes and the ideology.

An important point to make here is that part of the reason that women submit to the exploitation inflicted upon them in the first place is that they are not conversant with the formal, literate world, and that many of them live and deal in a limited circumscribed environment which does not promote unifying with people outside.

How then, have they managed to organize, and make inroads into the formal systems? This obviously requires the help of people who *are* conversant with that formal world, or poor and illiterate women would have come together long ago and SEWA would not be so unusual. The general experience of the self-employed, however, is that people who are conversant with both worlds are the ones who exploit them, milking benefits from both sides.

The initial inspiration for devoting the kinds of skills which would bridge the gap between these two worlds came from Ela Bhatt. Her concern with women's labour problems and the degraded conditions under which their families were forced to live gave her the strong conviction that self-employed women should learn themselves how to deal with the two worlds in order to change these conditions. The headloaders who approached her in 1971 were the kindling to her fire. They came to meet her with Gal Baji, their *thekedar* (contractor). Although he was concerned that the women were living on the street, he was still very obviously controlling them. He wanted charity, not justice. The initial insight Ela gained from her contact with them—that the best way to change situations of poverty was through struggling for justice in women's work lives—has proved a powerful organizing tool which eliminates any sense of charity in the organization.

The success of her strategy gained its first widespread recognition in 1977 when she was awarded Asia's prestigious Ramon Magsaysay Award for 'making a reality of the Gandhian principle of self-help among the depressed workforce of self-employed women.' Now, after 20 years as the leader of SEWA, her belief in women's self-reliance through self-employment has grown into her belief that the future of India lies in the hands of rural and poor women. She constantly reiterates that if India wants to pull itself out of poverty, it is through giving these persevering women access to resources, decision-making, planning, and implementing of their own programmes, that this will be accomplished.

In SEWA's 20 years of existence, over 46,000 women have joined Bhatt's work, dedicating their individual skills to facilitate interfacing the formal and informal worlds. The majority of SEWA's organizers are working class women themselves. Some with special leadership qualities have come to represent their trades in the union, and others who are literate bring this skill with their first-hand understanding to forge bridges. A few middle class and elite professional women have also been drawn to SEWA, leaving outside jobs in business management, as physicians, and lawyers, to contribute their skills to the organization. Others have come from different parts of India with skills of union organizing, public health management, and economics, to settle down in Ahmedabad specifically to work with SEWA. And some have come from other countries, to stay for a short time and teach skills developed elsewhere. One such contributor was Martha Stuart, who came from 'Are You Listening?' based in New York. She began the process of training self-employed women in the use of video equipment, so that they could communicate their work life and struggles to the larger world from their own perspective. From this start, SEWA has begun extending this training to illiterate communities all over the world.

This is the basis of SEWA's ideology—that women from all levels of society join together to plan *with* rather than planning *for* poor women. The strength of the organization is in its membership, which generates the understanding and ideas which the middle class women can help convey. SEWA does not engage lawyers, doctors and managers simply to provide services to the organization. Lawyers, doctors and managers who believe in the work come to learn from the self-employed the context of their problems. They provide their services while they *pass on* their skills. The idea is holding hands in mutual respect while they shift control. Out of this ideology, 60 women from various trade groups are now providing basic health care services to their communities. Other self-employed women are learning to prepare and represent their own legal cases. Artisans have grown from exploited piece-rate workers, to partners in business in their own cooperatives. From these cooperatives, certain women have risen as managers of the cooperatives. When women workers assume these positions, SEWA sees policy change become a reality. There is conviction in the demands when they are voiced by the workers themselves.

Through this kind of interaction and growth, SEWA has paved the way for putting self-employed workers on the world labour map. During the course of building SEWA on the experiences of self-employed women in Gujarat, it became increasingly apparent that many women across India and other parts of the world were likewise economically active while remaining poor, marginalized, unprotected and even invisible as workers. While labour unions in the west were lobbying against putting out work into workers' homes, SEWA's home-based workers recognized that centralized, industrial modelled workplaces would never suit their need. They began demanding to be legitimated and protected at home. The International Labour Organization (ILO), which sets standards for international labour laws, and the International Confederation of Free Trade Unions (ICFTU) which represents 96 million workers in 81 countries, have begun to respond to SEWA's demands by initiating an ILO Convention (1990) for the recognition and protection of home-based workers.

Besides working to reorient modern trends toward validating home-based artisans, labourers or cultivators who are traditionally self-employed, SEWA also promotes traditional ways of trading that have been marginalized by the modern, western, urban models. Street vendors provide important daily services to consumers, supplying them with fresh vegetables, fruits, fish, eggs, milk, and cooked snacks, yet there is hardly an urban development plan in the country which incorporates them. These vendors ask nothing except their right to ply the streets or squat in the markets with their two baskets or small hand-cart. Because they are not officially allotted space or given licences, they are labelled 'encroachers', harassed and beaten by the police, their goods confiscated, and bribes extorted from them to let them sit unharassed for a day or two.

For years, the municipal authorities and the police were not responsive to SEWA's requests to allocate space and issue licences to these women vendors. Some vendors' families had been selling in the main market for up to three generations, but nonetheless found themselves evicted. SEWA organizers decided to take their case to the Supreme Court. They were successful in getting a ruling in favour of the women hawkers, who now sit with the security of licences to back up their refusal to move or pay 'fines.' This ruling has also set the stage for the National Policy on Hawkers and Vendors which SEWA is currently lobbying to push through Parliament. This policy formally legitimates this traditional way of trading, by providing licences, space, and facilities for vendors in both urban and rural markets across the country. SEWA is constantly challenging the relics of colonialism and western influence which marginalize Indian ways of life and work, and demanding that society at large also examine its policies and priorities.

SEWA's major achievements in this regard at the national level came when the Prime Minister agreed to appoint a National Commission on Self-Employed Women to study the problems of such women across the country and develop an agenda for change. The President of India nominated Ela Bhatt to Parliament and appointed her to head that Commission. The Commission's year and a half study across the nation included 800 public hearings— meeting women in their workplaces, in the fields and mines, on construction sites, in the streets and markets. The Commission's research revealed that the problems of self-employed women in Gujarat reflect women's situation nationwide. In late 1988, the Commission's *Shramshakti* ('women's labour power') report was published, aimed at bringing visibility and positive change in the lives of tens of millions of women. These changes are outlined through the policy recommendations which largely promote the grassroots strategies SEWA has found effective in its work, while revamping social services, protective legislation, and the labour monitoring bureaucracies. SEWA organizers were actively disseminating the findings of the Commission, pursuing translations into all the Indian languages, and organizing working groups to carry out the recommendations when the National Front Government was elected to power in late 1989. When Ela Bhatt was appointed as the first woman to sit on the national Planning Commission which drafts the long-term Five-Year Plans, it became clear that the agenda of poor, working women had finally won some of the policy attention they had begun struggling for 17 years earlier.

That SEWA has succeeded in building a union which reflects its grassroots sensibilities is reflected in comments I have heard from dozens of SEWA women. Time and again they say, 'SEWA is my mother,' or 'The bank is like my mother,' or, 'When we have a difficulty, we go home to SEWA.' This has special significance in Indian culture, where a girl goes to live at her in-laws' house after marriage. She usually thinks of her mother's home as the place of warmth and safety, where she can be free, relaxed, and more herself. At home she is usually listened to, protected, and helped in whatever manner her family can offer to solve her problems.

One reason SEWA members ascribe maternal attributes to their work organization is because of the philosophy of struggle to which SEWA adheres. It is an especially feminine philosophy which adheres to non-violence, to arbitration and reconciliation, and most importantly, to a quiet, fiercely determined resistance to exploitation. When SEWA women formulate their demands, they agree to what they consider just and minimum, and then they remain firm till their demands are met. They inform their opponents of all their plans before they take action. These strategies gain them credibility not only in their opponents' eyes, but also in the eyes of the general public. SEWA has seen time and again how important the support of the general public is in its struggles for poor women who have little status in society, if the scales are to be tipped in their favour. When SEWA bidi workers marched by the thousands in protest of exploitative practices and low wages, citizens sympathized with their demands. When the vegetable vendors peacefully occupied their vending spaces, from which they had been evicted, the public responded and told them that they had missed buying from them in their absence. The women's refusal to employ violent means, combined with the support of the public, renders the authorities powerless to declare a law and order problem, and their opponents are compelled to respond to their demands.[4]

One can recognize here the resonance with Gandhi's philosophy of non-violent struggle for India's independence from Britain. SEWA draws a great deal of inspiration from Gandhi's work, and believes that he was instrumental in getting Indian society to recognize women's importance in the world of work and social change. Gandhi himself ascribed the tactics employed in the freedom struggle to the tactics he had observed his wife and mother using at home to resist their own exploitation. While the organization reinforces the philosophy of non-violent organizing, the women practise it from the experience of their day-to-day lives.

I do not want to oversimplify here, or promote the idea that all women are generous and transcendent to violence. But during the year and a half I spent at SEWA, I did witness women's faith and experience in the process of change through conciliation and compromise, rather than through aggression. Their conscious application to the public sphere of the negotiating and nurturing qualities women are conditioned to practise within the Indian family arise from the same practical incentives. Because they are the poorest in society, their families, homes, and occupations are the most obvious and immediate targets of any violence in both rural and urban areas. Poor women in Ahmedabad have experienced several intense and destructive waves of caste and communal violence in which they have lost children, relatives, their homes, and their work. Their experience of these tragedies gives them reason to recognize the benefits of non-violence. Their inspiring example has come not only by recognizing the benefits, however, but also by being able to practise non-violence under extremely oppressive circumstances.

I once heard Ela Bhatt talk on why SEWA has found inspiration in Gandhi's practices. She said one reason was because Gandhi did not rely on miracles in his work against powerful social forces. SEWA women also recognize that no miracles will change their lives, and they persevere in their day-to-day struggle toward self-reliance. They continue to gather women by trade group, to learn about their specific problems and develop solutions to overcome them. Collectively they distil problems common to several trade groups, and work out ways to alleviate them. They continue to respect the *process* as much as any result. They say that gaining a demand is useful only if it leads to more organizing, only if it inspires travelling further in the process of change.

A woman who 10 years ago never ventured out of her house, but sent her son to collect tobacco and tendu leaves from the contractor so that she could support herself and her children by rolling bidis would not have even been able to introduce herself. She would have told us that she did not work if we asked her about what occupation she was engaged in. She would have described herself as a wife, or mother, or widow. Since her alliance with SEWA, however, she has grown from being able to speak her own name into the definition of a bidi *worker*. Meeting so many sister workers gives her the courage to not only collect the supplies and return her products herself, but also to ask her contractor to pay her the legal minimum wage. Then her consciousness expands to recognize herself as a *unionized worker*, along with all the women who stitch garments, weave cloth, process food, make incense, produce baskets and brooms, and who work as smiths, potters, and carpenters. Once she sees she is one of so many, she comes to understand how deeply the exploitation runs in the system, and how she, along with so many sisters, should be getting a better deal for their labour. From her slum in Ahmedabad, she moves out to other neighbourhoods where women also practise her trade, to other trade groups with whom she shares her religion, to other states, to the local *Panchayat* (elected government representing about five villages), to state governments, to courts, to the Parliament, to the International Labour Organization. She then says loudly, clearly, 'I am a worker. Recognize me. I work at home. (Or in the market. Or in the fields.) Recognize my workplace. Grant us the protection we need in our work. We want dignity, not desperation—our work should provide us this.' And from this place, her strength becomes infectious, and she stands with her sisters saying, '*We* will plan the agenda for change. *We* will sit and decide our priorities. And *we* will manifest the changes!'

SEWA women have a vision of governing bodies of the near future: From village level Panchayats to Parliament to organizations like the ILO, they see their tribal, Muslim, Harijan, poor, low-caste, calloused, articulate selves sitting on those bodies, making decisions, no longer the recipients of policies and plans made by others.

This movement from the private, individual, circumscribed world to a broader consciousness of collective, public, political worlds is reflected on some level in all the women who have been associated with SEWA for any length of time. To generate the self-respect needed to resist exploitation, to demand change collectively and refrain from violence under such oppressive economic and social situations, requires a great deal of inspiration. The blooming strength and emergence of these women from their limited communities and desperate economic situations speak for the inspiration they cull from coming together.

This strength and emergence are creating what is perhaps SEWA's most important contribution. In the shift from traditional to modern worlds, from verbal interactions to highly sophisticated technologies, voids are created which individuals cannot muster the resources to span. Poverty is only one of the repercussions of these voids. Communalism and fundamentalism, with their resulting violence, also enter in attempts to hold onto the old, understood systems which are irreversibly retreating. The persistent work of a sisterhood—which for 20 years has crossed over definitions of poverty and wealth, of the boundaries of different communities, of literacy and illiteracy, of who can use services and technologies—now holds out viable, positive values and models which can serve as starting points to fill those voids in a healing, Indian way.

END NOTES

1. This account is drawn from Usha Jumani's 'The Informal Sector as "People's Economy": Seven Individual Views from Women of Ahmedabad,' July 1988, pp. 35–39.
2. Bhatt, Ela, 'Women and Small Scale Enterprise Development in a New Era.' Paper presented at the International Institute of Development, Ottowa, October 1987, p. 10.
3. These trends are noted in *Shramshakti*, the Report of the National Commission on Self-Employed Women, Government of India, 1988. For further discussion of these issues, see 'The Grind of Work,' preface in that Report.
4. These ideas on SEWA's reliance on Gandhian ideas are drawn from Ela Bhatt's introduction in Pushpa Joshi (ed.), *Gandhi On Women*. Ahmedabad: Navajivan Publishing House, 1988.

2

Emergence

In 1972, when we started SEWA, we had no idea how to do it, or where to start, but two things I saw clearly: In our country, most of the production of goods and services are done through the self-employed sector. Eighty-nine per cent of our labour force is self-employed. Unless they are brought into the mainstream of the labour movement, it is no movement worth its name.

Secondly, I recognized that 80 per cent of Indian women are poor, illiterate, and economically very active. It is these working class women who should be taking a leading role in the women's movement of our country. Ninety per cent of these women's time is taken up in their work. Work is their priority. If we bring these women into the movement on the basis of work, it is strategically the most effective way of organizing large numbers of women according to issues which are relevant to them.

Ela Bhatt in an interview, May 1988

Ahmedabad, the birthplace of SEWA, is the textile mill city where Mahatma Gandhi organized labour in accordance with his principles of non-violence and passive resistance. The city's vibrancy is due, in great part, to the previous lure of the mills. Since the beginning of this century, industrialized jobs have drawn people in from villages not only all over Gujarat, but also from Uttar Pradesh,

Rajasthan, Maharashtra, Andhra Pradesh and Madhya Pradesh. While some of those migrating to Ahmedabad found jobs in mills, many people in need of employment adapted their skills to other niches of life in the city. The kinds of occupations that have evolved around the mills portray a graphic picture of the way self-employed women have carved economic niches out of whatever kinds of opportunities exist.

In the city's large wholesale cloth market where the textile mills' products are sold, women work as headloaders, carrying the bales of cloth to retail merchants whenever an order is received. For heavier or bulkier loads, women and men work in pairs pulling huge carts loaded with up to 1000 kg of cloth, steel, wood, chemical, and oil freight. Garments and quilt covers stitched by women in their homes from the waste of textile mills line many of the streets and stalls in the crowded, old walled city. Blacksmith and carpenter women recycle much of the waste of the mills: large chemical barrels are cut and hammered into pots, pans, stoves, utensils, and tools. Waste wood is used for tables, shelves, small stools, and cupboards for low income customers.

Independent of the textile mills are the kind of self-employed trades which exist in every Indian city. Fruits and vegetables are hawked by small-scale vendors who squat behind their baskets in the busy markets or business centres, or who push *laris* full of produce through the streets. Alongside several of the city's markets, thousands of used garments are hawked at low prices to consumers every day.

Since the mid-thirties there has been a serious decline in the number of women workers in the textile mills, due to technological modernization which has displaced low skilled women's labour. Although men were also engaged in low skilled jobs, they were reabsorbed into the industry and trained in the use of more technical equipment, but women were generally excluded from this upgrading. While in 1925 women accounted for 20 per cent of the textile workers in the mills, in 1975, SEWA found that there were only 2.5 per cent women workers in the same industry.[1]

Following the early technological displacement of women workers, there was an overall decline in the textile industry, beginning in the sixties. Because of both the outdated processes and machinery of India's oldest mills and the strength of the textile unions, some mill-owners began to give out work to home-based or shed-based power-looms where protective legislation could not be enforced, while others have pulled out of the industry altogether. In the last decade, 30 of the 61 large mills of the city have closed down.

Families who have migrated and have no land to return to have had to adopt whatever means of livelihood they could for survival. Many women in retrenched weavers' families have turned to waste paper picking—an unhealthy and, as they consider it, degrading job—culling any recyclable waste from the city's garbage heaps. Other women have taken up occupations—like rolling incense sticks or bidis or the grain wafers known as *papad*—to supplement the family income. For up to one-third of these families, these are now the only sources of income. Though originally the prosperous mills had attracted people from the villages to Ahmedabad, the inward migration has not declined with the decline of the mills. On the contrary, successive droughts, increasing landlessness, and displacement of traditional skills in the villages have contributed to a growth in immigration of people in search of jobs.

This pull of the city has made certain areas of Ahmedabad an amalgamation of rural India, somewhat urbanized—Hindus, Muslims, Harijans and tribals all cluster in their own communities. As people enter the city, new hutments are erected in barren lots, or along canals or railway tracks. Trades are taken up, domestic animals are herded there and huts are made increasingly permanent. Gradually that area is absorbed into the consciousness and spread of the city, which continues to grow and absorb other such colonies.

These hutments and the relatively unskilled trades of people who have left behind subsistence lives in the village exist side by side with the most modern developed face of Ahmedabad. India's leading institutes of architecture, management, space research, and design are situated here. These modern and traditional worlds, formal and informal, are by no means mutually exclusive. The high rise industrial and commercial complexes which are growing across the length and breadth of the city are built by the labour of women who carry headloads of bricks and cement and use them to construct walls with the help of their men and children. The roads, water, and electricity systems are also constructed by these labourers. Home-based piece-rate workers are the basis of viability for many thriving industries like garments, incense, prepared foods, toys, and electronics. Some of Ahmedabad's most popular fast-food restaurants draw their appeal from the multitude of vendors who sit outside them, vending their traditional Gujarati textiles and handicrafts. A woman who owns a pot, a dozen tea cups, and a kerosene stove as her tools of trade makes her living by squatting outside the modern State Bank of India complex, and sending her son in with tea whenever anyone in the bank orders it. Camel carts bring vegetables from the villages to urban consumers and vie for space on the traffic tangled roads with hand-carts, motorcycles, and Maruti-Suzuki sports cars.

These traditional and modern aspects which are characteristic of cities all over India, also create conflicts the consequences of which are most often borne by the poor and unskilled. They lead their lives in public through sheer necessity. They have no choice but to bathe at public taps and to cook outside their huts on the roadsides. They use the roads themselves to do their production work on, to store their materials on, to sleep on; they use them as their children's playgrounds, or as their toilets. Planning ideas for clean and beautiful cities are more often attempted by demolishing the slums rather than installing water, sewage, and drainage systems. In the place of slums high-rise buildings are constructed which only the elite can afford, while the displaced families migrate to another open space and construct new living and working spaces under similar conditions. Open spaces where hawkers have carried out their business for years, and sometimes even for decades, are swallowed by car parking or modern shopping centres. While doctors transplant kidneys and perform heart bypass surgery in the medical research hospital, a woman smith sits in front of her hut, beating a piece of sheet-metal 10 or 15 times to make one hole. And as new satellites are being designed in the modern Indian Space Research Organization, women's legs are being broken by their heavy handcarts which have no brakes. The modern and traditional aspects of the city, the urban and the rural, are still struggling to co-exist and productively complement each other.

It was against this background that Ela Bhatt became increasingly aware of the complexities and contradictions of modern India finding niches for its traditional and industrial aspects. Bhatt had been deeply affected by Gandhi's non-violent movement in the independence struggle which she experienced in Surat, Gujarat, through her grandparents' participation. During college she worked on the 1951 Census and saw face-to-face the degraded conditions in which innumerable families were living. In 1955, after following in her father's and grandfather's footsteps by attending law school, she began to look for a Gandhian job as a way to work on some of the problems of poverty and injustice. After a meeting with Ansuyabehn Sarabhai, the President of the Textile Labour Association who had founded the union along with Mahatma Gandhi in 1917, Bhatt decided to use her legal skills to represent the labour problems of the TLA workers.

Ansuyabehn's work had begun similarly in 1914 when she started visiting the workers' slums at night to educate them. She thought literacy would help solve their problems of poverty and exploitation. When she confronted the realities of their 15 hour work days and the toll of the plague on their communities, however, she realized that what they needed more immediately was to organize and negotiate for more tenable conditions.

In the course of her work, she sometimes had to agitate against her own brother who was a large mill-owner. When the Ahmedabad mill workers who had kept the mills open throughout a year of disease and death learned that their plague bonus had been withdrawn, Ansuyabehn called on Mahatma Gandhi to help her organize workers and negotiate fair solutions. Gandhi's and Ansuyabehn's early work of arbitration and negotiation between the owners and the workers led to the birth of the TLA, which was India's first union of textile workers. These two leaders worked together to inculcate the ideals that a labour union has a social responsibility, and that the union should work to develop the *whole* human being—not just the worker.[2]

As President of the TLA, Ansuyabehn continued to represent mill workers—both through their work and their families' home life—until she died in 1972. For her, a union meant strength for building up the workers' capabilities. She believed that workers and owners were equal classes, and worked with Gandhi on his 'Constructive Programme' for women's participation in the independent nation. Ansuyabehn insisted on a women's component in the TLA. It was on her initiative that women's programmes in the Women's Wing were introduced until Bhatt took the torch.

'Ansuyabehn is always portrayed as conventional, but she was actually a very radical person,' said Bhatt in an interview 15 years after Ansuyabehn's death. 'She wanted women to be fearless. She herself was fearless, and she had an intuitive sense about labour organizing. During their first strike over the plague bonus, she tore a page from her diary, wrote down the workers demands, and gave 48 hours notice to the ₃mill-owners before striking. Her spontaneous early practices are now laws of unionizing in India. There just was not any other person doing work like she was in the urban slums, or with labour, at that time. And until the end of her life, she was always committed to working with the poorest people.'

Bhatt's initial three years at the TLA (1955–58) were spent preparing proposals which were later translated into labour laws, and representing the TLA in Labour Court. After her marriage to Ramesh Bhatt—a committed activist and professor of economics—and the birth of their two children, she returned to work in 1961 with the Ministry of Labour of Gujarat. By 1968, when the TLA offered her the position to head the Women's Wing, she knew she wanted to work specifically on the labour problems of women. At the time, the Women's Wing was engaged in imparting training in stitching, typing, embroidery, and other conventional skills to the wives and daughters of mill-workers. Bhatt was convinced, however, that poor working women in the city needed access to a workers' union and more comprehensive training and social services.

The first chance for such organizing came in 1971 when a group of migrant women headloaders and cartpullers who were living on the footpath without shelter approached the TLA for assistance in housing. Bhatt went with them to their work and camping places where many women crowded along the busy roads with their empty hand-carts or headcloths waiting for a call from a merchant. As Bhatt questioned them about their housing needs, other issues began to surface: they earned only 10 to 15 paise per trip, never amounting to more than Rs. 3 per day (then equivalent to about US 30 cents).

'The traders lose track of how many loads we carry,' one woman told her. 'Then they pay us less than they owe us.'

'We get paid the same amount whether we carry bales to the next road or to the market two hours' walk away,' another said.

Then a third: 'I often have to sit all day, and get only one or two trips. All day the children are alone, and I cannot even bring *roti* (flat breads) from only two trips.'

Supabehn, a cartpuller added: 'Most of our earnings go to the pocket of the contractor who owns these carts. We need our own carts.'

The organizers of the Women's Wing called a meeting for all the women working in the cloth market. After discussing these problems, they decided to form themselves into a group and try to work together to improve their situation. Following Supabehn's lead, each woman paid her first monthly membership fee of 25 paise.

After this meeting ended, Ela went back to the TLA and wrote a newspaper article outlining the problems the cloth market head-loaders had articulated. The merchants quickly countered the charges in their own article. The Women's Wing reprinted the merchants' claims of fair treatment on cards, and distributed them to the newly formed group of headloaders to use as leverage. They were going to try to hold the merchants to their claims.

In the meantime, Chanda Papu took a day off from her used-garments trading to meet Ela Bhatt at the TLA. Chanda had heard from TLA workers that Elabehn* was working with women like her on their problems. She went hoping she could get help with a loan.

Used-clothes vendors walk 10-20 kilometres every day with a *topla* (large shallow head-basket) filled with stainless steel vessels and plastic basins taken on credit from a local shopkeeper. They pay 10 per cent interest per month on the retail priced vessels which form   the basis of their trade. They yell out *Pialla-burnee wallah!* ('Glass and jar trader!') as they move through the middle class housing colonies, where they trade vessels for the residents' old clothes.

Most used-garments dealers are Vaghari women, many of whom live and work in the crowded lanes of Raikhad, an inner city slum of Ahmedabad. Chanda's house is like most in this neighbourhood—light only comes from the open doorway and the places where the wall is broken or the bamboo mats are torn. The dirt lane is usually muddy from the open drains which pool here. In this lane, husbands and sons and brothers help Vaghari women mend the clothing the women have traded for. They use the hems and unworn pockets to invisibly patch holes. They replace broken zippers, hooks, and

---

* *Behn* is Gujarati for sister, and connotes respect and familiarity. Members of SEWA always attach behn to organizers' names, and as members become older or become leaders, they too become referred to as behn (or 'bibi'—Urdu for sister). In referring to Ela in the context of her interactions in the organization, I will identify her as her colleagues so fondly do, as Elabehn; in the outside political forum, as Bhatt. In referring to her generally, I will identify her as Ela, in the spirit of the open familiarity she grants all who come to meet her.

buttons, and often turn the entire garment inside out and restitch the old seams in to make a new looking garment. These vendors sit in the daily and Sunday markets in both urban and rural areas, hawking the clean, repaired garments to low income customers. Millions of people in India have never worn a new garment in their lives, and depend on the trade of Chanda and others like her for their clothing.

Chandabehn's composure reflects her years as a shrewd bargainer. When she is with her customers, her eyes narrow in concentration and her mouth is stern as she explains how long the garment will take to repair, how little exchange it will bring. She repeatedly juts her chin and says, *Bolo!* ('Speak!'), meaning, 'What is your offer?'

The day she approached Elabehn in the TLA office with the problems of her trade, however, Chanda could barely say her name. She wanted to sit on the floor, not on the chair (which would put her at Elabehn's level). She did not know where to spit her snuff. No one had ever asked her, her name before. She is known in her own family and community as the mother of one of her sons, or the wife of her husband. Outside of that, she is simply a nameless Vaghari—one of the tribes the government has designated as a 'backward caste,' and whom many urban dwellers think of as semi-criminal, because they are wanderers and traders.

In 1971, Chanda related to Elabehn the difficulties of the garment trade fraught with debts and police harassment, juggled between feeding the family, pregnancies, and the problems of family life in the slums.[3] British laws are still found in Indian books which relegate small traders to the ranks of illegal 'encroachers', even though it is the most widespread, traditional way of trading.[4] With the fingerhold of these laws, policemen threaten vendors with arrest or confiscation of their wares, keeping them sufficiently terrified to pay a small 'fine' into the hands of the policemen. When arrested, they are often severely beaten until they 'confess' their theft, for which much larger sums are levelled against them. Because of the widespread belief that they are thieves, Vagharis can be arrested, beaten, sentenced, and fined summarily, without evidence to implicate their guilt.

Their loss of income to fines and arrest is compounded by their debts to merchants and money-lenders. They pay an interest varying from 10 per cent per month to as high as 10 per cent per day on borrowed capital. In 1972, most families trading in used-garments had an average income of only Rs. 225 per month. More than half the families who were earning this much were over Rs. 1700 in debt.[5]

During this initial meeting, Chanda and her sister workers asked Elabehn why she could not help used-garments traders get some of the benefits the TLA was helping the textile workers get. They decided to contact other women with similar problems and organize a meeting. Within a week the meeting was called in a nearby garden, Trikhoonia Bagiche (the Three-cornered Garden), and over 100 women attended—headloaders and cartpullers who had already organized themselves in the cloth market, used-garments dealers, vegetable vendors, carpenters and smiths.

Chanda recalled her experience of that meeting: 'As the day passed, I heard things from the other sisters which began to raise heat inside me. Those women were also dirt poor—like I was— harassed, working 16 hours a day, using their children's labour, barely making ends meet. Finally, I could not stop myself. My anger at the police boiled over. I stood up and spoke for the first time in such a group. "Why do the police beat us and arrest us?" I asked the other sisters. "Why do they take bribes? We are not criminals, we are business women!" '

'All the other sisters were equally stirred up. I suddenly understood what Elabehn meant, and I shouted, "Let's make our own organization and do something about these problems!" '

All the other women cheered and shouted their assent, and began pulling out their membership fees. On 3 December 1971, the Self-Employed Women's Association was born. Ela Bhatt was made General Secretary, and Arvind Buch, TLA's President, was made President of SEWA. The acronymn which means 'service' was appropriate to the spirit of their union.

'Who would have guessed on that day how much we all had to learn?' Ela recalled about that first meeting. 'For the first hour, we could not get the meeting going because all the women were shouting at the others, "Sssh, ssshh! Let the behn (meaning me) speak! Ssshh! Ssshh!" After waiting a long time and no one heeding anyone else's advice, I finally shouted "Quiet!!!" We were all finding different voices to deal with each other with,' she chuckled. Organizing had begun, and the first self-employed leaders were emerging.

The same definitions of labour unions that SEWA set out to

change posed the first obstacle: Indian labour laws only recognized unions where specific employer–employee relationships existed. SEWA upheld that unions did not have to be formed *against* an employer, but were equally valid as unions *for* the worker. After four months of negotiations with the government, the authorities finally agreed to SEWA's broader interpretation and registered it as a legitimate trade union in April 1972. This would prove to be only the first of innumerable policy constraints or conceptual blocks which SEWA would come up against in trying to make laws and policies responsive to the needs of poor self-employed women.

SEWA's main goals *for* its members were to bring visibility to women as *workers*; and to improve women's economic position by giving them access to resources and control over their own income. Besides fair credit, women needed their own tools of trade, access to raw materials at fair prices, and access to markets so that the middleman would not corner all their profits. The organizers recognized that these objectives would only be met if SEWA brought social and political visibility to these women as workers.

SURVEYING FOR THE BOTTOM LINE

To begin, they conducted large-scale surveys of the working and living conditions of women in the slum areas of Ahmedabad.

'First of all we just needed to know what kind of occupations women were doing out there,' said Nirubehn Jadav, Secretary of SEWA. She has been an organizer since SEWA's inception, and is popularly known as 'SEWA's Police Commissioner,' because of her reputation for keeping abusive policemen in line. As a garment stitcher, she first came to the Women's Wing of the TLA when her husband worked in the mills to conduct sewing classes. She readily shifted from teacher to organizer when Elabehn began to get involved with self-employed women.

'When we came across new trade groups during our surveys, we kept our eyes open for one or two outspoken women with some fire,' she said, explaining the organizing process. 'We would get these women to go amongst their sister workers and find out what their problems were. They conveyed the problems and priorities of their trade group so that we could call these women together for a meeting.'

From hundreds of meetings it became clear how many problems cut across occupations. Again and again women's vulnerability surfaced due to their lack of protection in employment. SEWA began to tackle these problems one by one.

'For the used-garments traders, we called a big meeting in the garden near Puri Bazar,' Nirubehn explained. 'We invited the Police Superintendent and 500 garment vendors came. Chanda gave her first real speech and it was stunning. It was the first meeting of this kind, and the first time the police ever considered the problems of the garment vendors. The Superintendent responded by allotting the vendors space in several markets in the old city where our women were selling.'

For the vegetable vendors who were losing to bribes or fines anywhere from Rs. 2–Rs. 5 out of their daily earnings of Rs. 10–Rs. 15, SEWA started confronting the officers who were extorting money from the sellers. Rajibehn, a tough, hefty vendor who was forced onto the footpath when the open lot where she used to sell was enclosed and built on, recalled the day Nirubehn, equally solid and self-composed, appeared on her daily rounds of the members' workplaces.

'The usual payoff was going on when I saw Nirubehn come into our lane,' Rajibehn related. 'The officer was going down the line of sellers sticking out his hand. We each put Rs. 2 in it. If we do not, he starts roughing us up with his stick, or kicking our vegetables. If he gets especially perturbed, he calls the municipal van and confiscates our vegetables or arrests us. All of a sudden, Nirubehn grabbed the policeman's hand as he was taking a two rupee note. She said, "What are you doing?" He said, "Nothing." She said, "You are extorting from these poor vendors again!" He said, "How will you prove that?" She reached her hand in his pocket, and a whole wad of crumpled one and two rupee notes fell out. She called a rickshaw, and told the policeman to get into it. She was holding him by his arm, and said, "We are going to go visit the Police Superintendent and see if he still wants you to wear that badge." '

'He was really frightened, and called two other officers to help him. They came and pleaded with Nirubehn, saying "Please leave him, he has small children at home!" '

'Nirubehn said, "Does he ever leave these vendors? Don't they also have small children?" '

'They said, "Please! We will never bother these vendors again!" Ever since that day, they have not even entered this lane. When they walk by this street, they join their hands in "Namaste" and keep going!'

Once some effective action like this has been taken, self-employed women begin to feel that SEWA is really *their* organization. Rajibehn said that 'after this incident, I walked to every market in the city to bring new members into the union.'

Knowing that they had this backing, other vendors also began to resist the extortion of the police. It happened for Valumbehn, a woman who sold vegetables in the Jamapura area. An officer began harassing her for a bribe around 5 o'clock in the evening, which is the peak period for vegetable vendors. She told him to come back later after the peak period was over, but he persisted, so she simply snatched his sash with his badge and sat on it. This police-man kept calling SEWA and hovering around Valumbehn, but she and Nirubehn had decided that they were not in any hurry to return the badge. When the Superintendent called to apologize, Nirubehn officially earned her 'Commissioner' title—she obliged him by returning the badge on his pledge to let the vendors sell peacefully.

During its initial surveys and struggles, SEWA found that 97 per cent of the members were slum-dwellers, 93 per cent were illiterate, and on an average each woman had four living children. The bottom line for every woman they met was that she did not have enough money. Vendors, who generally had a higher income than most of the other groups of self-employed women, attributed their financial problems to their daily losses to the police or muni-cipality and the high interest they paid on working capital. For instance, it was not unusual for a vendor to borrow Rs. 50 each morning to purchase vegetables, return Rs. 55 to the money-lender in the evening, and repeat the same cycle indefinitely. While pro-viders of labour and services earn the median income of the self-employed trade groups, home-based workers, despite being skilled artisans, earned the lowest income of any group of self-employed women, contributing to their lack of self-esteem as workers. Among the women who were stitching garments, cartpulling and making wood and metal utility items, the most common problem was that they did not own their own tools of trade or production. Besides complaining about the exorbitant rate at which they hired their tools, they all said, when asked about their priorities: 'We need more work, more work!' Some of them were already working 16 hours a day!

Out of this statement, countless issues were distilled. Despite long hours of tedious or strenuous work, their incomes were simply insufficient for their families' needs. While 78 per cent of the women did not own their tools of trade, none of the producers had wholesale access to raw materials. Earning only enough each day for that day's food meant 60 per cent of the women SEWA came in contact with were in debt. In case of an emergency, they were compelled to borrow money. If they used their daily working capital to buy food for their family, they had to borrow money at high rates of interest to do their business the next day. For women who were the sole supporters of their family—30 per cent of the women surveyed were—these circumstances were manifested in acutely desperate situations. It was also observed that 70 per cent of the surveyed women had to carry their children along with them to the work site. Children of market vendors were exposed to filthy street conditions and the danger of traffic on the roads where their mothers sold goods. Children of cartpullers were exposed to extreme heat and vehicular pollution, as they were slung in cradles below the carts, or rode on top of loads if they were slightly older.

For these and countless other issues, these women did not have either the leverage or the awareness to ask for a better deal from anyone. Their only choice was to accept the interest rate fixed by the money-lender or not to borrow. They had to pay the asking retail price for their raw materials, or not work. They had to take their children along, or leave them alone. They had to accept the piece-rate offered by the trader for production work, or he would give the work to someone else. They had to pay the rental fees fixed by the contractors for their tools, or not produce. Thus the only solution they could see to their problems in their isolation and vulnerability was 'more work.'

SEWA retaliated by developing generalized strategies to overcome these conditions. They articulated their goals in a small pamphlet they published, 'Profiles of Self-Employed Women':

There are certain practical truths they (self-employed women) need to realize in their own interests, (i) to be healthy in order to avoid loss of work days, (ii) to be literate enough to avoid being trapped into corrupt practices, (iii) to improve their skills by better training in the modern sense, in order to increase their bargaining power, (iv) to learn to save in order to build their own capital or to make use of credit facilities for productive purposes.[6]

Organizing around these goals helped hundreds and then thousands of women come together as *workers* to begin shattering the myths of their isolation. They stopped reiterating fictitious middle class perceptions that 'women are in the home,' and that 'women do not work.' They stopped believing that they were at the mercy of the contractors, or passively accepting the violence and harassment of the police. They started believing that through their struggle, they *could* stop police harassment or secure minimum wages, or get other relevant demands met.

THE FIRST INTERVENTION: CREDIT

The initial gains were seen when SEWA secured self-employed women access to institutional sources of credit at fair interest rates. Fair credit acted as a huge membership draw for the organization, immediately solving women's problems of working capital by giving them sufficient resources to buy their own equipment or raw materials. SEWA's credit plan was benefited by the central government's poverty eradication campaign of the early seventies. Under Prime Minister Indira Gandhi, the government put pressure on the nationalized banks to allocate up to 1 per cent of their loan portfolios to families falling below the official poverty line. Since the banks had no previous models to go by and SEWA was a recognized organization representing the poor, the banks agreed to lend money through SEWA. After some initial success with the Bank of India, the State Bank of India approached SEWA to help link them to clientele.

SEWA organized group leaders to contact women from their trades to come to SEWA and fill out loan applications. Time was spent educating women about what banks did, how they worked, and what women would be responsible for if they were granted a loan. SEWA designed the application form for the banks, helped the members complete them, and upon approval accompanied the woman to the bank which was granting the loan to help her secure the money.

'Through this programme, our membership suddenly swelled to almost 3000 members,' Ela recalled. 'Sometimes it was overwhelming. A group of 20 vendors would come together in a group. They were so excited, they would all rush toward me and begin shouting at once, no matter if I was dealing with another group. Sometimes fights would break out when people got impatient with waiting. Sometimes the other organizers and I would have to go into my office and bolt the door. For five minutes we would catch our breath, and then go out to face the crowds again. By the end of the day, the TLA hall was a mess from discarded bidi butts, snuff spit, and children's messes. Each day we would sit and work out solutions to the problems we encountered that day.'

Chanda, who by this time had become an active group leader and brought many used-garments traders to the union for loans, later commented, 'I could see how much trouble the *behns* were having controlling the crowds, so I helped them keep order. For me it was just what I had to do everyday in the market!'

Once women began receiving their loans, the nationalized banks experienced identical problems with a little less patience. SEWA women visited the banks in large groups and took along all their children. Since the only buildings they generally entered were other people's houses, and where they would ask for water when they were thirsty, they would also ask the bank tellers for water. They came in their dirty work clothes. They often went to the wrong bank because they got confused about which branch or which bank they were responsible to. They stood in the wrong queues, and the tellers had to fill out all their receipts for them. Bank employees did not understand women's work schedules and how difficult it was to get away from the market or from their production work. They were impatient if their clients showed up at the wrong time, or gave vague addresses like, 'Laxmibehn from Jamapura.' A few hundred women fit that identity, which led to confusion. If a woman came with money and could not deposit it, it was often spent on the way home to buy some essentials, or in retaliation for being refused.

As SEWA organizers and group leaders worked to sort out these difficulties, they also found that because the size of the loan was large (Rs. 500–Rs. 1500—about US $50–150), women often deposited their money with the very same traders or money-lenders from whom SEWA was trying to free its members. If women did not deposit the money somewhere, it was often spent by their husbands or other family members for unproductive purposes.

At one meeting called to discuss some of the difficulties women were facing with their loans, several hundred women stood up one after another recounting their problems with the banks. Chanda, who was quickly becoming an articulate spokeswoman for the self-employed, again voiced a popular opinion. She said, 'Behn, why can't we have our *own* bank?'

A few other women also picked up the idea, and started echoing the request.

Elabehn responded, 'How will we have a bank, we are so poor? It will take at least Rs. 100,000—that's a hundred rupees a thousand times—for share capital.'

Another vendor said, 'Behn we are poor, but look how many we are!' Once again, spontaneous cheering broke out in consensus. Following this meeting, the members started visiting all the small lanes of the slums and selling places of the markets, raising the necessary share capital to launch a cooperative bank.

In the meantime, the Registrar of Cooperative Banks expressed scepticism and resistance to the idea of a bank for poor, illiterate women. First of all he asked, 'How can you have a bank of *women*, who do not have any control of income in the family?' Once SEWA women disillusioned him of that middle class idea, he argued that illiterate people could never manage a bank, and that it would be a suicidal attempt. As SEWA developed the strategy of putting a photograph of every woman holding a slate with her account number on her pass-book, Elabehn was working in her own shrewd and gentle way of demonstrating the needs of SEWA's members to officials who had conceptual blocks.

Chanda had Rs. 350 of basically rotten money. Some of it was in coins which had been stored in a tin, they had become wet and defaced with rust. The rest was torn and soiled rupee notes which people had traded her for used clothes. Chandabehn took the money to SEWA and asked Elabehn if she could help her exchange them in the bank. Elabehn took the money to the Cooperative

Bank department and asked them to change it. They asked her, 'How can we accept this ruined money?' She responded, 'As long as you do not give us our own bank, this is what happens to poor women's money in their *kaccha* (temporary, mud, grass, salvaged material) houses!'

With these kinds of persuasions, and SEWA's concrete display of intention by raising the share money within six months, the state registered them as the Mahila SEWA Sahakari Bank in July 1974. This was accomplished after 15 members sat up the entire night prior to registration, learning how to sign their names, so that they could be promoting members of the bank.

SEWA Bank would continue to act as an intermediary for the nationalized bank loans for the next two years, but now women could carry out all their transactions at their own bank. Illiteracy was no longer a barrier, and now women had a safe place to deposit their money which their husbands did not have access to. Many women kept their pass-books at the bank itself, so that their families did not even know about their loans or savings.

While this work was going on at home, SEWA played an important role in the globally growing women's movement. Bhatt attended the Mexico City Conference in 1975 for the United Nations International Women's Year, sitting on panels and sharing the experiences of the union and banking work, as SEWA was one of the few groups represented which had some experience. With the subsequent Decade for Women, this conference marked the beginning of international organizations turning to SEWA as a resource in the women's movement.

At that meeting, Bhatt met Michela Walsh, a US Wall Street investment broker. Based on inspiration generated at that meeting, Walsh went on to launch Women's World Banking (WWB), which since 1981 has been extending loan guarantees to women around the world who previously did not have access to credit. Both SEWA and Bhatt (who now chairs the WWB's Board of Directors) have had a long lasting working relationship with the WWB.

PROBLEMS FOR THE BANK

In spite of giving inspiration to others to extend credit to poor women, SEWA Bank was still young and had its own share of difficulties to face and solutions to work out. Largely because of the push given by the government to extend credit, in 1976 almost 9000 loans had been extended through SEWA. As repayment problems began to surface, and SEWA organizers tried to follow up, they found that many women were simply not in a position to repay. This was for a variety of reasons: frequent illness in the family; unsteady employment situation of the husband, or no husband; frequent pregnancies leading to loss of work; social customs involving heavy expenditure—marriages, deaths, religious festivals; no access to cheap raw materials; no access to markets, and thus forced to sell to traders at lower rates; old debts which kept them bonded to previous traders or money-lenders; and the expense of hiring their tools of trade.

'While those loans were a boon to us, we still had many problems,' said Santokbehn Pritviraj—a gaunt, weathered looking carpenter—when asked about repayment problems for junk-smiths in the early years of SEWA Bank. 'I used the loan I took to buy a month's worth of wood at wholesale. I made good profits and could pay back my loan easily. My husband was in Trivandrum, so I did not have troubles. My sister had many problems with her loan, though. Her husband was unemployed and took half of her money to pay off some old debts. On top of that, many of our men drink. If they are unemployed, they drink even more. Where was this liquor money to come from? We would save what we could to give the bank, but what could we tell the *behns* when my sister's husband beat her to take that money for his own use? Or, when her children fell sick and the money meant for her loan went to buy them medicine? When our lives are like this, how can we repay regularly?'

The challenges facing SEWA Bank at this juncture were obviously many. They realized that self-employed women's lives needed to be viable before their loans would be viable. Further, the bank's repayment difficulties were compounded during the years of the Emergency by a government moratorium on repayment of debts by the rural poor. The moratorium announced in July 1975 only pardoned those indebted to money-lenders, but many SEWA borrowers interpreted this to cover government-sponsored loans as well and stopped repaying. All of SEWA's fieldworkers had to work full time to rectify the situation. It was both a painful and an educational experience for SEWA. As Nirubehn recalled:

'We were trying to convince all the women who had taken loans that all of us were responsible to repay. Half were repaying regularly. Some of the others understood, and wanted to repay, but they just could not. If one of them gave us Rs. 10 or Rs. 20 to put toward her instalment, we wanted to give half back to her, so that she could buy food for that day. Others said, "Why are you pressuring us for this money when even the government is saying we do not have to pay?" Afterwards we realized it was sometimes easier to say "the government has excused us" than it was to admit that they *could not* pay. And though SEWA was trying to get the banks to clarify that people *were* responsible for their loans, they would not take any stand. This made it very difficult. The women who were repaying would point to their neighbours and say, "Look, she is not repaying, and nothing is happening to her. Why should I?" '

'This was the first time we came under criticism from our membership, and it was painful. Even more sobering than this criticism, though, was seeing how deeply our members' economic problems ran. From that point our *real* work began and we have built a much stronger bank based on that difficult year.'

Over the next few years, in an attempt to be responsive to its members' needs, the bank along with the union began to develop an integrated set of services for self-employed women, aimed at making their loans more productive and their lives more viable. Supportive services included helping loan applicants find the cheapest source of raw materials, and when possible, better marketing outlets. Women in the same occupations were grouped together to do bulk buying. They helped women find and negotiate production space, and linked them to government subsidies for helping them purchase their own tools of trade. In 1976, SEWA Bank had enough deposits to begin advancing loans from its own funds. This also helped repayment because women viewed the money as SEWA's, rather than the government's.

The bank also became better at assessing and verifying women's ability to repay a loan. If a used-garments dealer who was earning Rs. 250 per month wanted a Rs. 1000 loan to go to Bombay and purchase a surplus of cheaper garments, this kind of loan was generally sanctioned. If a woman who earned Rs. 150 per month requested a Rs. 3000 loan for her daughter's marriage, she was usually refused. One of SEWA Bank's commitments at this time was to create a climate in which women could break the old social customs which perpetuated their unproductive debts.†

The major accomplishments of the bank by the late seventies were that many women owned their own tools of production; they had been freed from their old private debts at high interest rates; and many had recovered their valuable jewellery—often a woman's only asset which is pawned at a fraction of its value, and which many poor women are usually never able to free themselves from debt enough to repossess.

SOCIAL SECURITY NEEDS

This phase of SEWA Bank coincided with their survey of defaulters which revealed a high incidence of maternal deaths amongst SEWA borrowers (see chapter 1). To address this problem SEWA attempted to link its members to social security benefits through governmental or institutional sources of insurance benefits. The Life Insurance Corporation of India denied them coverage, saying that poor women were not a 'profitable proposition.' As SEWA members and organizers discussed how to initiate some social security services, the members were adamant that they could not afford to pay regular premium for insurance. Ela suggested that they all donate one day's wages. From this small beginning and a contribution from the TLA, they established the Mahila SEWA Trust in 1975 to support social services and development programmes for the members.

From the Maternal Protection Scheme—the Trust's first project

† Though subsequently SEWA has given in on this. These customs die hard in tightly knit poor communities which depend on social approval and support. There has been a gradual trend toward sanctioning even these loans—if the woman has proved herself a good repayer—to help keep her free of the private lenders. While Bhatt is self-critical of this leniency, it is also a strength of the organization, that they give women access to skills, resources, and education while leaving them free to their own decisions. It reduces the dependencies that develop when others dictate, and avoids setting up the same power relationships women had with private lenders or contractors who dictated their lives through controlling their money.

(see chapter 1)—they went on to offer a widowhood assistance scheme to help a member survive in the period immediately following her husband's death, when most Indian women stay at home to observe a month of mourning. Following on the heels of this, they established a long succession of creches and *aanganwadis* (nursery schools) which would offer mothers and their children other options than the street or the cramped working environments which their tiny homes turn into when production work takes place. When Bhatt received the Magsaysay Award in 1977, she donated the award money of $20,000 to the Trust, which gave it its first major source of income.

On other health fronts, SEWA concentrated on changing the conditions which contributed to women's poor health. SEWA struggled for four years to get members out of the slums and into low cost government housing, but it failed to move the government to allocate houses from low income schemes to women workers.

SEWA negotiated for fair wages so that a woman and her family could consistently have enough to eat. It linked members to the most appropriate health care available. SEWA worked to improve their occupational health conditions—an enormous task, as self-employed women often are involved in the most strenuous physical tasks using the crudest equipment, or are continuously exposed to harmful chemical substances.

In SEWA's first decade they repeatedly tried literacy training, but met with limited response. As Ela described it, 'I knocked my head against the wall for years.' Self-employed women were too busy in their day-to-day struggle for income and caring for their families to spare time for something which they could not immediately perceive the benefits of.

'It was difficult to even show up for a reading session if that day's food money was not earned yet,' Ela said. In later years literacy training achieved greater success when the training was relevant to a specific need, but really the effect has been generational. The daughters of SEWA members are encouraged to attend and stay in school (which they are able to do only if their mothers' work lives are made more remunerative), and younger women from self-employed trades are the ones now entering positions where literacy skills are needed. Even this, however, has been more of an urban than rural trend. In 1990, Ela still chastised herself for not protesting enough over girls' withdrawal or exclusion from school.

While SEWA challenged the paradigms of welfare versus empowerment, of unions organizing only industrial workers at the expense of the self-employed, and of a women's movement focused mainly on issues of middle class and elite women, the women SEWA represented were still mired in a low skilled, low asset reality. Despite significant gains, the daily hunger reality drew the lines around the vision of change that these women were able to project for themselves.

END NOTES

1. Renana Jhabvala, *Closing Doors: A Study on the Decline in Women Workers in the Textile Mills of Ahmedabad*. SETU. New Delhi: Tej Press, 1985.
2. This history of the TLA taken from their pamphlet, 'Six Decades of Textile Labour Association, Ahmedabad', 1977.
3. This account of Vaghari trades and work problems compiled from 1988–89 interviews with many Vaghari women in Ahmedabad who helped build SEWA in its first decade.
4. The major laws relating to hawkers are the Indian Railway Act, 1819, and the Bombay Municipal Act, 1882. SEWA's legal advisor points out that these laws have hardly been changed since their inception, despite 40 years of Independence from the instigators of these laws.
5. These figures are taken from a SEWA study of 500 used-garments vendors in 1980.
6. Ela Bhatt, *Profiles of Self-Employed Women*. Ahmedabad: SEWA, 1976, p. 19.

3

Independence

In all my life, I have never worn a gold earring or nosepin. I have never worn new clothes any day of my life. I wore your frock, somebody else's salwar and somebody else's odni. I am surprised at this age to say that I have never worn new clothes any day of my life . . . . All I want from Allah is a full-time job so that I can feed my children.
Khatoon Abdulla Golaiwalla, firewood collector and nursery worker of Junagadh.[1]

While SEWA brought public visibility to the exploitation women were facing and created pressure on the system to change some of these conditions, it also became clear that struggle in conventional trade union terms would not suffice. It was not clear at first, however, that developing alternatives would push them out of the conventional trade union structure that originally inspired them. The shortcomings of conventional tactics came home to SEWA most forcefully in two situations in the early years: the first was in 1976 when agricultural workers from Zamp village came to Ahmedabad seeking help from the TLA. They had heard on the radio that minimum wages had been fixed by the state for agricultural labour, and were wondering who could help them secure these wages. SEWA organizers went along with the TLA organizers to assess the problems of the rural labourers. While organizing them into a union called the Agricultural Labour Association (ALA), SEWA noticed that there were no women members. At SEWA's insistence, they registered women labourers only to find that they outnumbered the men!

The events that followed revealed the difficulties they would face working in rural areas. Caste, feudal, and gender hierarchies were stronger in the villages than in most urban communities. In 1976, the employment situation in 25 villages of Ahmedabad district where they conducted surveys and held meetings was dismal: the land was stony, extremely saline, and drought-prone. There was only 4–10 inches of annual rainfall. Further, 81 per cent of the households were landless, yet 78 per cent of them depended on agricultural labour for their income. Most of these landless labourers experienced 200 days of unemployment every year. Women outnumbered men as labourers because many men migrated to Ahmedabad in search of work, leaving the women to manage the family in the village.

The minimum wages at that time were Rs. 5.50 per day, but most women labourers were earning Rs. 3. Meetings were held every night to discuss low wages, non-payment of wages, extremely long hours of work during transplanting and harvesting followed by uncertainty of work for the remaining eight months. Despite the meetings being stoned by unknown boys, labourers and organizers drafted a charter of demands for minimum wages which they sent to the Labour Commissioner.

In the meantime, the union organizers met local employers to demand minimum wages. In the village Bhayla, the 'landlords verbally agreed but proceeded to terrorize the labourers. The ALA asked the Labour department to mediate. The employers were required to pay minimum wages to workers in the presence of the officers. That night, SEWA organizers heard a noise and saw a fire in the fields. They found that their members were being beaten by a police party called by the landlords. After the immediate violence, the employers continued to victimize the local women by hiring labour from outside the village.

In another village, Devdholera, where the landlords tried to hire people from outside, the women were strong in the union. They did not allow any outside labourer to enter the fields by keeping a vigil for three weeks during the harvest season. Though they were successful in keeping their work, they were still a long way from receiving the minimum wages. The physical blows and the threats of no work made the organizers realize that the main cause of labourers' low wages was their lack of employment opportunities. Conventional union-style work would never be effective under these circumstances.

RURAL ALTERNATIVES

The ALA moved on, but SEWA stayed on to try other strategies of organizing rural women. They found 27 families who had previously been weavers working as labourers on farms or digging roads. Increasingly impoverished, they had lost the means to purchase raw materials for weaving. SEWA sent a weaving teacher to help them get their looms working again, and linked the weavers to rural banks, for credit for purchasing wool.* The weavers resumed producing woollen blankets, selling them in their traditional markets and earning about Rs. 150 per month. No one will argue that this is a large income, but for people who were previously earning Rs. 70–Rs. 90 cash income per month for only part of the year, consistent income was a blessing. It served to pressurize the landlords to raise the daily agricultural labour wages also. When offered only Rs. 3 to work in the fields for the day, the re-established weavers would stay home to weave. The landlords offered better wages without any demands being stated simply because they needed their work done.[2]

This experience set the stage for SEWA exploring more extensively the need for a strong multiple-occupation base for families with little or no land to enable them to earn income throughout the year.

URBAN ALTERNATIVES FOR STITCHERS

While this work was unfolding in rural areas, a kind of parallel struggle was going on in the Muslim community of Dariapur in

---

* Not until 1988 did SEWA Bank get government permission to extend its scope to direct lending and savings in rural areas.

Ahmedabad's inner city, with different results. Dariapur is an old neighbourhood, with thousands of tiny houses built next to and on top of each other. Most of the women in this neighbourhood are engaged in stitching, or some other home-based activity, as there is a general observation of *purdah*. Although many of the houses have been made permanent over the years—often by using the severance pay of the retrenched mill workers—majority of them are no larger than 8' x 10' in size. The temporary houses are even smaller, with neither any natural light nor any facilities. Thus the narrow footpaths that snake through this community form a large part of the production space for stitchers.

In 1978, women who stitched *khols* for local contractors were earning Re. 0.60 (then about US $0.06) per quilt. Khols are quilts patched together from small scraps of textile waste and sold in the open market to the urban and rural poor. Each khol requires one to two hours of work, with the women stitchers bearing the costs of thread, sewing machine, and oil themselves. After these deductions, a woman was barely earning Rs. 3 after 10 hours of labour.

Karimabibi, presently Vice-President of the union, was a major catalyst for getting these women organized. She is a short rounding woman, who has worn spectacles ever since her eyesight deteriorated because of stitching. She laughs freely while she speaks—just one of the courageous gestures she evinces in surroundings of poverty.

She was forced to leave school when she was 11, to contribute her labour to winding bobbins and adding to the family's income. She attests that despite leaving school, she was clever at math and continued practising her calculating skills in the family businesses. She moved from bobbin winding, to garment stitching, and then when traders began to see the profitability of stitching quilts from the mill waste, she took up that work. When she saw her production costs just about equalling her income, she approached her contractor to ask for higher wages. One of her relatives who worked in the TLA's Dariapur centre heard her arguments with her contractor, and suggested she visit SEWA. She and a few other women went to the TLA and told Elabehn their grievances.

SEWA organizers went to their *mohulla* and spent time with the stitchers for 10 days, holding meetings and talking about their problems. They organized 600 khol stitchers and set out to make a demand for Rs. 1.25 per quilt.

'We negotiated unsuccessfully for weeks,' Karima related in an interview, 'so we staged a strike. After striking 10 days the merchants finally agreed to Re. 1 per quilt. It became clear within one day, though, that they were not going to honour their agreement. What they did instead was to harass us. They gave bad materials to sew and then rejected the quilts we made from them. Or they would say, "Today there is no chindi. Come back tomorrow," when we could see tons of chindi behind them. After 10 days of strike we were hungry. I was just widowed and like many others, completely supporting myself and my two daughters on my stitching income.'

She was not the only woman whose position worsened after they voiced their demands for a wage increase. The traders chose the most vulnerable women to victimize. SEWA used its TLA contact to get a small quantity of chindi from the mills, and gave the most victimized women work independent of the traders. Thirty-five per cent of those who got together to form this new production unit were widows, divorced, or deserted women, and 58 per cent had husbands who were unemployed or only sporadically employed.[3]

Innumerable problems arose in the course of this chindi venture. Although these women were good stitchers, neither they nor any of the organizers had experience in the other aspects of the trade. The acquisition of chindi from the mills, the grading and sorting, distributing it to women by weight, collecting the finished product, selling the khols, and maintaining accounts—these had never been dealt with by the stitchers who were largely home-bound by gender and religious constraints. While SEWA provided employment to the victimized women for some time, it did not want to become another trader—it had a larger vision in mind.

Since Bhatt had attended the Afro-Asian Institute of Labor and Cooperatives in Tel Aviv in 1971, and had seen the Israeli example of the joint action of the union and the cooperatives, she believed this was the way to empower poor women. 'Gandhiji gave us our indigenous example of struggle alongside of the constructive programme,' she related, 'but this workshop crystallized for me *how* to manifest it.'

The union was strong, supported by the TLA experience and contacts and their own successful cooperative banking venture. SEWA now saw the chindi women's struggle as the next place to build a cooperative. Their struggles in this venture were not small nor did success come quickly. The shift in consciousness from piece-rate workers to worker-owners was a monumental one. For women who had never ventured out of their community to learn to deal with male mill agents as the only women in the city purchasing chindi, for illiterate women to learn accounting, for stitchers to learn sound business strategies, and for a small production unit to break into the larger market represented no small odds.[4]

'We all got first-hand experience in how to resist the attempts of vested interests to break us,' Karimabibi recalled. 'Traders undercut our prices. They could sustain short term losses in the interest of long term profits if they put us out of business. They kept interrupting our chindi supply through their old deals with mill managers by giving them a cut to get our materials. Then they bribed some of our chindi stitchers out of the coop with offers of cuts and higher wages. When these tactics did not break us, the traders started to spread defamatory rumours about us. We were breaking social customs by going out to purchase chindi and run our shop, so it was easy to spread other stories about our behaviour.'

All the women who got together at the time of the khol crises in 1977, with no models or experience to work from, can now say that they have shaped a concrete model for other women's cooperatives to work from. Bilquish Bano was one of these women. The brief history she gave of herself reveals how vulnerable women are to the decisions of others over their lives.

'I was married when I was 14. Not until four years later, when I was describing my husband to a friend, did I discover that he was a hermaphrodite. My father got me divorced then and married me to another man. This man used to beat me and lock me in the house, sometimes for a few days at a time. After slowly selling off all of my things, he took us out one day, ordered tea, and just walked away. We never heard from him again.'

After this, occupying a *kaccha* hut, Bilquish supported her two children and her mother by hawking and cleaning houses in the slums. She previously had sorted chindi for a khol trader, but quit when he refused to pay her Rs. 2 per day for her work. One day she passed the SEWA shop and saw that the sorters did not know what they were doing. No one asked her to help, she just sat down and started sorting. After they saw her skill, no one asked her to leave. The losses the unit was suffering due to low quality production were suddenly reduced and Bilquish just stayed on. She had both business acumen and an insider's awarenesss of which women most desperately needed work. SEWA hired a tutor to teach her math and literacy skills. She eventually learned to manage the shop which the SEWA cooperative purchased in the row of shops where their former contractors sold khols, and was nominated to the Board of Directors of the SEWA Bank.

Renana Jhabvala, who now heads the union, took this chindi struggle on as her first organizing project when she left her doctoral studies at Yale to work with SEWA. She is an intense, articulate woman who has the unusual capacity for immediate thoughtful action. Her paternal grandparents were leading figures in the freedom struggle, and her fair looks borrow partly from her Polish-born mother, Ruth Prawer Jhabvala, the famous novelist. Though Renana now thinks seriously before she speaks, her colleagues attest that in her early years at SEWA, she was less tempered in her speaking—impetuous and angry at the injustices she saw. Then or now, she always speaks what she thinks.

Renana was the first young, 'modern', highly educated woman to come to work at SEWA. When she arrived in Ahmedabad, she almost immediately abandoned the theoretical research she had come to do for the Indian Council of Social Science Research to get down to the practical business that needed attention. She is adept at culling the relevant points out of issues and information, which makes her a sharp organizer. She is guarded about her personal self, and subsumes the personal for SEWA work. Ela commented about her: 'She is not an intellectual—though she is so intelligent—because she is an activist in the true sense of the word. I think she never returned to complete her Ph.D. for the reason that she believed it would be only a personal gain, but not that useful to SEWA.'

As a full-time organizer she has first-hand knowledge about the critical issues of the self-employed which need research. In the decade since joining, Renana has contributed several important studies on the retrenchment of women workers in industry, and on the conditions and legal status of many trades of home-based workers, including the chindi workers.

The chindi workers' experiences were some of the earliest to define for SEWA the importance of policy change which favours poor women. The supply of chindi is extremely limited, especially since the closure of many mills. SEWA requested the government to give priority to chindi *producers* (rather than merchants) in supplying raw material from government mills. Members say that their cooperative would not have survived the vested interests' tactics if the government had not agreed to this policy in their favour.

Through the chindi project, SEWA found confirmation of the importance of cooperatives as an organizing tool. For the first time in their lives, these women *owned* something and had decision-making power over it. Women were earning steady incomes which, even if still meagre, lent stability to their day-to-day lives. They saw that along with the union lobbying for policy change or negotiating with employers, cooperatives could be a political force. Two strategic moves on Sabina Cooperative's part compelled the merchants in the city to pay higher rates to *all* the women khol stitchers—organized or not—and illustrated the leverage cooperatives could exert.

'Whenever we approached the merchants for a wage hike,' Karima described, 'they always protested that they were barely breaking even. They said that if they had to give a raise it would close them down. "Then *no* stitchers will get work," they always said. Well, here we were as proof that you *could* pay fairer wages and not go under.' Because the cooperative was paying more, the merchants had to relent.

'The smartest thing we did to work a substantial raise for all the chindi stitchers happened when the traders were facing economic troubles. The government wanted to impose a tax on all the chindi taken from the mills. The chindi traders who originally broke our agreement for a wage increase now approached *us*, asking for *our* help in opposing the tax! They claimed that this higher cost for raw materials would further cut into poor women's wages. We had a hard time believing that they were suddenly so concerned for our welfare! We went to the Labour Minister and demanded that he *not* lift the imposed tax unless the traders agreed to pay higher piece-rates to their stitchers. He agreed, and the traders were compelled to give a raise. This made us feel our strength. We had finally found our leverage points.'

Women were also experiencing non-economic benefits through their union and cooperatives. Due to her on-going negotiations with the Labour Commissioner, labour officers, and chindi merchants, Karima acquired a reputation for following the footsteps of Ansuyabehn Sarabhai. While Ansuyabehn represented the interests

of workers against mill-owners who included her brother half a
century earlier, Karimabibi was representing the interests of her
sister workers against merchants who included her brother.

She described the shift in attitudes her work with SEWA effected
in her community: 'For years my neighbours' tongues wagged
against me as I went openly about my business—"She has no
shame", "She likes to roam about"—things like that. Now they
have seen that I sit with important officials and that I am Vice-
President of a big union. They see how this work has improved the
lives of their families. Now those same people sometimes come to
me for advice. *That* is something for a widow in this place!'

DISPLACED ARTISANS

By 1978, SEWA was moving quickly, pursuing several alternative
economic ventures for its members. Through the surveys and
contacts with women approaching the bank, SEWA had come into
contact with the many problems traditional artisans were facing.
Their products were rapidly being displaced by modern goods
which they did not have the skills or opportunities to produce.

Saira Bukhari, a woman who does traditional handblock printing
of cotton fabrics, described the problems her community (Chhipas)
faced in the seventies: 'We were all working for a trader, only
doing the printing work. Our designs were somewhat crude, mostly
for bedsheets. We could not earn more than Rs. 2 or Rs. 3 per
day. Screen printing had taken most of our market. Who wanted
this work when the mass produced bedsheets were cheaper? Also,
customs had changed from the days when my parents were blocking
cloth. Hardly anyone was wearing this traditional cloth anymore.
Like widows—how many widows do you see in the old block
printed mourning saris anymore? So some of us came to SEWA to
get loans for sewing machines. All we could think to do was learn a
new trade.'

SEWA's response, rather than giving loans for sewing machines,
was to train these women in more refined block printing techniques
which appealed to a modern middle class market. With support
from the All India Handicrafts Board, these women were given

training in the entire production process so that they could do their own work. Previously they knew only one aspect of the production process (the printing) which they did on a piece-rate basis, making contractors' strongholds practically impossible to resist.

Saira and other artisans who took training participated in a three-day camp sponsored by the Handicrafts Board in Delhi, where each woman artisan role played as the Chief Minister of State and spoke about the changes she would make to help women artisans like herself. Ela attributes this role-playing by SEWA women to be a major factor in bringing visibility to women artisans.

'What the bamboo, block printing, and chindi women said at that meeting became a kind of policy statement,' she recalled in an interview. 'The Vice Chairman of the Indian Planning Commission, M.S. Swaminathan, had come to deliver the valedictory address on the closing day. He was overwhelmed by what the women said, and asked us to send him a memorandum of what they suggested. From that workshop and memorandum, a chapter for "A Fair Deal for the Self-employed" came for the first time in the Sixth Five-Year Plan (1980).' Policy changes were surfacing.

THE DAIRY MOVEMENT

In 1978, looking for ways to strengthen rural women's existing employment and create new opportunities, SEWA approached the National Dairy Development Board, which was networking dairy cooperatives throughout the state. Ela wanted to know why there were no women's dairy cooperatives, and why women had been excluded from the numerous training programmes sponsored by the NDDB. SEWA organizers pointed out that women were entirely responsible for cattle care and milking, yet none of the income from this work reached them. The NDDB proffered several excuses: that women could not understand the written training material; that the sophisticated techniques of cattle care and co-operative management would be too difficult for them; and that women could not come so far or spend the night for the training sessions.

SEWA offered to send women who would disprove these assumptions, if the NDDB would develop non-formal training materials. The NDDB agreed, and SEWA brought 25 women from Zhamp village to Ahmedabad for the training. The women thrived on both the training and their first exposure to the world outside of the village.

Over the next eight years 35 more groups of women were exposed to this training. With funds from the International Confederation of Free Trade Unions, SEWA set up a rural training headquarters in the village of Devdholera, from where it organized 15 dairy cooperatives. Only three of these original 15 survived against the forces of male domination, caste hierarchy, and political and private vested interests which could not tolerate women cornering the ever increasing milk market, but the number highlights how eager women were to start new ventures which might improve their economic situation. The number also gave SEWA some in-depth experience in how to deal with the many defiant heads rearing against rural women's empowerment. Like the bank, SEWA has now set up stronger milk cooperatives based on the experiences of those initial years. SEWA's early all-women's models lent inspiration to other state dairies and the NDDB, and women's dairy cooperatives now stretch extensively across Andhra Pradesh and Bihar as well.

VENDORS' PROTESTS

While many rapid gains were being achieved through SEWA on women's work fronts, they were still experiencing other blatant insensitivity and setbacks. In Ahmedabad, the municipality decided that kerosene vendors in the city needed to be licensed. When SEWA vendors went to apply, they were refused licences simply because they were women. The licensing officer said that women did not vend kerosene, and if they did, they should not—they should be at home.

The other vendors, too, were still facing severe harassment by the police and municipality. Though the used-clothes vendors had evolved some effective ways of dealing with harassment, they still faced problems. Whenever one of them was arrested, Chandabehn was called.

'Once a sister got arrested because the police thought she had stolen the expensive sari she was trying to sell,' Chandabehn described. 'I rounded up many Vagharis and sent them to the jail. Then I went to the house where the sister had traded for the sari. I got that *behn* to come with me to the police station. She testified that she had traded that sari with my sister for vessels, but the police did not want to believe us. They looked from me, to this rich *behn*, to all the Vagharis standing outside. What could they do but release my sister? Even then, they insult us. Do you think they said they were sorry for the mistake? No. They said, "This is the first time we have ever released one of you without a confession. You Vagharis are all thieves."'

Discrimination against the vendors persisted. Vegetable vendors in the main market experienced this most intensely and persistently. Since 1973, SEWA has been working with women in markets across Ahmedabad to secure licences and delineated, legal vending spots. By 1978, having received no consideration of their demands or applications, the vendors decided to make their petitions and protests public. Nearly 2000 vendors gathered in the main market on Independence Day and marched in protest against police harassment.

These processions, though infrequent, always create one of the strongest impacts of any of SEWA's strategies. Observers witness thousands of poor women marching together, carrying their children in their arms and in the case of vendors, with their vegetable baskets on their heads. Those without children wield placards decrying police extortion and brutality, or demanding licences. Many come barefoot or in their old, torn clothes. Strength and defiance are clearly visible in their voices and gestures as they shout slogans demanding recognition and justice.

This first procession of vendors wound through the city past the Municipal Corporation to the Parade Grounds next to the main police station. They invited the Chief Minister to address their demands at this meeting. They were again affronted by official insensitivity when he stood up and asked why they did not go back to the villages they had come from![5]

Despite this remark, he later organized meetings in which the city officials verbally agreed to SEWA's demand for allotting selling space to the vendors. However, when licences were still not forthcoming, SEWA members began to present their union cards whenever an officer confronted them. These cards worked as a sort of talisman against harassment. Officers were increasingly reluctant to deal with the union which was now known to press legal charges for assault and to approach the higher authorities when bribes were taken.

The situation came to a head for the main market vendors, however, in 1980, when a cyclist was assaulted in the market and a riot ensued. The authorities clamped a curfew on Manek Chowk, and for two days, the entire market was closed. Ela Bhatt maintains that the incident with the bicyclist was just a pretext to forward the authorities' plan to clear the market of vendors once and for all. On the third day, when the shops were allowed to reopen, any vendor who tried to sit in her spot had her goods confiscated and was thrown out of the market.

Most of these vendors have been sitting in this market for several years. Some are vending from the spots their grandmothers sold from when the local ruler first allocated vendors spots in the large open market. These vendors have the potential to do a lucrative business here because their goods are cheap and fresh, and they sit in the heart of the market where all the lanes of the gold and silver and cloth markets converge. As the market has increasingly expanded with shops and crowded with traffic, the authorities covet the diminished open space where these vendors sit for vehicle parking. The authorities are fuelled in their persistent harassment of the vendors by the shopkeepers occupying the adjacent permanent vegetable market whose business is undercut by the street vendors.

Laxmibehn, the wiry, toughened group leader of the Manek Chowk vendors who appears older than her 55 years due to poor health, recalled the chain of events that followed their eviction from the market.

'I went straight to SEWA and told Elabehn what was happening to us. How would we earn? I had been sitting in that market since I was a baby with my mother. I had been selling there myself since I was 12. How could we get back our spaces? Elabehn tried phoning the Police Commissioner. He told her that it was not in his hands, that the municipality was in charge of this issue. The next day she came with us to see the Municipal Commissioner. He told us it was a police decision. We went back to the police. The Commissioner was not in. For four days he was not in, while we were getting desperate. We had been out of work for one week. Every night we were meeting, discussing, what to do? Then 20 of us along with Elabehn and Renabehn went to the Police Commissioner's office. They told Elabehn, "He is out," but she said, "That's all right. We will wait for him." After a few hours, he came—though we don't believe he was ever "out".'

'He was upset at Elabehn. He said we were a law and order problem. But she is a good talker. She told him about our problems. She told him we had not been involved in the violence the week before. Those were the days she would speak up for us everywhere, "Don't these vendors in their bright clothes with their fresh vegetables look much nicer than parked cars?" she would say. "Shouldn't we give priority to their earning their living? All they are asking from you is two baskets worth of space." Like this she convinced him, and he finally agreed to try and help us.'

'Even after that, they kept us out. For another week we tried everyday to return to our spaces, and everyday they threw us out. We were selling the vessels from our houses to buy food. We went again to the Commissioner, and Elabehn asked, "When everybody else is allowed to do their business, all the banks and schools are open, how can you keep these vendors out?" '

'Again he only promised to "see," so Elabehn politely said, "We are going to start our work tomorrow at 8 a.m." '

'We called a big meeting at the TLA that evening. About 400 vendors came. I told them everything we had tried, and everything the police had said but not done. Everyone was very agitated. Elabehn asked, "Shall we brave the police? Are you ready to claim what is yours?" Everyone shouted "Yes!" Anything was better than this slow starvation. We decided to occupy our old spaces in the market early the next morning.'

The next day happened to be the death anniversary of Gandhiji. SEWA vendors thought a *satyagraha* ('insistence on truth') would be a fitting tribute, and set out to inform Mr. Buch, SEWA's President, the Police and Municipal Commissioners, and the Mayor. All the authorities tried to dissuade Ela from going ahead with the plan. Neither Mr. Buch, the President of both SEWA and the TLA, nor Mr. Barot, TLA Secretary who was then the Labour Minister, wanted the TLA to be blamed for any action which might be construed as anti-government. They tried to convince her not to go ahead. But, as Elabehn recalled: 'We had tried every possible channel of finding a solution and no one was moving. There was simply no other option left. To anyone who called me that night, appealing to me not to go ahead, I asked, "What will you promise to do for the vendors, then?" With nothing concrete offered, we simply proceeded.'

'We were fired for action, but also a little afraid of what might happen,' Laxmibehn recounted. 'We went to the market early. All the SEWA organizers were with us, and we sat in our usual places. Our baskets were empty though, because we did not know what would happen. None of us could afford to lose any vegetables. The organizers stood between and behind us. Many of us were nervous. After everything that had happened to us, we were terrified of the police. I have been badly beaten up many times. Elabehn kept reminding us to stay calm. She told us if we were arrested, to just go quietly. Five police vans pulled up full of constables. Pretty soon a crowd gathered, everyone looking at what was going on. A few people started harassing us and stirring up the situation. The behns kept reminding us to stay calm. The policemen acted like they were maintaining law and order, but wherever they went, there the fights would start. Also, the shopkeepers were shouting at us. They do not like us here. It was difficult not to fight. This was *our* place. But we could also see this was just what everyone wanted to happen. If we fought, they would arrest us, and we would be out of the market again.'

According to the other organizers, at this point in time the Police Superindentent of Traffic came to Elabehn and told her that if the vendors left now, he would 'see' later. Ela said the vendors had come to do their work today, and could not leave yet. He told her, 'Even your President did not want you to do this, and you went ahead. You are disobedient!'

She continued to engage the police officers in discussion so that the vendors could fill their baskets unnoticed and begin business. The Superintendent was trying to reason with Bhatt. He said to her, 'If you honour me, I will honour you.' He used the Hindi word *izzat*, which means one's social standing, and links a family's honour with the conduct of the women of that family. A family's public position is lost if the honour of a woman is lost.

Therefore, when Elabehn replied, 'I have no honour', he was absolutely shocked. This was *not* what a self-respecting woman was supposed to say. He did not know how to deal with this, and said 'Then I am leaving, and *you* can take care of the traffic and deal with any problems that arise.'

With that, he and all the officers withdrew. Rather than facing problems, however, SEWA vendors watched the tension and crowds withdraw with the police. All the vendors went into the wholesale market and returned with full baskets. The market filled up with customers who were glad to see the vendors back. SEWA members from all over the city came to sit with their sisters in the market, amidst cries of 'Long live SEWA!', 'Gandhiji lives!', 'We are all one!', 'Long live Elabehn!'

When traffic jams became a problem, SEWA women stationed themselves and began directing traffic. For the next five days, SEWA was in charge of Manek Chowk. Elabehn recalled, 'My observation of that week was that my skin turned black from directing traffic. The vendors' observation was that their income increased dramatically, because no one was extorting bribes!'

In 1980, SEWA had constructed its own buildings—one next to Ellisbridge in Ahmedabad, and the other in the village Devdholera. These were used for holding meetings and conducting training, with the main offices still located in the TLA. SEWA was organizing righteous struggles for the lowest castes and economic classes of women, and was successful on many fronts. Developing economic units and cooperatives of handblock printers, chindi workers, vegetable vendors, dairy producers, handloom weavers, bamboo workers, industrial cleaners and waste pickers led SEWA to establish a Rural Wing and an Economic Wing in the organization. Even if each effort did not lead to immediate economic gains, each represented an important step in carving concrete models for change.

These women started from a position of extreme vulnerability—with no means to organize; a precarious economic existence recurring every day; ill-health compounded by physically exhausting work; the physical and emotional burden of housework; faced with the humiliation and indignity of the caste system; politically invisible, illiterate, and their lives controlled by others' decisions. After eight years of collective struggle, these women were pooling their internal resources of courage and strength to emerge from this morass for the first time. Their skills, confidence, and consciousness shifts were becoming apparent at this point in time. Leaders like Chandabehn, Santokbehn, Nirubehn, Laxmibehn,

Karimabibi, and Bilqish Banu had acquired new skills to enter formal worlds they had previously been marginal to or victimized by.

As they organized around the crunch immediately surrounding their personal lives, these women began to realize how inter-dependent all the problems they faced in their poverty were. Even after acquiring a fair loan, they had to face harassment by the police. After successfully bargaining to have their piece-rate wages raised, they still faced the problems of polluted water, infectious diseases, and communal tensions—resulting from overcrowded conditions in the slums. Their immediate and extended families' perception of women's appropriate roles and activities, was still slow, if not outright reticent, to change. Each trade group was recognizing the discriminatory laws and policies that were obstruct-ing their ability to earn a decent living. Out of their personal struggles, their collectivity was giving them a political conscious-ness—not a party consciousness—but rather a conviction that if the present system was untenable, then they needed to seek political alternatives.

They effected one such alternative in 1980. SEWA and other Gujarati women's groups successfully petitioned the government to support women's employment through a resolution that all government institutions give priority to women's groups in buying goods. SEWA interpreted this resolution creatively for the more victimized and harassed vendors who left their vulnerable market spots to begin supplying fresh produce to government jails, hospi-tals, and schools on a daily basis. SEWA bamboo workers supplied brooms and waste-baskets to government offices under the new mandate.

A GROWING RIFT

While the women's union was gaining ground, tensions had been mounting between SEWA and the TLA, which had much of their executive leadership in common. Most SEWA organizers trace the emergence of the tension to Ela Bhatt's reception of the Magsaysay Award in 1977. They believed that the TLA leaders wanted credit for the work of SEWA, since they represented the older, parent organization. The TLA blamed Bhatt for travelling abroad more and more often, and they charged her with neglecting her duties in the Women's Wing sewing classes. Also, SEWA's work in developing the self-employed was sometimes perceived as clashing with the interests of the TLA: advancing credit and building alternative economic structures were not considered union work. Some of the people whom SEWA had to confront directly because of their exploitation of the self-employed were allied to the TLA. The growing personal and political strength of all the women in the organization was disconcerting to the TLA leadership in a society where women are taught to defer to men. The underlying tension surfaced into a real crisis between the two organizations over an incident in the city on which the two took very different stands.

Ahmedabad has a history of serious caste and communal tensions, which have often erupted into violence. In 1981, the tensions and resulting violence in the city stemmed from a conflict over reservation of seats in the medical college for Harijans. Higher caste medical students and their supporters launched an agitation to do away with the reservations. Both indiscriminate and targeted violence between the two groups became widespread. The city was sucked into three months of curfews, closures, demonstrations, and destruction, during which over 40 people were killed. No one was speaking up in favour of the Harijans.

Ela, citing the TLA's commitment to Gandhian principles, pointed out the struggles they had previously launched under Gandhi to remove untouchability. She wondered how they could remain silent on this issue. A large number of both TLA and SEWA members were from communities which would directly benefit from the reservations. The TLA, however, also had common leadership with the National Labour Organization's, whose members included more middle class and white collar workers. The TLA leadership, therefore, did not want to speak up for either side, fearing conflicts in the larger union body, and was maintaining a policy of silence.

The primary, immediate need for SEWA in such times, however, was peace. Women who earn daily wages could not survive the curfew and closure of the city for long. Their trades depended on markets being open, on being able to procure their raw materials, and on the streets being safe for them. All of them were losing more and more income, and many, when they tried to work, were victims of violence.

The time came for SEWA's Annual General Body Meeting, which was usually held outdoors so that all the women could participate. There was an ordinance, however, prohibiting any meeting in the open due to the violence, so a smaller group met at SEWA to discuss their problems. These women, including the Executive Committee and the trade group leaders, passed a resolution asking all members of society to bring peace so that the self-employed could resume their work and feed their families.[6]

This action on the part of SEWA caused the situation to erupt. The TLA rebuked Ela for passing such a resolution and allowing it to be reported in the press. Things came to a head when Ela was asked to participate in a peace meeting organized by some of Ahmedabad's Gandhian leaders. She warned them that she was pro-Harijan. They said that they wanted someone who would reflect that viewpoint. The Chief Minister, the Home Minister, the Minister of Health, representatives of the medical establishment, student representatives, some Gandhian leaders, and many journalists were present at the meeting.

During the meeting, the Chief Minister took the stand of refusing to rescind the Harijan seats, but offered instead to give the upper castes extra seats. Representatives of the upper castes and the medical establishment insisted on denying any seats at all to the lower caste students.

While listening to the participants quarrelling over and regurgitating the same issues which had kept the city at war for three months, Ela kept thinking about what she had seen in her work with so many poor women—the number of maternal and infant deaths she had seen, and the mercenary manner of the doctors towards poor women. Her bitterness overflowed as she stood up and quoted the figures SEWA had estimated for maternal mortality. She said, 'The *real* problem is medical care! Even today the umbilical cord is cut with a sickle and that sickle is not even sterilized in the fire. We have not yet been able to put a proper knife or scissors in the hands of the village midwife. This is the condition in the country, and what are you people fighting about— your few seats and your attachment and your grant! It is so irrelevant!'[7]

'The reservation must stay! This is a war between unequals. It is

the Harijan women in rural areas who lose their lives, and as soon
as there is any curfew, it is Harijans who are beaten up. They
suffer the most. The reservation must stay!'

As the only public leader to take such a forthright stand, Bhatt
was widely quoted in the press, since her views gave support to the
government stand. She publicly advocated meeting the people
who were victims of the violence, and trying to bring peace from
their perspective. Following this coverage, her house was stoned
for several nights.

Bhatt recalled the incidents immediately following her public
statement: 'My members had been telling me for months about the
terror of the violence, and I had sympathized with them. But now I
understood the sleepless nights surrounded by fear—that terror of
lying in the dark and fearing the stones from an unidentified, mass
anger . . . .'

'Then we discovered that the assailants were boys from our own
neighbourhood . . . . There was just nowhere to go. If I went to
the labour neighbourhoods, I was a hero. I did not want to be a
hero. And in my own neighbourhood, no one would speak to us
. . . and the stones . . . .'

Bhatt was also held in contempt by the TLA for 'extreme
indiscipline.' Indeed, SEWA had breached 'discipline' on many
counts, as far as the status quo was concerned. Organizationally,
the TLA was built on a hierarchical structure. Decisions were
made from top down and were highly politicized. SEWA members
and organizers on the other hand made joint decisions, democrati-
cally, on all aspects of the organization, and strictly avoided any
alliance with a political party. And here, SEWA's spokeswoman
was advocating meeting the people who were victims of the violence
—not taking a political decision amongst leaders.

SEWA was also thinking about social work. Social work in India
has a history of being paternalistic and welfare-oriented—a kind of
'we'll help you by *giving* you these things you need'—treating the
symptoms rather than the sickness, and often not even perceiving
the symptoms accurately. Women, moreover, are often viewed as
'objects of reform,'[8] rather than active participants in change or
development. SEWA's commitment to an economic agenda which
gave poor women control over their own resources had similar
implications to allotting Harijans reservations in education and
jobs—it meant empowerment, not welfare.

After SEWA's stand on the reservation issue, internal pressure was increased by the TLA leadership against Ela and her colleagues, though the TLA could not immediately take any overt action which might be construed as openly anti-Harijan.

A month and a half later, in May 1981, Ela returned from a Board meeting of the Women's World Banking in San Remo to find her office telephone disconnected and a letter from the TLA leadership advising SEWA to vacate the TLA premises. Within a month the TLA leaders resigned from the executive positions they held in SEWA, the TLA deposits to the tune of Rs. 300,000 were withdrawn from SEWA Bank, Ela was expelled as an honorary member of the TLA, and the TLA resolved to sever all links with SEWA.[9]

This is SEWA's side of the story. The reasons given by the TLA a few months later when they consented to speak to the press after a lot of negative coverage against them were these: (*a*) that it was simply a matter of indiscipline on Bhatt's part— too many foreign trips without permission, and violating the silence policy on the reservation issue; and (*b*) that SEWA was not ordered to leave, but gladly accepted their advice in a usual weaning process 'after their initial teething problems were over.'[10]

The final blow of disaffiliation which came in August that year casts doubts on the validity of the TLA's assertions, however. It occurred at the General Council meeting of the National Labour Organization, a Gujarat-based federation of 36 unions. All 36 unions had as their President one of the TLA office bearers, except for SEWA—now that Buch and his successor, Manharlal Shukla, had resigned.

SEWA knew fairly well what its fate would be, since the office bearers of the NLO were also the office bearers of the TLA. SEWA wanted to bring along a delegation of 25 of its organizers and group leaders to observe the proceedings of the meeting, which they sensed might be undemocratic. The observers had been denied permission to attend, but based on rumours that they were to be disaffiliated, they went anyway. Due to a flat tyre, they arrived late in a dramatic setting of torrential monsoon rains. They were all granted permission to enter the chamber, but were subsequently ridiculed when trying to represent the issues of home-based workers under the Contract Labour Act. One TLA delegate provoked laughter from the Council by asking, 'How can we ask

for bathrooms and latrines for them when they work at home?'
(not even considering that that might *be* the point for workers
whose conditions are so exploitative that they are forced to live in
slums without sanitation facilities). Following this, some TLA
office bearers became verbally aggressive, asking why SEWA
observers had been let into the hall, then again accusing Bhatt of
indiscipline, and demanding an apology or dismissal. All the SEWA
observers and delegates left the meeting in the face of what Bhatt
called 'the brute majority. They told us, "You have had your
snacks, now go." '

'I was most upset by what happened next, though,' she said in a
later interview. 'I considered all of these people as my mentors, I
had respected them like my own parents, I had been groomed by
them in union work. As we were waiting outside the meeting on
the terrace balcony, we heard them bring up the resolution to
disaffiliate us. They did not say more than two lines and the issue
was closed. To this day we do not know if they did it constitutionally.
The only thing we heard was Mr. Buch quote a proverb, "A
golden dagger should be worn for decoration, but not for killing
yourself." Then he said, "I built a wall of poor women around
TLA to protect us from Indiraji's attacks, but now that the Emergency is over, we no longer need them." '†

'I just had no idea,' she said, 'that anyone was using SEWA for
some political gain. We were all raw with the wound of the
insult—first of all feeling foolish to have been so naive, and then
angry to have been so used.'

Here SEWA suddenly realized the fate which many women's
movements that are part of larger organizations of men would face
in the next decade. What Madhu Kishwar in 1988 observed as a
trend in rural women's movements was SEWA's experience a
decade earlier:

> In most cases, the leadership begins to make a special appeal to
> women to join when the movement is facing a crisis like govern-
> ment and police repression or a backlash from oppressive forces.
> At such times, the leaders call on women more easily because

† In the early seventies, when Indira Gandhi split the Congress party, the TLA
was associated with the old party which was ousted from power. In the sweeping
socialist reforms which followed, groups like the TLA had to shore themselves up
against policies which threatened to undercut their old political control.

the community is compelled to suspend the normal rules of behaviour in order to cope with the emergency and the men become more willing to encourage women's participation.[11]

Although the TLA did not need to make a 'special appeal' due to Bhatt's vision and the organizing women's strength, they only tolerated the growing union of women as long as it served their purpose of political protection. Now that they perceived their strength as a threat, the alliance was severed.

Elabehn recalled the rally of solidarity which followed: 'We called all our members for a big meeting at Akhandanand Hall three days after this meeting. We had to put loudspeakers outside, because about 2000 women came, and everyone could not be accommodated inside. The majority of them were Harijans, and there was fire in their heart and eyes. Everyone who had been there (at the NLO meeting) spoke with great courage and indignation about what they had heard and seen. Both leaders and working class women took turns speaking with equal assertiveness. There was such a sense of liberation that there was no man heading the meeting and telling us what to do or think. There was no one we had to be careful not to hurt if we did not pay him enough respect. It was our first meeting without a *topee* (literally "hat", but meaning, male leader). We passed a resolution that day that men would not be allowed as members or as office bearers of our union. Although insulted at the way we had been thrown out, really, we felt most powerfully, an incredible sense of freedom. It felt like a daughter's righteous struggle. We had left the nest.'

END NOTES

1. Vijaya A. Pastala, excerpted from unpublished case studies, Mount Holyoke College, October 1987.
2. This account was compiled by interviews with Ela Bhatt and statistics were taken from her paper 'A Strategy for Wage Revision,' based on SEWA and ALA studies in 25 villages of Dholka taluk (unpublished mimeo).
3. Jennifer Sebstad, *Struggle and Development Among Self-Employed Women*. USAID Report, 1982, p. 166.

4. This account of the chindi struggle drawn from my interviews with chindi stitchers and organizers; from Sebstad, *op.cit.*, 1982, pp. 159–73; and from Lalita Krisnnaswami's ILO paper, 'Rags Ring in a Revolution,' 1987.

5. This account of the vegetable vendors' struggle was drawn from interviews with vegetable vendors, organizers, Ela Bhatt, and an unpublished paper by Renana Jhabvala, 'SEWA's Struggles,' 1985, which was later published as an article in *Manushi* magazine.

6. Sebstad, 1982, *op. cit.*, p. 226.

7. Debashish Mukerjee, 'Ela Bhatt, an Interview,' *Debonaire*, July 1981, p. 14, as quoted in Sebstad, *op. cit.*

8. Madhu Kishwar, 'Gandhi on Women,' *The Economic and Political Weekly*, 5 October 1985, p. 1695.

9. Sebstad, 1982, *op.cit.*, pp. 231–33.

10. *Economic Times*, 8 June 1981, as cited in Sebstad, 1982, *op. cit.*

11. Madhu Kishwar, 'Nature of Women's Mobilisation in Rural India,' *The Economic and Political Weekly*, Vol. XXIII, Nos. 52 and 53, 24–31 December 1988.

Figure 3.1
The SEWA Tree
A Women's Support Network

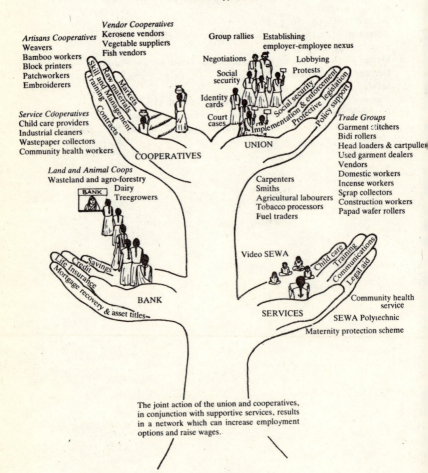

Artisans Cooperatives
Weavers
Bamboo workers
Block printers
Patchworkers
Embroiderers

Vendor Cooperatives
Kerosene vendors
Vegetable suppliers
Fish vendors

Group rallies   Establishing
employer-employee nexus

Negotiations   Lobbying
Social   Protests
security

Identity
cards
Court
cases

Skill and Management Training
Raw materials
Markets
Contracts

Social security
Implementation & enforcement
Protective legislation
Policy support

Service Cooperatives
Child care providers
Industrial cleaners
Wastepaper collectors
Community health workers

COOPERATIVES   UNION

Trade Groups
Garment stitchers
Bidi rollers
Head loaders & cartpullers
Used garment dealers
Vendors
Domestic workers
Incense workers
Scrap collectors
Construction workers
Papad wafer rollers

Land and Animal Coops
Wasteland and agro-forestry
Dairy
Treegrowers

BANK

Carpenters
Smiths
Agricultural labourers
Tobacco processors
Fuel traders

Video SEWA

Child care
Training
Communications
Legal aid

Savings
Credit
Life Insurance
Mortgage recovery & asset titles

BANK

SERVICES

Community health
service
SEWA Polytechnic
Maternity protection scheme

The joint action of the union and cooperatives,
in conjunction with supportive services, results
in a network which can increase employment
options and raise wages.

4

SEWA's Shakti: Growing Up and Leading Out

Duryodhana was wretchedly unhappy, full of discontent and envy that his kingdom was so poor and ordinary, while his rival cousins the Pandavas lived amidst beauty and the devotion of their subjects. He decided to challenge the eldest king brother, Yudhishthira, to a gambling match, knowing it to be the one weakness of this warrior king. When Yudhishthira accepted, Duryodhana pitted him against his clever and unscrupulous uncle. Yudhishthira slowly lost jewels, gold, chariots, elephants, horses, slaves, servants. Yudhishthira was seized with a kind of madness and could not stop. He pledged the wealth of the kingdom, the villages, his lordship, and lost these too. Then he staked his four brothers, one by one, then himself, and finally Draupadi, his beautiful wife. When she was lost, Duryodhana laughed, 'Now she is our slave and will sweep the palace floors!' She refused to come, saying that as soon as her husband became a slave, she ceased to be his wife. They dragged her before the assembly, her large eyes flaming. Duryodhana ordered her clothes stripped from her in front of the assembly to bring the proud queen shame. As she heard the order, she knew no one in the world who could come to her aid. She turned all her thoughts to God, reaching out to Him for help.

Lord Krishna came to help her work a miracle. As each garment was stripped, another appeared in its place. As her sari was unwound, it grew continually longer, never exposing her. When she opened her eyes from the concentration of her prayers, the pile of glittering garments burst into flame. Duryodhana's father grew afraid of the folly of his son, and offered Draupadi a wish. She took her husbands' freedom, and her own, and left the hall with her eyes blazing fire.

from the popular Hindu epic, *The Mahabharata*

Bhatt still recalls feeling like Draupadi in that NLO assembly from which SEWA was heckled out, her elders and mentors in trade union work standing by watching as she and her colleagues were publicly humiliated. 'I felt like I was being stripped in front of the people I had respected most, with no one speaking up for me.'

The modesty she evinced by referring only to her feeling of vulnerability is characteristic of Ela Bhatt, but the further analogy of Draupadi's story is also apt. Bhatt likewise rose powerfully from this low moment through her positive strength and the solidarity of members and organizers who rallied to combat the TLA's attempts to break the women's union.

After the TLA revoked the old contracts and withdrew building space, SEWA located new production space and mill contacts for chindi supply. SEWA rebuilt bank deposits withdrawn by the TLA through mobilizing members' deposits. When rumours began floating that the bank was going to close down, Bhatt broke her silence with the press and gave extensive interviews presenting SEWA's side of the story. As over 60 articles appeared in the press across the country, largely condemning the TLA action, national and international support poured into SEWA. Women's groups and trade unions sent messages of solidarity. It became clear that they would not only survive the split, but also would, in fact, be stronger.

Missing the connection they had with Ansuyabehn Sarabhai after their departure from the TLA, they launched a fortnightly newsletter which they named 'Ansuya.'

'Like Hindus who have a rebirth because they want to continue their life,' said Bhatt, 'I felt I should continue the work begun by her in this new context. We chose her name for our paper because

Ansuya means, literally, "without rancour". We needed to send out that kind of message at that time. Shankarlal Banker, who started the TLA with Ansuyabehn and Gandhiji, inaugurated it for us. We wanted to put out a sign that we were going ahead in that spirit.'

Bhatt's leadership qualities have contributed greatly not only to SEWA's successful separation from the TLA, but also to its ability to work successfully through government bureaucracies; through the polarized interests of employers, government and workers; and through the international trade union establishment which could have, like the TLA, felt threatened at the prospect of empowering informal sector workers.

Her reputation for mediating tension not necessarily by changing her position, but more often by getting others to think differently about their position, dates from her pre-SEWA days as a lawyer for the TLA in the fifties. She was the only woman in the union not to cover her head with her sari. When she sensed that it was creating unspoken tensions, she dispelled them by saying to the union's Secretaries who were upset: 'This is like my parents' place (where daughters do not cover their heads), not my in-laws'. I have come here to grow and learn.'

She strikes most people who meet and work with her as a very sincere, simple, wise, and calm person. Although 'streamlined' may not seem an appropriate adjective for a khadi-clad Gandhian, it aptly describes her mental temperament. She knows what is important, focuses adeptly on it, and lets the rest go, remaining uncluttered. When she was appointed to the central government Planning Commission in 1990, occupying a large government bungalow in New Delhi, there was no sign of her status or gender. Large tables stacked neatly with files, simple block printed bed-sheets covering beds, a desk, and a wall chart of tasks characterized her living quarters.

Dr. Anandalaxmi, President of Mobile Creches in Delhi and Principal of Lady Irwin College characterized Bhatt's intuitive intelligence in a Hindu way when she said, 'She is an old soul. You can see the wisdom of many lifetimes in her eyes.'

When Ela tries to clarify a point through the many interviews and public speeches she gives, she often focuses on the memory of a woman whose circumstances she narrates as an example. She appears to recall individually thousands of poor women she has met, making her 'wisdom of many lifetimes' not only that of her own successive lifetimes, but also that of many other women's experiences which she has deeply internalized and gained insight through.

Michela Walsh, the American President and founder of Women's World Banking, has travelled with Bhatt to many countries, to assess women's economic status and needs. Bhatt is the Chairperson of the WWB's Board of Directors. In an interview, Walsh said of Bhatt, 'The thing about her is you can never tell where she is uncomfortable. She wears the same face everywhere. In the slums of Ahmedabad, singing Gujarati songs to workers in the streets of China, addressing heads of state and parliaments—she wears the same face. And she is the shrewdest political person I know. She never confronts an issue head on, but she can walk, for example, through the aisles of the World Bank, drop an idea, you might not even know she said anything, but minds will start to change.'

A special leadership quality for which Bhatt is credited is her commitment to empowering others. She repeatedly credits SEWA members with having the best understanding of how to run the bank, and is constantly urging SEWA members towards greater self-sufficiency—both financially and managerially. All SEWA organizers seem to be constantly balancing the members' need for support with their need for autonomy. Bhatt characterized this in an interview with Jennifer Sebstad in 1981 when she said 'We have to be careful not to grab power and control, but in any small programme taken up we must also be prepared to follow through and take the final responsibility. Only creating awareness is not enough. We must also prepare leaders. But until they are ready to assume power, we must assume final responsibility for action. If we don't, we fail. If the poor had that capacity already, they would not have been exploited for so long.'[1]

These leadership qualities and the attention she has attracted to the problems of self-employed women have brought her a great deal of acclaim. In the decade following her reception of the Magsaysay Award, she received three other prestigious international awards: the Susan B. Anthony Award for Communal Harmony; the Right Livelihood Award (December 1984), which is also known as the alternate Nobel Peace Prize, presented in the Swedish Parliament the day before the Nobel Prize 'to bring recognition to human endeavour that strives to better the quality of life'; and the Women and Creation Honor from the Femme Alliance in Paris (1990).

Nationally she was conferred with the highest honours of state by the President of India in two successive years, with the orders of Padmashri and Padmabhushan (1985, 1986) and with the Best Entrepreneurs Award, Delhi (1982). While she acknowledges that the awards have brought positive attention to SEWA work, she also cites them as examples of how invisible the self-employed are, that people know about and acknowledge her, but still do not recognize what the work is really about.

Bhatt attributes SEWA's well-established success to the strength and courage of working women. What she clearly lends all the women she works with, however—which allows their strength and courage to manifest—is her fundamental belief that people can grow. Instilling confidence in women that they can do any kind of job successfully is no small feat. During interviews for this book, I was sometimes interrupted by men of the family and told that their wives were like buffaloes and could not think. This attitude is the one that keeps women off of any kind of equipment like looms or potter's wheels, it is what renders them unemployed when their formerly manual tasks of spinning or tobacco leaf processing are mechanized (How, after all, can buffaloes operate machines?), and it likewise emboldens men to try to assume leadership control of women's cooperatives. It takes committed, consistent backing by alternative attitudes like Bhatt's to successfully counter these forces.

While Bhatt instils confidence in all women, her clear vision of building a unique women's support system gives women the means to translate their innate strength into action. Her penchant for organizing stems from her belief that organizing lends strength, which is the most obvious thing Ela Bhatt thrives on—women showing their strength.

AN ALL-WOMEN'S FORUM

Since its split with the TLA in 1981, SEWA has been made up solely of women. Observers often question if an organization with only women members is the best way to bring about social change. SEWA emphasizes women's need for confidence in order to grow, and cites the cultural conditioning which dictates that women defer to men and which hampers women's confidence in a mixed forum. On several occasions, SEWA has seriously discussed allowing male members into the union, since many issues of the self-employed are common to both sexes. Ultimately, however, they have decided against it, believing if men are admitted, they will simply take over and SEWA's purpose will be lost. Also, a woman's participation in an all-women's organization is more easily accepted by her extended family than it would be in a mixed forum.

SEWA is not trying to work through an exclusionary vision. The organization believes that by improving the conditions for the woman, it can improve the conditions of the entire family, and hence the society. Since poverty takes the hardest toll on women, the organizers assert, let their relief from it be managed by them. When a woman's income is increased, it benefits the entire family. As many occupations are family occupations, setting up networks and support for women contributes to the work of the entire family. For instance, when the family land is recovered from mortgage and placed in a woman's name, or jointly in both names, it also protects the entire family from vulnerability, migration, separation, and starvation. Or, when the union demands identity cards for bidi workers, their entire family gains access to the medical clinic. Or, when the prolonged drought was decimating the animal herds of the families, SEWA's provision of fodder, diesel for pumping water, and deepening of village wells obviously benefited the entire community which was in need of these resources. If a vendor-member's husband has been harassed by the police, for example, SEWA *will* take up his case also. The balance which has been shifted through an all-women's membership, however, is *which* family member gets access for the family. That resources are channelled through the women's hands is the radical difference.

As an all-women's union, SEWA makes an important contribution by representing women's work issues in the larger trade union networks. After they were disaffiliated from the NLO, they secured other international affiliations. Through their bidi membership they were affiliated with the International Federation of Food, Beverages, Tobacco and Allied Workers (IUF) in 1983, and through their agricultural labourers, they joined the International Federation of Plantation, Agricultural and Allied Workers (IFPAAW) in 1985. In these forums, SEWA specifically represents women's issues, which helps reorient the male dominated unions towards women's work issues.

SEWA's all-female membership adds another bonus: it provides its members and women everywhere strong female role models. It would be difficult to find another instance in the world of women from such diverse educational, class, religious, and occupational backgrounds working together as colleagues. Bhatt's ability to learn from anyone sets an inspiring example for all of how to share experience and overcome inappropriate limitations. A woman who has studied land tenure rights in the university has a lot to learn from women who actually cultivate the land and who understand village land politics. They are essential to each other in developing new models of women's collective access to land. Whoever they have to approach to apply, register, challenge, or pressure for their new model, they watch themselves—all women—making the negotiations, and it imbues their pursuit of Gandhi's 'self-reliance' with a new meaning.

SOME OF THE LEADERS

Once SEWA had split from the TLA and was no longer sharing leadership with it, tensions about democratic leadership quickly dissolved. The fiery group of women leaders who rallied after the separation and assumed responsibility contribute an unusual strength to the organization by giving it decentralized second and third levels of leadership after Bhatt—unusual in most Indian women's organizations, which largely depend on one central leader. The everyday leaders housed within the organization are the 'Standing Committee', mobilized in 1981 and comprising: Ela Bhatt as General Secretary; 'Police Commissioner' Nirubehn Jadav and Renana Jhabvala as Secretaries (see profiles in chapters 2 and 3, respectively); Usha Jumani, who joined in 1980 with a doctoral degree in Management, wanted to work and evolve management systems which suited the self-employed; Anila Dholakia who headed the rural wing; Lalita Krishnaswami who was overseeing the economic units; Ranjan Desai whose colleagues refer to her as the 'conscience keeper' of SEWA; and Hansa Mehta, the hard-headed and practical clerk whose frugality and clean accounting helped her rise to the position of the head accountant. This Committee meets daily to discuss work progress and collectively decide how to proceed.

Usha Jumani—sometimes an impatient catalyst in the process of change—gave up her position teaching cooperative management at the Institute of Rural Management in Anand to join SEWA a year before the split. She earned her doctoral degree from Ahmedabad's prestigious Indian Institute of Management, but coming from a family of textile traders, she felt discontented with all the focus on formal systems which disregarded what she perceives as India's traditional work systems. Regarded as a rebel, she is renowned for her question, 'Why impose an alien culture on our culture and take that as a measure of our progress?' She aggressively promotes self-employment and its reliance on verbal systems of communication. As a full-time Management Consultant to a union of the self-employed, she is defining new territory.

After the split she assumed the role of Managing Director of the bank for four years to help develop better working models—although she considered this as only part of the job of Management Consultant and a kind of exercise to help them all think in new ways about what kinds of services they needed. She joined the Standing Committee in 1988, to help integrate SEWA with formal channels and develop appropriate training models in the organization. She edits the English publications including Annual Reports and *We, The Self Employed*, a journal for activists and policy-makers. Usha Jumani is a critical thinker and conceptualizer for the organization, distilling their experiences into proverbs and diagrams. For example: 'All actions—raising women's consciousness, sensitizing the government and the public, and striving for economic viability—have to be *simultaneous*, not sequential.'

Anila Dholakia is a high-strung woman who is perpetually in a rush. A native Gujarati, she gave up her career as professor of psychology to join SEWA. At the time of the split, she was coordinating what was then known in SEWA as its 'Rural Wing'. She facilitated hundreds of women organizing into dairy cooperatives and fiercely resisted the pressure of vested interests in the village which tried to break them. Though she took up a government job in 1989, everyone at SEWA still enjoys the articulate legacy of organizing and empowerment songs she composed and set to popular folk tunes which inspire thousands of women to a collective spirit.

Lalita Krishnaswami is a tall, strong-looking woman with a flair of style, who came to SEWA in 1978 to help coordinate the training and skill upgrading for block printers, bamboo workers, and chindi stitchers. Her interest in traditional crafts and her artistic sensibility drew her into full-time management of the then 'Economic Wing'. She has developed extensive training programmes to help fill the gaps in knowledge and confidence which inhibit women from managing their own cooperatives, and she supervises colourful nationwide exhibitions at which SEWA artisans sell their products.

Ranjan Desai earned her 'conscience keeper' reputation because she is a social worker by nature. She worked for the Red Cross before joining SEWA. She would still work for no pay if asked, and will definitely wear khadi to the end. Her skill is good use of her heart, and she has dedicated long years to educating women on health and fertility issues and to organizing paper pickers—perhaps the most difficult trade group to organize. She is usually serious and talks in a small voice in the midst of the swarm of activity around her—until she smiles. Her warm laughter and the lines around her eyes and mouth attest to the frequency with which she responds with humour and patience to difficult situations.

Hansa Mehta is a solid, sturdy woman who does not believe that one can spend poor women's money 'just any old way.' She has moved up through the ranks of skills, from her initial job as filing and errand clerk, to doing accounts on a part-time basis (on Ela's insistence) and making rounds of the city to collect membership fees. After the split from the TLA, she was made in charge of all the accounts. She now manages 10 other accountants and keeps track of Rs. 40–Rs. 50 lakh (4–5 million) a year, constantly juggling funds coming in from government, from international organizations, from private donations, and from membership fees; and funds going out to nine projects, to cover organizational expenses, to cover services offered to 30,000 members, to finance training and research, buildings, and vehicles. Her colleagues attest that she is relentless in making certain that the funds are used legitimately and wisely.

This Standing Committee was joined in 1988 by Arvinda Bhatt, a seasoned SEWA organizer, and Mirai Chatterjee from Bombay, who joined SEWA in 1984. Arvindabehn, like 'Police Commissioner' Nirubehn, quit her job as a sewing instructor for the TLA after the split and joined SEWA. She manages the khol stitchers' cooperative and organizes similar production centres in the rural districts of Mehsana and Kheda. She is loyal, reliable, and steadfast on the premise that women need to be organized, and brings a decade of organizing experience to the Committee.

Mirai is a frank, open woman, always ready to discuss the issues and ethics of the projects she is developing. After receiving her postgraduate degree in Public Health from Johns Hopkins University she came to SEWA and revived the maternity benefits scheme. She helped launch SEWA's Jagruti (Awareness), Community Health Programme, designed to train self-employed women to become community health workers, helping women to be in control of their bodies and health. She coordinates occupational health studies in specific work related conditions, and helped set up a SEWA pharmacy that provides poor families access to cheap, safe medicines.

While each Standing Committee member grew into her role as an administrator of one department of the organization, the Executive Committee was also activated in the months following the split. The members of the Executive Committee—whose profiles are scattered through all the narratives of the trade struggles—are considered the heart and soul of the organization. They meet once a month to assess how things are progressing. Since 1981 they have shared increasingly more responsibilities with the organizers, and are considered the final arbiters, whose consensus gives direction to the organization. Most embrace a profound commitment of service to the membership, which is striking in the face of the simultaneously heavy demands of their occupations. A couple of members have misused the power of their positions and had to leave under exposure of corruption—a healthy sign that women are actually moving into places of power. There are 25 Executive Members, 21 of whom are self-employed women elected from the membership, and four are full-time organizers who are also on the Standing Committee. The Standing Committee carries the Executive Committee's mandates back to the paid organizers of the union, and oversees their implementation.

In its regrouping after the split, SEWA officially separated its union activities from its development activities. 'We were not doing either thing well by having everyone working on everything,' Jhabvala explained. 'The two activities need different kinds of organizers, with different temperaments. Union struggle means being ready at any hour to take any necessary action. Organizers have to be sharp, able to negotiate through sticky situations, willing to fight and confront malpractices—go to jail if necessary. Those who work on economic development have to be good managers. They have to establish business relationships by working diplomatically through the community. They have to develop markets and material outlets.'

To strengthen their union strategies, they hired several literate women from each working class trade community as full-time organizers. While the union organizers had SEWA and TLA experience as a foundation to work from, the cooperatives had no such background. Each cooperative needed a good manager if it was to compete in the market with its products. This need projected many problems. Professional managers are expensive. How would they interact with the old working class organizers who had brought all these women together? Would professionals be dedicated to the cause of organizing the self-employed? How would they find managers who would not only manage, but also pass on management skills so the workers, over time, could assume those positions themselves? Salaries have gradually increased at SEWA with the rise in the cost of living, but even today, the highest monthly salary any SEWA worker earns is Rs. 1500 (US $90.00). No one wants to emphasize the difference between educated skills and worker skills, but rather respect the unique contributions and responsibility of each member and organizer.

The problem resolves itself somewhat through SEWA's reputation of being an interesting place to work and through patience—basically, waiting for the right woman with enthusiasm for a particular job to turn up. This has happened in the case of non-professional managers as well as professional managers. Bhatt attests that the working class organizers have been the most effective over the long term. 'They have the rapport and strategizing ability to work with the members, and they have patience to see problems through,' she said.

Almost every woman working in the organization attests that

her work is personally challenging and always changing, although several did complain about salary levels. One young woman defected from the industrial textile sector where she worked as a designer and has helped turnaround the floundering weaving projects by bridging the gap between village women's traditional wool weaving skills and the demands of the urban cotton handloom market. 'I was bored and unsatisfied at my old job in the industry,' said Sukruti. 'I think like many organizers here, we all know we want to do *something* about the problems we see around us. We just do not know *what*. Here there is a place just to start, and it is challenging on every level—personally, occupationally, socially.'

One of her rural colleagues, Balubehn, who began work with SEWA as a very poor spinner for her husband's weaving work, has even greater conviction about the challenges of her work. In May 1989, she had just returned from a three week tour her weaving cooperative made to South India to see some of India's finest weavers at work. In her 10-year association with SEWA, she has developed from a spinner into their most skilled weaver, and in place of her tiny empty hut, she has earned her family a two-room house whose verandah protects her two large looms. 'From that place of begging for spinning work to earn a few rupees, I never knew how to *imagine* being inspired,' she said in an interview. 'From the day I began learning weaving, I have wanted to weave new designs, more beautiful cloth. How can your mind ever stretch that far sitting in the dirt, grateful to spin white thread?'

MOVING INTERNATIONAL

SEWA's first decade developed women's self-esteem, solidarity, their concept of being workers, and the revolutionary idea for women that they could run their own services and production units. In the decade following the split, SEWA began to project these developments in national and international forums. As they began to strengthen their vision in 1981, it became apparent that serious policy change and legal justice were imperative. They were not just trying to get access to systems like unions and cooperatives as they existed. They wanted these structures themselves to change in order to meet their realities.

In 1983, Bhatt went to Oslo, Norway, as an observer to the World Labor Congress of the International Confederation of Free Trade Unions (ICFTU) which represents 96 million workers in 81 countries. In an introductory speech to the Congress she outlined the problems of the self-employed. One Norwegian journalist reported that 'she (Bhatt) shook up complacent world trade leaders with her well-timed speech, telling them that their movement ignored the labourers most in need of protections.'

A constructive dialogue ensued, generating the idea that the self-employed in India needed official documentation about their conditions. At SEWA's Annual General Body Meeting in 1984, the women formulated a resolution to lobby the state government for a Commission to focus specifically on *self-employed women*. They demanded something similar to the Royal Commission on Labour (also known as the Wheatley Commission) of the thirties which had led to massive reforms and legal protections for workers in the industrial sector in India.

In 1985, SEWA submitted a similar resolution to the central government. The simply worded resolution highlighted their conditions of poverty, their invisibility in national statistics and policies, and their large contribution to the Gross National Product. They demanded a Commission to investigate means to rectify these problems.

Concurrent with national and international policy lobbying, SEWA networked out to strengthen women at the grassroots level in other parts of the country. A 'spearhead team' comprising a few SEWA organizers made its first foray in 1982 to meet groups who had expressed an interest in sharing ideas or had requested help in starting SEWAs in their areas. The spearhead team headed by Jhabvala lent experience in organizing new members, and helping conduct surveys.

New SEWAs in Bihar, Delhi, Madhya Pradesh, Haryana and Uttar Pradesh, together with the older SEWA in Ahmedabad formed an affiliation called SEWA Bharat. They wanted to use their affiliation to strengthen their ideas, affect information collection, lobby collectively, etc. Not all of the member groups considered themselves Gandhian, but they agreed to common principles for their association: they would adhere to non-violence, all women, and working with the poorest or most outcaste groups such as the Mithila painters, tribal silk spinners in Bihar, and the Muslim embroiderers of Lucknow. They made a sort of pact to fight the evil, not the evil-doer, the system and not just individual small employers.

Each SEWA organized around different issues. For some the major issue was income generation for destitute women and families. For others it was delinking skilled women from exploitative middlemen into their own production units. A few wanted to strengthen union activities, and some actively fought unjust social practices against women, like dowry and child marriage.[2]

This networking concretized for SEWA the wide spread of home-based workers' problems. Karimabibi, who has travelled with the Executive Committee to help the organizing efforts of other SEWAs, commented on her experience: 'After meeting so many other women working at home like me, I really believed there should be some law which would protect all of us. We decided to pursue national laws that would cover us.'

Thus in 1985, when SEWA women attended the UN Decade on Women's Conference in Nairobi, one of the top priorities on their agenda was to work on furthering the cause of home-based workers. Bhatt is a Founding Committee Member of DAWN (Development Alternatives with Women in a New Era), a group organized in 1983 by Devaki Jain, an eminent social scientist and friend, whom Bhatt credits for great inspiration and support to SEWA. The panels DAWN held on home-based workers in Nairobi led to the subsequent national level workshop sponsored by SEWA and the Gandhi Labour Institute to pool experience on the social, economic and legal problems of women home-based workers. The consensus of participants was to focus on more studies and greater organizing efforts.

Subsequently, the ILO approached SEWA to collaborate on studies of women-headed households. SEWA informed the ILO that their priority was to survey and organize home-based workers, of whom a large percentage are household heads. The ILO agreed to shift its focus to home-based workers and collaborated on projects in four states. They held organizing 'camps' which the bidi workers of Indore, the chikan (embroidery) workers of Lucknow, the ready-made garment workers of Ahmedabad, and the leather workers of Agra attended for a week. They explored the socio-economic, legal, and occupational health issues of each trade group and emphasized workers' needs to unite.

All labour organizations in the eighties have had to acknowledge the vast proportions of workers in the informal sector, especially in developing countries where an increasing amount of the world's production work takes place. This reality caused home-based workers' issues to attract interest in other parts of the ILO bureaucracy, promoting more studies and funding.

The SEWA–ILO camps culminated in a workshop in 1987, at which everyone who had been involved agreed—now that workers were organizing, they needed to focus on the primary need for national legislation. The extremely limited legislation which did exist to protect some home-based trades was largely failing. It depended on proof of the employer–employee relationship, which the employer usually denies, thwarting enforcement. Without national legislation, any attempts within one state to initiate protection would mean a shifting of establishment to an unprotected state.

Indira Jaisingh of the Lawyers Collective of Bombay collaborated with workers, researchers, government labour officers and organizers to draw up a National Draft Bill on Home-based Workers to submit to Parliament. The Bill promotes decentralized tripartite boards of workers, employers, and government which would establish the relationship between workers and employers by registering both, making payment of wages, ensuring social security benefits, etc.

While Jaisingh was collaborating on policy at home, Bhatt discussed the problem with world trade unions. Her 1984 address to the World Labor Congress of the ICFTU had outlined the general problems of the self-employed. At the 1988 Congress in Melbourne, Australia, she specifically advanced the cause of home-based workers. At the seminar on women preceding the Congress, Bhatt got European delegates from Sweden, the Netherlands, and Britain interested in SEWA's resolution, and they helped her lobby with other European delegates. In the main Congress, Bhatt made an appeal to each trade union represented to recognize home-based workers and to conduct research into their conditions in each respective country. She challenged the unions to build up a relationship of solidarity with such workers by bringing new legislation and providing them access to training and other collective bargaining processes. The Congress passed SEWA's resolution, radically altering the former western biased views that home-based work should be abolished. Their resolution reinforced the signals to the ILO that serious international concern was growing.

NATIONAL LEVEL STRUGGLES

While the grassroots camps and the international trade unions provided the forums to begin effecting a policy on home-based workers, SEWA's vendors pursued other networks. SEWA and other local voluntary groups in Ahmedabad had been arranging forums since 1981, bringing together hawkers, vendors, data collectors, activists, planners, police and government authorities to share perspectives. Despite these forums and the Supreme Court judgement in favour of the Manek Chowk vendors, harassment continued against them.

In 1986 SEWA called a National Workshop on Hawkers and Vendors, for which hawkers' groups from all over India met in Delhi. The meeting was organized to formulate a resolution for a national policy for hawkers and vendors, and to raise their demand again for a Commission to study the problems of women in the informal sector. SEWA wanted good press coverage to make this a high profile meeting, which was achieved when the then Prime Minister Rajiv Gandhi accepted their invitation to inaugurate the workshop. Famidabibi, a vendor from SEWA Bhopal, Laxmibehn from Ahmedabad, and many other hawkers spoke forcefully about their conditions, their experience in the Supreme Court, and the authorities' disregard of the judgement and stay orders against them. The vendors were jubilant when the Prime Minister responded to their demands with his announcement of the government's decision to appoint the Commission on Self-Employed Women.

Karimabibi recalled her experience of the appointment of the Commission: 'We are still surprised every time when our demands get heard. Saying we want a Commission, or realizing there should be a law for home-based workers is one thing. Anyone can ask. But being *heard*—being called as the experts on the issue—let us say that that is new experience for us . . . .'

Karimabibi along with the other members of the Executive

Committee was invited to Delhi to meet the Labour Minister, Shri Anjiaih, and the Minister for Women, Margaret Alva. 'These Ministers asked us about our problems and what we wanted the Commission to do for us,' she related. 'We spoke out on everything we had been discussing for years in SEWA.'

Nine months later, in January 1987, the entire SEWA membership considered it their personal victory when Bhatt was appointed by the then Prime Minister Rajiv Gandhi as a Member of Parliament in the Rajya Sabha (the Upper House), and was asked to chair the Commission. She would occupy the distinguished position of being the first Member to represent an all women's constituency, and would give SEWA a direct conduit to national policy channels. SEWA members boasted proudly, '*Our* sister is an MP, and she will talk about our problems in Delhi.'

Bhatt shifted her residence to Delhi, initiated Commission activities, sat on the Labour Ministry, and brought up the problems of rag-pickers, women labourers, home-based workers and hawkers for the first time on the floor of the House. From the beginning she spoke from her SEWA experience, but as the Commission conducted its nationwide studies, she gathered more fuel for her fire to speak on the similar conditions existing nationwide.

The all-women Commission of five members and one Government Secretary proceeded to tour 18 states of the country, organizing 800 public hearings of working women, as well as stopping on the roadsides to interview women they saw at work. The Commission members visited all the workplaces of women—mines, construction sites, fields, factories, homes, markets, and anywhere else they found women at work. They set up specific task forces to study the current status of self-employed women and their work conditions; the existing macro-policies which affect impoverished women working in the informal sector; the existing legislative protection for such women and its enforcement; the health issues for self-employed women; the communication channels that reach women workers and the images and information they project; the specific problems and exploitation that poor labouring women face; and their organizing experiences which combat these forces.

The extensive research of the different task forces and the public hearings with working women, voluntary agencies, government officials, activists, trade unions, and research organizations contributed to the Commission's report, *Shramshakti: Report of the*

National Commission on Self-Employed Women and Women in the Informal Sector. 'Shramshakti' means women's labour power. It is a powerful report, opening poignantly with the documentation of individual voices and group accounts of both the discrimination and exploitation women workers face, and the successful organizing strategies they have developed around these conditions for change and empowerment. Each chapter outlines the findings of one task force. While a few positive threads can be found, most of the existing conditions found by the Commission officially reflect what SEWA members in Gujarat already know. A brief summary here will locate the current position of India's self-employed women, and place SEWA's struggles in context.

Self-employed women's economic positions are misconceptualized. Census categories do not cover workers who are engaged in many varied activities. Women workers are under-reported by 30–40 per cent of their actual numbers. Because they do not fit into only one occupation classification, they are defined as marginal workers and rendered statistically invisible as far as their economic contribution is concerned. Almost 80 per cent of women workers are involved in agriculture, mainly as labourers. More than three-quarters of these women are daily wage earners, earning one-half or less than their male counterparts for the same work. Earnings for women in the unorganized sector average Rs. 227 per month in sharp contrast to women in the organized sector who net Rs. 963 per month.[3]

The demographic portrait which the Report draws from statistics collected throughout the eighties is disturbing: While there are only 975 females per 1000 males under 4 years of age, the number drops steadily to 896 for those between 10 and 14 years, which is attributed to inadequate nutrition and health care. The Report points out that in most countries of the world, women outnumber men. The low population ratio, ill health and mortality are perpetuated by early marriage—6.6 per cent of girls under 14 and 43 per cent of those under 19 years are married. These young women grow older to fill the profile the Report has drawn of the average rural woman who spends 16 years in pregnancy and lactation, who is pregnant six to eight times, and who gives birth to more than six children, of whom four survive; 418 women die per 100,000 live births.

Only 18 per cent of rural women are literate as opposed to 41 per cent of their male counterparts. Only 142 females per 1000 males are main workers. The activities where women outnumber men are the processing of cashew nuts, cotton and wool spinning outside of factories, rolling bidis, processing tobacco, and food processing. Most of women's occupations are traditional and largely unpaid: animal rearing, agriculture, free collection of household products like fuel, and making dung cakes. Of the modern skilled jobs like transport work, train manufacturing, electrical wiring, plumbing, and carpentry, women account for less than 1 per cent of the workers. Even modern agricultural skills are handled by less than 10 per cent women.[4]

Women's exclusion from training or access to modern skills means not only that their skills are redundant, but also that when new technology is introduced, they get replaced in their former jobs by men.[5] While their traditional opportunities decline, there are no corresponding openings for women in modern occupations. Women who do work in new industries are consistently engaged in the least skilled jobs. Of the estimated 90 per cent of India's poor women working in the informal sector, nearly two-thirds of their enterprises operate from a fixed capital of less than Rs. 50 (US $3). More than 80 per cent of these workers earn less than Rs. 500 per month (US $30).

Workers who are in the informal sector are the basis of viability for many formal sector industries. The home-based piece-rate informal workers absorb all the risks and fluctuations of the market. When any technological upgradation is introduced which displaces these workers, unemployment levels then further depress wage rates. The Commission emphasized that organized and unorganized labour are *not* separate phenomena. Policies which favour subsidy, raw material supply, and technology upgradation adversely affect the unorganized sector workers whose products become uncompetitive on the market without such subsidies, or whose skills become obsolete in the face of new machinery.

Many forces combine to keep women in less skilled low paid work, but a major one is their lack of access to resources, the primary one being land. When men have land titles in their names, it is they who receive the benefits of agricultural extension services, credit, training in new technologies, and inputs like irrigation and fertilizers. As women remain on the periphery of these new processes, their role in production and management continues to be confined to unskilled tasks and largely defined by men.

Another intense constraint for women is that as long as their access to a resource like water is severely limited, they will never be free from subsistence tasks to undertake more skilled jobs which could positively affect their quality of life.[6] A revealing study in Gujarat showed that 78 per cent of the women of one taluka spent four hours daily fetching water, yet 92 per cent of the women stated that they had never been consulted about the site of the borewell, the water spikets, or the hours during which water would be available in their village when a water supply project was undertaken there.

Women face different crises when their customary rights to resources like forests are lost with the enactment of statutory law. The problem is most acute for tribal women whose entire existence depends on forest products, but it is also severe for women in landed villages who depend on this access for fuel and fodder. These closures are concurrent with vast encroachments and privitizations of the common lands traditionally used for grazing, fodder, and fuel collection. Thus, all the resources which women previously collected with only the cost of their labour become commercialized.[7]

The national policies which attempt to alleviate poverty through special programmes were reviewed by the Commission and found largely inadequate. The programmes do not meet the needs of the poorest women because they lack other support services to back up the loan or training they receive. Many such women are unaware that there are such programmes to benefit them. Those who are aware are often dependent on rich, literate, high caste male leaders of their community to access the benefits for them.[8]

The power of this Report is the articulation of how interdependent each aspect of women's social and economic position is, and how crucial an integrated approach is to effect any change. For example, the provision of child care services is not only necessary for a woman to take training in a new skill and then have time to carry out her occupation, it is also vital if her daughter is to be freed from the household duties including the care of her younger siblings. If this facility is provided, a woman can then engage in more skilled jobs where she is less subject to exploitative wages. If she earns better income, there is less need for her children to also be wage earners, and they can be free to attend school. The current government schemes for child care, however, offer a salary of only Rs. 275 per month ($16) for full-time child care providers who are, of course, women. This salary keeps them below the official poverty line, and they too face the compulsions of having their children contribute to the family income.

The task force covering occupational health disclosed a daunting report. With all the subsistence work, family care, and household tasks in addition to income generating work, most women work 15–16 hour days, largely under debilitating conditions. They face exposure to tobacco dust, fumes, toxic chemicals including pesticides, long hours at machines under poor lighting conditions and in poor postural positions, doing endless piece-work without ventilation, toilets, fixed hours, or protective equipment. They are undernourished, anaemic, often pregnant while continuing such arduous tasks, physically and mentally harassed by in-laws or an alcoholic husband, with little or no access to basic amenities like potable drinking water or safe health care. Even where poor women do live in proximity to medical facilities, they face extreme discrimination and lack of understanding by the medical staff of their social or work situations and how these affect their health conditions.[9]

The Report takes the government to task for its oppression of women through its family planning policy. This policy places all the burden of contraception on women, and promotes dangerous methods which are beyond the control of women, like injectable contraceptives, or insertion of IUDs or tubal ligations under unsterile conditions in large camps without adequate follow-up. They argue that access to safe family planning is necessary and important, but not to the exclusion of all other health care facilities, which discredits the public health care system and causes poor women to turn to private, often exploitative, practitioners.

Obviously, since women as workers have been invisible to date, not much work has been done on their occupational health problems. *Shramshakti* makes a start by not only documenting women's occupations, related health problems, and recommendations for change, but also by emphasizing the necessity of certain minimal conditions if their health is to improve: a living wage, regulation of working hours, maternity benefits, the need for affordable health insurance and access to workers' accident compensation, and a safe work environment with appropriate protective equipment.

Since many of these issues are to some extent covered in the present government policy, the Commission undertook to find out how many women were aware of the schemes that could effect change for them, and how they found out about these schemes. They examined all the channels of media and questioned rural and urban women in the unorganized sector to find out what channels of communication reached them. The overall impression that emerges from these interviews is that first, unorganized women's problems are barely reflected in any of the media. Radio programmes for women account for 1.4 per cent of total broadcasting time. The specific women's hour programme has been denigrated by calling it 'purdah hour' (veil hour) and it is largely entertainment-oriented. Furthermore, the few relevant programmes are broadcast in the afternoon, when only women who do not work can listen.[10]

Films by and large project distorted images of poor women: they are the sacrificing vehicles for their sons' or husbands' success; they are the complaining maid-servants who are projected in order to place the status of the protagonists; or they are in some transitory phase of work before manifestation of a 'just society' when they can become housewives. Poverty is sentimentalized, and viewers are not exposed to the real issues of squalid living conditions, overcrowding, poor sanitation, etc. Television programmes intended to extend education to poor women are often condescending. Juxtaposed with condescending advice come advertisements projecting women as sex symbols and glamourizing conspicuous consumption.

Reviews of primers used for adult education programmes revealed that they do include images of self-employed women, but they do not place adequate emphasis on women's work—middle class household work is still the largest reflected image. For regular readers in the formal education system, men are referred to between two and six times more than women, and references to self-employed women are virtually absent.

The second major impression is that dissemination of information to women through any of these media channels is largely influenced by family and neighbourhood-based communication channels. Lower caste and poor women are in general not exposed either to media channels or to public meetings at which information about development programmes is exchanged, and they find out about these only when men deem it important to communicate the message.

The Commission called for restructuring media dissemination by integrating socially aware members into planning groups to evolve a network which not only can reach the large number of women in question, but can also project relevant and representative images of them so that the other sections of society get a more realistic picture and have a more grounded appraisal of these women's contribution to the life of the country.

The final task force report outlines the history of women's organizing in the country, particularly tracing poor women's participation in the large nationalist and labour movements and their present-day local struggles over specific issues. While poor women were involved in the independence movement, their participation dropped sharply after independence as they were not included in the leadership which was focusing on governing a new country, nor did the All-India Women's Conference focus on the issues of the self-employed. In the mid-seventies many other women's groups besides SEWA began to emerge, and women began to portray themselves as militant and aware and determined to struggle for their rights. The kinds of issues around which women successfully organized were protesting ecological destruction of village resources, loss of employment to mechanization, discontinuation of alcohol licensing and closing down existing vends, and peasant uprisings for land rights. The one point which the Report indicated, however, about the majority of these struggles was that they were unsustainable: once the particular issue around which women organized was solved, the organization dissipated, and further issues were not addressed.[11]

This sets the stage, then, for the Commission's recommendations for policies which will favour the self-employed and unorganized women and help them organize. They acknowledge the difficulty poor women face in challenging the status quo, opposing vested interests, confronting their own fears and weaknesses which are a result of years of long conditioning. In their attempts to overcome these obstacles, women face humiliation, ridicule, hostility, violence, the alliances of power groups against them, loss of work, and other forms of intimidation like sexual harassment. Within themselves arise caste conflicts and religious differences which they have no living experience of transcending until they successfully organize across these barriers. The Commission recommends ways the state can help women to come together—through their village

Mahila Mandals (women's societies), through savings groups, through unions and cooperatives. Communities' attitudes toward women change when they successfully organize, which gradually change perceptions in larger spheres. They further advocate devolving decision-making power to these groups for defining development priorities, and implementing them.

The policy recommendations which became a major focus of SEWA's adolescence will be discussed in detail later. The strength of their own organizing had become apparent to them, but the distance they had to travel is obvious based on the foregoing Report. Bhatt, who oversaw the entire Report, was not the only SEWA representative to contribute to it. Many SEWA activists mobilized research and collaborated with other workers and researchers to contribute to the study. This work further reinforced that the situation in Gujarat was not unique—either in the extremes of vulnerability and invisibility that self-employed women were facing, or in women's extreme eagerness to change their situation.

Before Bhatt's term as MP expired, she submitted this landmark Report and two Private Member Bills for national policies to cover Home-based Workers and Hawkers and Vendors. In early 1989 SEWA organized a joint meeting of private voluntary organizations and trade unionists at the Gandhi Labour Institute to develop strategies for national minimum wage legislation to cover all occupations. The different groups recognized the need to develop a coalition of the organizations working with the self-employed if they wanted to advance their policy priorities. This goal prompted Jhabvala and 10 other Indian activists representing voluntary organizations to travel to Washington D.C. in 1989 and 1990 to work with political action groups and study lobbying techniques. In other efforts, several voluntary and intermediate action groups including SEWA have formed an association called the Voluntary Action Network of India (VANI, meaning 'speech') to develop their constituency.

With the Congress-I government at the centre taking little action on the *Shramshakti* Report, SEWA published the recommendations in English and lobbied outside for regional language translations. SEWA organizers continue networking across the country to consult other organizations and governments on how to implement the recommendations in their respective states. In May 1989, SEWA, the Gandhi Labour Institute and the Ford Foundation organized an international conference on Home-based Workers' Research. Twenty-six researchers from Africa, Asia, and South America met in Ahmedabad to chart the direction of their research so as to present sufficient evidence to the ILO in 1990 to merit decisive global legislation. In early 1990, the ILO's *Work Digest* covered the conditions of home-based workers for the first time. Later that year, Bhatt called on the IRENE Women's Commission in Tilburg, Holland to press for an ILO meeting to set standards for home-work. The ILO subsequently set up a tripartite expert group committee to determine if world standards should be set in a Convention. Bhatt was appointed to that 18-member Commission, and we know what vote she will cast.

These are all exciting developments in the face of politics in the nineties. Voluntary organizations which emerged in the seventies to serve the populace which was being left out of development, or which was beyond the reach of government schemes, are now joining their small rivulets of experiences together to alter the quality and direction of the mainstream. That much of this re-orientation is taking place through women's experience bodes well for the hope that more integrated, humane development of people and resources will be the fruits of this alliance. The attractive quality of this movement is that it has laid down a path by which values deeper than industrial development at any cost may translate into action.

Most of these groups—like SEWA—are not associated with any political party, but are initiating policy change through what is known as a 'non-party political process.' SEWA has found it more conducive to its objectives not to be affiliated to a party which will rapidly come into and go out of power, but rather to hold whoever is in power responsible for responding to the needs of the poor self-employed population.

Jhabvala described their strategy: 'As a principle, we feel that the government *should* perform—they should deliver to poor weavers, etc., so we pursue them. How else will we get things done as poor women? Indira (Gandhi) legitimized channelling assets to the poor and we are trying to strengthen the forces which are pulling them to us (the poor).'

She attributes their ability to get the government to 'perform' while remaining non-aligned to political parties to their 'autonomy of goals' and their size. 'Small voluntary agencies who need money get caught by the government which is looking for non-governmental organizations (NGOs) to do some work which it will fund,' she said. 'The NGOs take up the work because of their need for funds, and then they have to make compromises. If you have autonomy of goals, and *some* financial resources, you will have to constantly manoeuvre to stay on your path, but you *can* take from the government what you need.'

Till 1988 SEWA manoeuvred for its needs through a strategy of initially setting up a project itself with resources from the Trust or from the funds provided by international organizations. This allowed SEWA to develop new models which the government often seemed inflexible towards. Since there are not many good working models for self-employed women, SEWA considered this freedom to develop new models essential. With their own funds and management, they could work together in an atmosphere of encouragement, rather than one of mistrust which the government often projects. They could do things immediately, which the extreme slowness or repeated delay of government funds does not permit. Once they had developed a sufficient model—like that of maternity benefits for landless agricultural workers, or for flexible child care services for self-employed mothers—they approached the government and lobbied them to support and expand the model, creating another way that SEWA affected policy and implementation.

This approach generally applies to their economic development as well as to their building of services for the self-employed. Although several government programmes provide self-employment support, most of them do not sufficiently cater to the needs of low skilled women. SEWA's economic policy lobby consists of promoting different kinds of economic activities for women, experiencing the constraints women encounter in the programmes, and then lobbying the government to revise state and central policies so that these schemes fit women's needs. Handlooms is one such example. Because women's level of skill is not able to withstand market competition, SEWA works to influence handloom development policy to support women's skill and technology training to the point that they can compete. It is not just weaving skills that women need, but also other skills to follow the entire process through to a remunerative conclusion—knowing the market, designing for it, weaving for it, having the ability to change with it, or to change it through innovative ideas.

SEWA's understanding of these constraints led to its reshaping of many government programmes for rural members, through what organizers call 'planning from a woman's perspective.' They developed informal dairy training material for illiterate women so that they could form producers' cooperatives and breed their own animals. They reoriented the kind of agricultural training women had access to so that they could learn relevant new skills. They developed extensive training models for women to acquire business and accounting skills to run their own cooperatives, and take on the responsibilities of democratic organizations. On the strength of their evolving rural programmes in Ahmedabad, Kheda, and Mehsana districts, they were invited in 1988 by the Dutch and Gujarat governments to formulate an entire district development programme for the Banaskantha district of north-eastern Gujarat. It is an important programme to follow in assessing SEWA's approach to rural development, as it provides a measure of their earlier rural programmes—which they continue simply because of women's dependence on them; or which they replicate and expand on in the new programme because they are successful models.

It is only two years since this Banaskantha project was launched, already there are signs that SEWA's rural approach is shifting: In Banaskantha, SEWA more actively seeks the support of Panchayats and existing government infrastructure, rather than establishing parallel alternative systems. In a 1990 interview, Bhatt expressed optimism over their dealings with the District Rural Development Agency's willingness and flexibility to redesign programmes in collaboration with SEWA. She thought that SEWA would further this direct pressure on the existing systems, now that SEWA women have gained mainstream credibility as programme and policy developers.

REORIENTING NEGATIVE VALUES

Obviously, all the policy change initiated by SEWA cannot exist in a vacuum. It needs to be supported by a change in societal values at every level. Bringing visibility at the public level is one place SEWA starts, but it is simultaneously supporting women through a consistent value network rooted in the community. There are hundreds of examples of how SEWA support has redirected the manifestation of negative values against women, but I will cite two examples here which took place during the eighties.

In 1987 an incident of *sati* (a woman who immolates herself in 'honour' of her dead husband) in Rajasthan focused national attention on Roop Kanwar, an 18 year old woman who sacrificed herself on her husband's funeral pyre. Despite the illegality and gruesomeness of the act, thousands of spectators had gathered to witness the event and receive the blessings of the sati. Hundreds of thousands of rupees were collected to construct a temple in her honour even as press reports began to surface which suggested that the young woman had been drugged, terrified, and forced into the fire by her in-laws. The events were unclear, but what became clear was that no one backed her up in life. The sati brought her husband's family fame and prestige. To them, her continued life would have meant one more mouth to feed. To herself, it could have meant ostracism, poverty, and the remainder of her life as a widow.

Shortly after the incident, at SEWA's General Body Meeting, the issue was brought up for discussion. SEWA's carpenters, smiths and cartpullers are largely of Rajasthani origin and orthodox in social practices. When Elabehn asked the members, 'Who among you is ready to commit sati?' the Executive Committee member, Mirabehn, raised her hand. Besides being an extremely skilled craftswoman, she is a gifted singer of religious epics.

The other women present got agitated and began chiding and condemning her. They spoke out about the negative pressure on women to commit these kinds of acts. They argued that women do useful work in society whether their husbands are drunkards, or hardworking, or honest, or unemployed, or dead or alive. Women's status did not just depend solely on men, as much of society tries to imply. They argued that they were valuable just as they are, for all the work and life they contribute. By the end of this discussion, Mirabehn stood up and said to Elabehn, 'I just raised my hand— but the sisters are right—I would not commit sati.'

What the members spoke in that meeting they formulated into a memorandum of protest condemning 'the outdated and inhuman ideal which victimized a young woman at the hands of her community.' A delegation went from SEWA to Jaipur and marched in silent protest with thousands of other women from all over the country, and presented their memorandum to the Chief Minister of Rajasthan.

These experiences are the kind which Ela cites as giving her confidence in the working women of India being the hope for change. 'There are so many negative values which put pressure on women in our society,' she said. 'But these women have shown me how, through the pressure of positive values, they can influence those negative values—they can generate positive attitudes of change.'

The most striking example of this ability was illustrated during the time when the self-employed women in Ahmedabad were facing extreme immediate crisis. Like the 1981 riots which triggered off SEWA's split from the TLA, reservation issues again erupted into violence throughout 1985–86. Trying to piece together the events and the causes that sparked them is difficult because there are no disinterested parties, and grief and tension still remain two years later. Most commentators agree that the government announced an increase in the reservations in schools and government jobs as an election ploy. Only 12–17 per cent of the existing 31 per cent reserved seats were being utilized, so the announcement of 18 per cent additional seats just prior to elections seems to substantiate the claim. The government was not focusing any effort on why the current reservations were not being fully utilized.

In February, upper caste students agitation against reservations began in the schools, soon joined by several thousand parents, and even members of the business community who were not affected by quotas, triggering off unprecedented violence all over the state and polarizing every community. What began as upper castes fighting lower castes, soon turned into Hindu–Muslim riots. The police got drawn in as targets of people's unrest, and soon they were inflicting violence against even innocent people in retribution. The army was called in to help control the situation, which they were not able to, and citizens of Ahmedabad lived through curfew being clamped on the city intermittently for five months.

When violence would erupt—throwing fire bombs, raiding and burning houses, shootings, and stabbings—a mass exodus from the affected areas of the walled city would follow. Out of 19,000 refugees who fled to relief camps, 98 per cent were Muslims. Long curfews followed, which as Ela described, were perhaps the worst violence against the poor. The relief camps were nightmares of poverty and loss. On several occasions the curfew extended round the clock for 10 days. One continued for 21 days. During the curfew, women were allowed out for brief periods to buy supplies, but as Karimabibi recalled, 'If we could not go out of our houses, how could we get work? If we did not have work, how could we buy supplies? It was a long, slow, dark starvation.'

Those in the relief camps were particularly demoralized because they had even lost their means of livelihood once the curfew was lifted. When they had to flee their homes, their tools of trade were looted or destroyed by the ensuing mobs. Even those who did not lose homes or tools were extremely affected by the curfew. Hawkers and vendors could not ply the streets to sell vegetables. Bidi workers, garment stitchers, incense rollers could not get raw materials. If they could obtain raw materials and produced them into finished goods, these were often destroyed in the subsequent violence, and they received no payment for their work. Paper pickers could not even think of combing the streets for recyclable waste. Union workers recalled painfully the experience of seeing SEWA members from the same occupations and same neighbourhoods in segregated relief camps—Hindus in one and Muslims in another. Garment workers from both communities who had been working concertedly for the preceding year on getting minimum wages passed for their work, suddenly saw their ranks divided and deep suspicion of one another.

Rahima, a garment stitcher and organizer, recalled the dejection and demoralization of her community in the relief camps. 'We had worked so long to make our numbers strong as stitchers,' she said. 'Now so many women were bitter and accusing. They would see me and say, "Where is your unity now?" While we were all sitting in relief camps, our men had been killed, and our houses burned. I knew there was nothing more important than healing this breach.'

This healing work was an important step to change the status of women in the crisis of violence. SEWA changed the shape of what relief meant for the self-employed. The first step toward rehabilitation was to provide riot victims with their lost tools of trade, or merchandise for hawking, or raw materials for their production work. SEWA recognized that everyone needed work in order to rebuild their lives out of the destruction, and over 500 families received sewing machines, or hand-carts, or hawking goods.

As they worked more and more closely with the victims, replacing their lost tools, helping them receive government compensation for rebuilding their houses, or for the injuries or death sustained in police firing or mob attacks, SEWA workers began to realize the necessity of putting an end to the violence and hatred, not only repairing the breach once it had occurred. As SEWA was the only secular organization providing relief work, the army began consulting SEWA on how to put an end to the violence. Both the politicians and the police had completely failed in controlling the situation.

Through these efforts, SEWA workers were issued the rare curfew passes which enabled them to go out during the curfew. Some SEWA members who were concerned but were not issued passes also came out to contribute to the relief efforts, and showed their SEWA membership cards, which the army honoured as legitimate passes. Their initial attempts at reconciliation concentrated on Raikhad, a crowded inner city neighbourhood. This neighbourhood housed Vaghari used-garments and vegetable vendors, the Hindu Bhois who hawk fish, and several Muslim communities of block printers, meat sellers, and garment workers.

Ela knew many of the Bhoi fish hawkers, so she and Renana first went to their houses and spoke to them. Usually these women sit in the same market place with the Muslim meat sellers, and they work closely together. One Bhoi woman wore a torn blouse, and was tense and afraid when she told them that she had been roughed up and they had been given an ultimatum to quit the market. All these Bhois were carrying their large fish knives, saying 'we cannot trust the police so we are protecting ourselves.'

After their meeting with these women, Ela and Renana went back to the desolate scene of destruction and desertion, groping for a way to make contact with the Muslim community behind the closed doors. Suddenly someone shouted, 'Behn! Behn!' It was a young SEWA member who had been trained in block printing. She called Ela and Renana into her house, and many women from her trade congregated there to talk frankly about their difficulties.

Thus began SEWA's mediation in the problem. For three days Ela and Renana continued meeting members of different communities, and the stories were the same. 'They' start the violence, 'they' throw stones, 'they' are going to attack us, we want peace but we heard 'they' are planning something—it was the same story from both sides. Chandabehn came along and spoke as a neighbour to the two communities and convinced them to have a joint meeting to dispel the rumours.

The army brought a vehicle to take the women to the neutral ground of SEWA for a meeting, and for the first sign of tolerance since the violence had erupted months earlier, women from both communities climbed into the vehicle together. The tension visibly lifted as all the neighbours watched.

The meeting began amidst accusations and anger after all the months of loss and violence, but the women gradually worked through their despair until they came to see one another's point of view. Once they were able to listen to each other's concerns and anger, they came to the conclusion that outside forces had been planting false rumours in order to perpetrate the violence. By the end of the meeting they vowed to rebuild their unity as workers. Karima recalled the end of the meeting when they sang unity songs which they usually sang to initiate meetings in the years prior to these tensions. 'Public meetings were prohibited in those days. When we were singing like this, some army officers came up to see what was going on. Everyone was surprised to see Hindus and Muslims sitting together singing prayers.'

This meeting marked an important beginning for strengthening bonds between the two communities. They then organized a meeting of men and boys to enable them to sort out their differences, and set up a peace committee for the two communities. These efforts quelled any subsequent violence in Raikhad, which many attest had been on the brink of serious eruption.

Another powerfully telling event about women's ability to lead as mediators of the violence happened in Dariapur, another pocket of the old city where the various communities have lived and worked side by side for generations. Curfew had been clamped down for almost the entire month of Ramzan (the longest Muslim religious holiday). The day on which they break their month-long daytime fast, Id-ul-Fitr, coincided that year with the Hindu festival of Rathyatra. The army had relaxed the curfew for a couple of hours that morning so that Muslims could go to their mosques and offer their prayers. Despite the curfew, the rathyatra procession broke the army cordon and followed its usual route through some of the tension-ridden areas. When it entered the Kalupur/Dariapur area, stones began flying over the small *kaccha* houses which line the street, more violence broke out, the army fired, and seven Muslims were killed.[12]

Muslim women began forcing their men off the streets to protect them and prevent furthering the violence. Some women grabbed the soldiers and began demanding explanations. Why had the Rathyatra been permitted to proceed on the day of their biggest festival, yet they were paying with their lives? Karima recalled being absolutely fed up—with the curfew, with the way the authorities were handling the situation, with the violence and victimization.

'I started organizing the women. I divided them into groups of five. Thousands of us all started marching together. When any army officer tried to get us back into our houses, we grabbed their sticks from them and threw them into the gutter. We all sat on the road, refusing to move, offering *satyagraha*. When the Major tried to convince us to move, we said we would only go home when he agreed once and for all to lift the curfew. We said they could shoot us if they would not lift the curfew. Do you know what it is like to have 10 people in our houses (they are mostly one tiny room), without doors or windows open, without work, without food? We did not care if they shot us under these conditions. He finally agreed to lift the curfew, but I made him sign a paper so that they would not enforce it again.' (Observers testified that this short woman convinced the towering officer while she had caught hold of his collar!)

Besides SEWA's critical role of providing relief and initiating reconciliaton efforts, which were the largest positive contributions to ending the violence, SEWA drew public attention to warped press coverage of the issues in the media. None of the papers had even covered the non-violent protest of thousands of Muslim women against the army action. Based on SEWA's information of these events, and their reporting that the worst victims of communal violence were the poor and self-employed, the *Indian Express* and *India Today*, leading national newspaper and magazine sent correspondents to report on poor families in the affected areas. A Bombay group called Women and Media sent a team of five women who wrote a special report on the impact of the disturbances on women, which appeared in the *Economic and Political Weekly*.

One of the women most severely victimized during this time was Rabiya Pathan. Her house was attacked by a mob including the police, who started beating her husband. When she tried to intervene they raped her and threw acid on her. Her husband was killed, and she was left with much deeper than physical scars from the incident. When *India Today* correspondents visited the relief camps, they photographed the six children she would have to support single-handedly after she was released from the hospital three months later. SEWA helped her secure Rs. 20,000 compensation from the government and provided her with a sewing machine to begin earning a living for her family. Her father saw the photographs of his grandchildren in the newspaper and came to Ahmedabad to help his daughter.

In June 1988 I met him in Ahmedabad. He returns periodically to try and convince Rabiya to return with him to Uttar Pradesh where he can look after her, or to send her eldest daughter, now 16, with him to get married in the village. Rabiya gently but firmly refuses him. She told me, 'I do not think I can see anything worse in my life, but I also will not move and be defeated. Here at least, I have my life with SEWA. Here there is some love and struggle which offsets that terror. I have realized how much I have to be able to work against all these forces. Here at least I have the dignity of my stitching, and my defiance against these odds.'

Her courage speaks everything about SEWA's second decade of existence. Rabiya's belief in uniting across such odds is what projects working women's values and determination for change further and further out. She is not only a victim of violence or a recipient of inadequate compensation; she is a woman who is once again marching with her sisters from both communities for minimum wages. She is living alone without any men to support her, to contribute to the lobby for a woman's support network. She is refusing to let her young daughter get married like she did so that she can also learn some skill through SEWA and earn her own income. Despite the terror she faced making a stand for her husband, she continues to stand as one of thousands of Ahmedabad women who demand a home-based workers bill which will protect women like her across the country, and—if successful with the ILO—women like her across the global map of women's vulnerability and invisibility.

END NOTES

1. Jennifer Sebstad, *op.cit.*, p. 244.
2. SEWA Haryana dropped out of the affiliation in 1984 when its leadership came

under indictments of extortion. The other SEWAs have varying amounts of interaction with the affiliation. See chapter 9 for more details.

3. *Shramshakti: Report of the National Commission on Self-Employed Women and Women in the Informal Sector*, Government of India, 1988, pp. 27–30.
4. *Ibid.*, pp. 15–57.
5. *Ibid.*, pp. 44–46.
6. *Ibid.*, pp. 61–63.
7. *Ibid.*, p. 59.
8. *Ibid.*, pp. 57–96.
9. *Ibid.*, pp. 136–73.
10. *Ibid.*, pp. 173–213.
11. *Ibid.*, pp. 213–49.
12. Ammu Joseph, Jyoti Punwani, Charu Shahane, and Kalpana Sharma, 'Impact of Ahmedabad Disturbances on Women, A Report,' *The Economic and Political Weekly*, 13 October 1985, pp. 1726–31.

5

The Union: Struggles of Solidarity

'This sister came to me crying. She said she had been trying to sell her bidis to the local trader for three days, but he kept refusing them. She was desperate to earn some money. For a week her family had only eaten what their neighbours gave them. I asked her to show her work. They were good bidis. They were fine. I said, 'Come on!' and we went straight over to that trader. I asked him, 'What is wrong with these bidis?'

He said, 'There is not enough tobacco inside them.'

So I said, 'Then please, show me the ones behind you which are made right.'

He handed me a bundle of 500 bidis. I took this sister's bundle of 500 from her hand and put them both on opposite sides of the trader's scale. This sister's were heavier!

I said, 'Look, if you do not accept her bidis, we also will not sell to you any longer!' He knew I spoke for 6000 bidi women, and meant what I said. He paid her on the spot for her bidis — full rate. He had been using this tactic so that she would come two or three more days, crying and hungry. Then he finally would have accepted her bidis, as though he was doing her a big favour. Her children would have been so starved that he would

*make her feel grateful to him even if he gave her a quarter of the
minimum wage.*

*. . . How do I know these things? I have worked in the bidi
industry for 25 years, and every trick has also been tried on me.*
      Godavari Padmashali, bidi worker and President of union

Godavaribehn is a gentle, thoughtful woman in her late 50s who
speaks alternately between a calm smile revealing betel-stained
teeth, and a stern frown expressing a conviction that leaves little
room for argument. She often refers to the need to change herself
before she can expect others to change as she speaks about her
work as the President of SEWA and leader of the bidi trade union
of about 6000 women. It is an important part of her leadership skill
that she does not simply blame outside forces for the vulnerability
they face as workers. While it is true for every trade group that a
shroud of invisibility and exploitation hampers all their efforts to
change, Godavaribehn also admits that women have been deeply
ingrained to believe that they are weak, and that they themselves
have to overcome this weakness before they can bring change.

The major focus of almost any SEWA meeting is unity building.
While this might seem obvious for most kinds of union work,
accomplishing a unified front of the self-employed is extremely
difficult. Organizing factory workers means bringing together
those who already have steady employment. When organizing the
self-employed, however, SEWA attempts to bring together women
who are often competing for the same jobs. For example, in the
limited market space available for used-clothes vendors, it is not
uncommon to see two vendors desperately fighting over one space.
Because piece-rate workers are so economically strained, they will
often undercut one another simply to get work, depressing wage
rates further. There is no limit to the labour pool willing to do jobs
at minimal wages. These problems are exacerbated by further
competition for water at the municipal taps and housing space in a
slum, and through historical communal and caste tensions which
condition people to attitudes of divisiveness and mistrust.

Along with these constraints is the looming power not only of
the contractors, traders, or landlords who employ these women,
but also of the community and its social strictures which limit
women's mobility and actions. Women who are hawkers, cartpullers
or paper pickers have overcome many obstacles which restrict

their movement, although they still face a great deal of harassment from residents in middle and upper class housing colonies and from authorities like the police. Home-based workers, however, especially Muslim women—because of social strictures which do not allow many of them to go out—are the most economically exploited groups SEWA has come across.[1] While some home-based workers are low skilled piece-workers, the majority are extremely skilled artisans. Women who have never left their neighbourhoods have no idea about the market value of what they produce, nor how to acquire raw materials or approach markets. A woman who does step forward in protest of her condition makes herself a target of social disapproval, which can result in ostracism, harassment, violence against her or her family members, or perhaps the worst recrimination for a family at the economic edge of survival—loss of employment.

These social conditions and practically non-existent or negative legal and policy climates contribute to the vulnerability and weakness of these women. Although it seems inappropriate to call them 'weak', because they are indomitable in the face of so many odds, it is correct to say they *are* weak individually in bargaining power, and weak initially in the belief that they have power to change anything.

That they have been able to break through these barriers and unify themselves in strength is short of a miracle only in the amount of work it involves. While unity enables them to press for policies and enforcement, they have also found it is difficult to unify until there actually is a policy backing them up which they can then rally around. Once they do achieve some legislative change in favour of the self-employed, *actual* change in conditions is further dependent upon the workers and their workers' organizations possessing the authority to identify the workers and enforce the laws. Self-employed women repeatedly have seen that without their participation, good laws within the existing bureaucracies have little impact on their lives.

SEWA's definition of union organizing is a continual process of distilling issues and building unity around them; raising the consciousness of workers, society, and government; pressing for policy change; and enforcing the policy so that women get their rights. Although the specific issues vary with each trade group, this process applies to all of them. The SEWA union organizes self-employed women from 33 trade groups. Each trade group fits into one of three general work categories: Home-based Producers; Hawkers and Vendors; and Providers of Labour or Services. To get some insight into the problems which these workers face, one or two trade groups from each category of workers will be discussed.

HOME-BASED WORKERS

Bidi Workers

Of the home-based producers, SEWA bidi workers have the most experience at making legislation work for them, although this was far from the case when SEWA began organizing them in 1978. Their successes after a decade of struggling for their rights have helped carve a path for all the other trade groups to follow— although it is never easy walking.

SEWA became aware about the bidi trade through Chandabibi, a woman from Patan, a town about 90 km outside of Ahmedabad. In 1978, she, like all the other Patan bidi workers, was getting barely Rs. 4 for a day's work. Her sick family members were being denied access to a medical centre set up by law specifically for bidi workers. To use the centre, she had to have a worker's identity card issued by her employer. In order to evade their legal responsibilities, most employers refuse to issue cards, entering fictitious names into their books, and registering women workers under male names so that no maternity benefits can be claimed. They change the fictitious names every few months, so that no one will be shown eligible for long-term benefits like gratuity or provident fund or scholarships.

Bidi rollers as a trade group suffer extremely poor health. These women sit in their tiny one-room houses, often without lights or windows. All day, every day, for many years these women and all the other family members breathe the tobacco dust. Surviving on family incomes as low as Rs. 4 per day (US $0.25), their nutritional levels are extremely poor. All these factors converge to make tuberculosis widespread among them. The medical facility set up in Patan for their use under the Bidi Welfare Act did not have patients day after day. Even the doctor had no work yet he refused to treat them because they did not have worker identity cards. Out of her frustration, Chandabibi became the first bidi worker to approach SEWA and request assistance in struggling for their rights.

When SEWA organizers went with Chandabibi to Patan,[2] they found about 500 women all reporting the same conditions, but reluctant to take any collective action. They distrusted outsiders. Many expressed resignation to their conditions of exploitation, disbelieving that they could be changed. They were fearful of the repercussions of both their employers and their community. Many women remembered the previous agricultural union organizer in the area who was murdered. As poor women, their social standing within the community was the only protection they had. They anticipated strong signals of disapproval if they put themselves forward publicly in direct opposition to their contractors who enjoyed high position in the same community.

A few women did initially come forward, however, to place themselves in a position of risking their income, their physical safety, and their social sanction within the community by asserting their demands for identity cards. They realized that these cards were their only hope to secure their legal benefits as workers—including the use of the medical clinic.

SEWA sought help from the Labour Commissioner and the Labour Minister who bullied some of the contractors into meeting SEWA organizers, bidi rollers, and some labour and welfare officers. When SEWA demanded that identity cards be issued to all the bidi workers, the contractors maintained that they did not have any regular workers on their rolls. Although everyone verbally agreed to a compromise, in which the labour inspectors would look at the employers' books and decide which workers should be issued identity cards, the contractors went ahead with their own agenda. They all 'lost' the keys to their safes where they kept their books, and began terrorizing the women. They threatened them with dismissal (even though none of the women were 'regular'), and made an example of Havabibi—a widow with no other means of support—by refusing her work. They told the others they would likewise be blacklisted if they talked to anyone from SEWA or the labour department, and they simply refused to issue any cards. These women became afraid that they would also lose their work, and many showed reluctance to pursue the issue.

Chandabibi, however, was not ready to give in. She suggested that the government issue the cards instead of the contractors. SEWA organizers approached the Welfare Commissioner, asking him to issue the identity cards, but met with no response. Everyone in Patan felt at a dead-end. The only work they could do was to try and get Havabibi and other victimized women reinstated in work. They *needed* their Rs. 4 a day, at least.

Godavaribehn became involved with SEWA shortly after this, when organizers decided to strengthen bidi membership by mobilizing workers in Ahmedabad. During her 25 years in the industry she had seen the enactment of protective legislation, the resulting closure of all the factories, and the returning home of all the women bidi workers. Godavaribehn had participated in a union as a young woman in Andhra Pradesh before migrating to Gujarat, and she and other Padmashali women who were getting none of their legal benefits immediately became interested in organizing with SEWA.

As a tobacco worker, Godavari works in the industry employing the largest number of women workers in the country after agriculture. Every morning she goes to a contractor in her neighbourhood who gives her raw materials of tendu leaves and prepared tobacco, supposedly enough for 1000 bidis. This amount of supplies provides work for about eight hours, including the labour of other family members—daughters, daughters-in-law, and grandchildren. Their work involves cutting the leaves to size with crude scissors, wetting them, filling and rolling the tobacco, folding the edges with a metal tool, and tying them with a thread. The women sit on the floor, with their materials on their laps in a flat tray, or in shallow baskets used to winnow grain. They are able to roll only about 800 bidis out of the amount of leaves and tobacco the contractor gives them.

'When we return them, he accuses us of keeping 200 ourselves,' Godavaribehn explained. 'Then he tells us that one or two hundred of the bidis we have brought are improperly rolled, and refuses to pay us for those. After 25 years I am still rolling improperly!'

Every deduction the contractor makes from the producers' wages means an increase in his profits. Some manufacturers go one step further to break the link between themselves and the women rollers. They run their business under the 'sale-purchase system,' making the woman 'purchase' the raw material, and then 'buying' the finished bidis back from her. Thus a woman becomes a 'small trader' herself, ineligible for benefits as a worker. Although the woman producer supposedly owns the raw materials, the contractor still appropriates all of them, but refuses to pay for the 'rejects', which often amount to a quarter of her day's output.

Prior to organizing, women's consciousness about these kinds of discrepancies was widely variant. Some women who recognized the manipulation and dishonesty of the system were angry and indignant about it, but were powerless to effect change alone. Others were aware about the situation but had resigned themselves to the existing conditions. Their energy was focused just on making ends meet *today*—there was no extra to expend on forces so much larger and more powerful than they. Many women did not even recognize the tactics of the contractors as malpractices because they were so pervasive and persistent and the contractor had worked so diligently to 'condition' these women. Surveyors often found bidi rollers quoting the contractors' stated price or even the minimum wage as what they received. Upon further questioning, however, they found that women were actually receiving as low as half of what they quoted after all the deductions and rejections.

Under all these conditions, and receiving an average of Rs. 5 per 1000 bidis when the minimum wage was Rs. 11, Ahmedabad bidi workers wanted to know exactly *what* their legal rights were. SEWA organizers asked the officer from the Central Board of Workers' Education to conduct classes for bidi workers on labour laws and labour court procedures. The Board agreed to conduct five-day worker education classes for groups of 50 women each, and to pay each woman a stipend to compensate her for days of lost work.

Though the women were goaded by their contractors not to eat or drink anything during these classes because they might be poisoned, the classes proved so successful that SEWA adopted them as a standard organizing tool. Besides educating women about their rights, these classes provide a forum conducive to unity building in the membership. These classes often mark the first time a woman interacts outside of her own family or immediate community. This exposure helps to allay her fears and to build her weak self-image, as well as to change the divisive patterns of behaviour which characterize the crowded communities where she lives.

What the bidi workers learned in these classes was that bidi work is one of the few home-based trades which is actually covered by protective legislation under the Minimum Wages Act (1966), the Bidi and Cigar Workers Act, and the Bidi and Cigar Welfare Fund Act (1977). These laws comprehensively cover the conditions of the workplace, maternity leave, creche facilities, scholarships for workers' children, medical services, housing, and minimum wages. Ahmedabad women were getting none of these. All they knew about the laws—for those women who were previously rolling in factories—was that they were encouraged to move home where none of these conditions could be enforced. For those women rolling bidis at home, they saw the emergence of a complex system of protection the large owners built around themselves by engaging contractors and sub-contractors. This system, as Godavaribehn described it, 'made it impossible to grab the *choti* (hair) of the principal employer.'

Godavaribehn recalled the spirited feelings of solidarity they felt at the close of these initial classes: 'We were fired up! We wanted to press for minimum wages. We wanted to show both the government and our contractors how many we were—and that we were not afraid to fight for our rights. I knew how much these traders needed us—how much their success depended on *our* labour. Kamla (her daughter who later became a paid organizer for the union) suggested a procession, and all the sisters started cheering and clapping. After all the years of grind, to feel like *something* was going to happen—it was an exciting moment.'

They spent two weeks preparing for the procession. Every possible moment and every available organizer contacted women bidi workers all over the city. The natural organizing ability which would eventually make Godavaribehn President of the union was called into play when she persuaded the Muslim bidi rollers to participate in the *morcha*. She had to convince their menfolk of the importance of the demonstration so that they would let the women come out of their houses.

In the Gandhian style it adheres to, SEWA notified the authorities well in advance of its plan. Some of the literate bidi workers made posters, and pasted them all over the city. They read, 'Give us minimum wage!', 'Down with the contractors' system!', 'Give us bonus!', 'We want our legal rights!'[3]

On the day of the procession hundreds of women and organizers gathered with their placards. Word spread quickly and press photographers began documenting about 700 women moving and shouting slogans and rapidly increasing in number. The bidi marchers were striking in appearance because of the diverse communities they represented. Some Muslim women were in their black burkhas. Padmashali (from Andhra Pradesh) and Kosti (from Madhya Pradesh) women came in large groups. Many women carried children in their arms, and a few were nine months pregnant. Some old bidi workers also walked with them. Some women joined the procession in their house dresses or came running barefoot as it passed through their neighbourhood. By the time they reached the shop of the biggest bidi owner, Jiveraj, there were about 1500 women. 'Give us minimum wages!' they shouted. He quickly pulled down his shutters. The procession moved on to the other owners' shops. Word had already reached them and they had pulled down their shutters.

Everyone on the streets wanted to know what was wrong. The public was unaware of the kinds of conditions the bidi workers faced. Women stopped to explain and rejoined another section of the long banner of workers winding through the streets.

'We did not even mind when the contractors shut their doors,' Godavariben related. 'We have been cowering before these bosses for 20 years. They were afraid of *us* for the first time. We just shouted our slogans louder and moved to the next place. When we arrived at the Labour Commissioner's office, even he got intimidated by our numbers. He asked us to send 10 women to talk to him. We represented 20 points against the merchants and their contractor system.'

'After that the labour department raided the contractors' shops, and filed cases against them. Our contractors started calling us for tea. They said to us, "You don't need to go to the union. Whatever you need, tell us directly."'

'So I said it again, "We want a wage increase!" With our pressure, and that of the labour department, they were forced to increase our rate by Rs. 2. And of course we *did* keep going to the union.'

Their spirited militancy and securing of concrete gains brought 6000 bidi workers into SEWA's fold in the next four years—now the largest trade group in SEWA. Women's collective strength and persistent struggle enabled them to negotiate their rates from Rs. 5 up to Rs. 13 per 1000 bidis by 1987.

'One thing we have seen is that you never know when a break-through will come,' Godavaribehn reiterated.

One such unexpected breakthrough came for the Patan bidi workers, three years after they had hit their 'dead-end', and reverberated into large scale changes for all the unionized bidi workers at SEWA. A Member of Parliament had noticed that the Bidi Welfare Fund had been steadily increasing, with very little expenditure being made. The Labour Minister was questioned about this on the floor of the House. He later summoned the Welfare Commissioner and ordered him to spend the money at once. In the Commissioner's rush to solve the identity card problem, he came to SEWA and consented to their 3-year old suggestion to issue cards. SEWA soon received a frantic request from the welfare officer in Patan for help. He had been ordered to issue as many cards as quickly as possible. SEWA organizers gladly complied with this request by identifying workers and issuing 1500 cards. The doctor in the medical clinic no longer found himself idle or able to refuse treatment.

The women who had assumed active roles as leaders and organizers recognized the critical importance of all self-employed women acquiring identity cards to prove that they *are* workers and eligible for benefits. The system which was evolved for issuing identity cards to Patan bidi workers proved the only tenable one for Ahmedabad bidi workers as well. In the face of the contractors and merchants' refusal to issue cards, SEWA became the recognized authority to identify women to whom the Bidi Welfare Department issued identity cards. Once these women were issued their cards, however, they still had to struggle to extract minimal compliance in acquiring their benefits. SEWA therefore developed a system of 'responsibility sharing' with the government which now ensures that the members do get their benefits.

Sharda Kosti, a former bidi roller turned organizer, explained how in her opinion this means that they virtually do the government's work for them. 'We fill all the forms for them to issue cards, we deliver all the scholarship cash to the schools of the workers' children, we bring in the women who are eligible for maternity benefits. Even after incurring all the costs which should be the government's, do they appreciate that we have done their work for them? No! Instead they see a worker who has on a decent sari, and they say, "How can *she* be a bidi worker?" and they try to disqualify her from the benefit. Isn't that the point—that these laws are supposed to begin giving workers a decent life?'

Despite persistent insensitivity towards the workers, they have got many of their rights. Ahmedabad women now not only have access to the Bidi Workers' medical centres, they also control the staffing of the centres. In 1988, SEWA workers stipulated that their centre employ a woman doctor. The government complied and appointed a woman doctor. However she proved to be rude and insensitive, and they staged a *dharna* (sit-in protest) in front of the centre and filed a petition for her removal with 2000 signatures on it. The doctor publicly apologized and asked them to withdraw their petition on her promise of respectful treatment. In the spirit of negotiation, SEWA workers agreed to grant her a trial period.

Another benefit of the identity cards is that they qualify the poorest bidi members for low cost government housing which is provided under the Bidi Welfare Act. SEWA members are not only the first to wrest this benefit from the government in Gujarat, but also the first to register such a bidi housing colony in women's names. Although the government is responsible for providing low income subsidized housing, they are so reticent to take any risk that they expect SEWA to make a fixed deposit guarantee against defaulters. While the conceptual blocks do not seem to diminish, SEWA's resources at least have risen to a point that it can counter some resistance to support members like Saraswati (the bidi roller with no door to her hut) to get access to her own legal housing.

The awareness of legal leverage is reflected widely in the consciousness of the bidi membership. The major bidi legal fight—and the one which promises major ramifications—is against the sale–purchase system. SEWA has called the largest bidi manufacturer in the state, Jiveraj, to court, placing the onus on him to prove all the women working for him are *not* his employees. Till now, the union only used the court defensively for home-based workers who were victimized. This time, however, they raised demands in the Industrial Tribunal from an offensive stance, claiming Jiveraj as their employer. If he does not want to meet their demands for increase in pay and social security benefits, he will be obliged to prove that they do not work for him. The outcome of this case will be critical for the bidi workers of Ahmedabad, because all the smaller contractors and sub-contractors follow his practices.

Godavaribehn's strategy reflected the sentiments of all the

more active bidi members of the union when she said, 'we want to organize women all over Gujarat. Maybe we are taking on a lot, but we have seen the contractors' shutters go down. We have seen the Labour Commissioner follow through on our demands. We have heard how good our voices sound *together*. We understand very clearly that the more women we bring into the union, the stronger we will be.'

In the decade since SEWA began organizing bidi workers, they have recorded tremendous gains which have laid the groundwork for other home-based trade groups in the union to work from. While other trade groups started one step behind bidi workers—with no protective legislation in place—the successes and solidarity of this group have led others to push for legislation and launch the struggle for their rights.

This process takes place on three levels. At the first grassroots level, the union women struggle against the direct exploiter, like the bidi contractors, or extorting policemen; at the second level, they struggle against an ineffective labour enforcement bureaucracy and legal system; and at the third level, against unfavourable or absent national and international policies and laws. SEWA's consistent work at the grassroots, government, and policy levels has helped to ground the changes it initiates in a consistent reality.

Leadership of the Union

The structure of the union which this process works through is based on trade groups. The 33 trade groups represent diverse communities of women who choose group leaders from among themselves. The group leaders for each trade meet every month as the Trade Committee, to discuss the ongoing problems and strategies of action. They are the main catalyst for action in each trade group. They in turn choose leaders to send to the Trade Council, which includes all the trade groups of SEWA. For every 100 members in a trade, one representative is sent to the annual Trade Council meeting to learn about the work of the other trades. From this 300-member Council, the Executive Committee of the union is elected.

The Executive Committee of 25 trade leaders and 4 staff organizers meets once a month to make the major political decisions of the organization—whether a trade group will strike, what resolutions they will put before the government or the public, etc. Their resolutions cover both work issues (demands for a Commission on self-employed women, and minimum wage notification), and social issues (alcohol prohibition and sati). The Executive Committee assigns work to the paid organizers of the union, who carry out their mandates. The Executive Committee members are the inspired leaders of SEWA—unanimously dedicated, articulate, and empowered women. The majority of the Executive members are in their 40s and 50s, due to their experience and the fact that—once relieved of the burden of child rearing—they have more time to devote to the unpaid work of the union.

Garment Stitchers

Everyone at SEWA is clear from the beginning that no one will abdicate the smallest part of his or her niche without pressure. Bidi manufacturers, paper processors, garment manufacturers, for example, are powerful economic forces. SEWA is not only struggling against the individual contractor or manufacturer; it inevitably is struggling against the policies of the industry as a whole. While SEWA seeks government support for fair labour practices through the labour and justice departments, the public sector branch of the government simultaneously experiences pressure to promote industry in the country. Characteristically, different branches and levels of the government find themselves with conflicting priorities. While the central government promotes artisans and traditional crafts through numerous schemes, the state—in contracting 20 years of bamboo supply to the paper industry—undermines the raw material supply to bamboo artisans. Likewise, when SEWA achieves a concrete gain in favour of certain workers, pressure on another arm of the government by vested interests can cause the benefits to be retracted.

While the bidi workers clearly had protective legislation which included those who worked at home, the home-based garment stitchers were existing in a sort of void—neither explicitly included nor excluded in any labour laws. The efforts of SEWA garment stitchers to get explicit protective laws passed inducted them into a struggle between the various branches of the government. Now emerging from five years of such struggle, they are well-informed about the effective measures to achieve the policy changes they require.

Rahima Shaikh, who organizes the home-based garment stitchers, is a thin, fiery woman whose determination is clearly visible. She was educated because her father was a priest, and from a young age she began to question him about the role of Muslim women in the community. She could not believe that the *Koran* relegated women to absolute submission to men's domination, however unreasonable it may be.

'When I questioned my father on this, he told me to read the Book for myself, and find the answers to my questions,' she said in an interview. 'Through doing that, I learned why they keep the women uneducated in our community. Then they can perpetrate their unjust practices against us, telling us it is written in our Holy Book. By reading, I saw how misconstrued the practices of our community are against women.'

It did not take long before her intellectual realizations became a concrete reality. She was married and carrying her first child, when her husband decided he wanted a divorce. All he had to say was 'talak, talak, talak,' and the divorce was accomplished. By this unilateral repetition of 'talak,' her community considers the woman officially divorced, without rights of support for the woman or her children. The *purdah* (cloistering) system which relegates women to the house imposes serious limitations on their ability to earn a living, as the mobility and skills needed for better paying jobs are simply inaccessible. When deserted by their husbands, many women and their children become destitute.

Rahima was sent back to her parents' house, to bear and care for her daughter on her own. 'I cannot explain how terrible I felt in those days. Already my parents were poor. Now I was back, with a child as well. I began stitching chindi quilts and cheap garments from waste cloth, for a trader in our area. I was earning about Rs. 4 for working all day. I heard that SEWA was working in our area, but I was not interested. All that was on my mind was work. I thought, if I take off two or three hours for a meeting, I will lose Re. 1. I could not even afford to sacrifice Re. 1.'

Her brother, who lived in a separate house and enforced observation of *purdah* in the family, asked Rahima to carry his wife's stitching work to the chindi shop where SEWA was organizing women. In agreeing to her brother's request, she came in contact with SEWA's work. SEWA organizers quickly recognized that Rahima's determination and her literacy skills could be a valuable link between the community and the organization. Ela asked her if she would like to be a half-time organizer.

'After seeing all the women who were selling their quilts at the SEWA shop, I felt the overwhelming need to *do* something about the injustices we were all facing. Because I had my parents to live with, I was better off. But I saw so many sisters whose husbands had said "talak" after they had four or five or six children—and they could not go back to their parents.'

Rahima saw the efficacy of organizing through the higher rates her sister-in-law was paid at the SEWA shop than women were making outside from the trader. Because of SEWA, the traders had to raise their rates so that their stitchers would continue to stitch for them.

'As one, no one will listen,' she explained. 'When we are many, the traders' ears open up. I saw that when I was only in my house, I also knew nothing. Now I want to get other sisters out of their houses, to at least get fair wages. The *Koran* says a woman should not stay hungry, nor her children. How will we abide by this, if we sit in our houses?'

At each stage, Rahima had to get her father's permission. Her organizing meant travelling to workers' houses in other parts of the city to tell them about the work of SEWA. Because she was from their own community, they were receptive to her ideas. Through the meetings she organized, she learned that there were at least 250 big traders in Ahmedabad alone.

'The thought of how many women must be stitching for these traders made my head spin,' she explained. 'We organized a survey. I would inquire until I could learn where the traders were sitting. Then we would wait near that place. When women brought their work, we stopped them. We asked them everything—what work they did, what rates they got, how many women stitched for their trader, what were their lives like, what did they need. Once we got into their neighbourhoods, we could always locate the workers—their houses are so small they have to pull their machines out onto the footpath.'

They surveyed 1000 women, and learned through them that

12,000 women were stitching ready-made garments in Ahmedabad alone. Men also stitch, but women were engaged in the lower paid, lower skilled work of making petticoats, children's suits, sari blouses, and undergarments. SEWA organized approximately 3000 of the garment stitchers. 'Some came readily, some with hesitation,' Rahima said. 'Some do not come—like I did not—until they see concrete results. That is all right—no one has to jump into the well without knowing how deep it is.'

SEWA began by appealing to the traders about the difficulties of the stitchers, but with no law backing them up, this had a limited effect. SEWA then informed the government about their circumstances, asking that minimum wages be fixed. Most stitchers were earning between Rs. 4–Rs. 10 per day, from which they deducted their expenses for thread, oil, and sewing machines.

'It became very clear to me that home-based workers bear all the costs of the building, the machinery, the electricity,' Rahima said. 'The employers spend nothing. They should actually be paying home-based workers *more* than factory workers, since *we* bear these expenses. With this little income, we keep our daughters home from school to stitch with us. How will the world change this way?'

Rahima's realizations were concretized during the years by SEWA's interaction with the ILO and their organization of home-based workers' camps. Besides Ahmedabad garment stitchers, they organized women in three other cities who were engaged in diverse home-based trades. Rahima was the key organizer of these camps, from which all the groups emerged determined to press for both minimum wage laws and for an enforcement machinery which included themselves.

For several years no progress was made on getting the minimum wages drafted. As a result of SEWA's constant interaction with the government offices, the union members became familiar with the lower level bureaucrats, who finally revealed why nothing was moving: the large clothing manufacturers who work in Gujarat's Free Trade Zone had submitted numerous representations to the government against minimum wages. On the other hand the pro-minimum wage file contained only a few letters from SEWA. Both the organizers and trade group leaders realized that if they wanted their file to move forward, they needed to show some strength. That was in 1985. As they planned to take out a procession as their show of strength, riots erupted in the city. The communal violence not only made all public action impossible, but also undermined the solidarity of the garment stitchers who were from both the Muslim and Hindu communities and housed in separate relief camps.

In 1986, when there was peace in the city, a meeting of the garment stitchers was organized. According to Jhabvala, the groups were suspicious of each other, but because of SEWA's relief work, they were willing to meet. In spite of the residual tension, they decided to march in demand of minimum wage rates. More than 2000 women from both the communities marched together. Three days later SEWA's file moved, and the government issued a draft for daily wage rates of garment workers.

Rahima described how their initial gain was tempered however: 'We were happy with our victory, but we were also afraid that the daily wage rates would not help us home-based stitchers much. Daily wage rates are useful for factory workers. But for home-based workers, the contractors will claim that we can stitch twice as many garments in a day as we possibly can, and continue underpaying us. It is a crucial issue for home-based workers of every trade that piece-rate wages be fixed.'

The garment stitchers continued in their efforts to push the piece-rate draft through the bureaucracy, while the ready-made garment manufacturers began their own pressuring of the government. They threatened to move their industries out of Gujarat if the government ratified the minimum wage scheme. SEWA continued undaunted with its own lobbying of government officers. When the Committee for Minimum Wages met, 200 women garment stitchers leafleted outside and succeeded in getting the wage actually ratified.

They organized a *sammelan* and 2500 garment workers came to celebrate the first victory of SEWA of getting a law enacted in their favour. They invited the entire staff from the Labour Commissioner's office and voiced their demands. They demanded help not only in implementing the wage rates immediately, but also in pushing the minimum piece-rate through. Union members and members of the Labour Commission worked out a piece-rate based on the time it takes to stitch each type of garment. After unanimous agreement, SEWA women were stunned two months later when the Labour Minister succumbed to pressure from the garment manufacturers and *suspended* the minimum wages.

'We were outraged!' Rahima said. 'The only time minimum wages have ever been suspended in Gujarat was when there was severe drought.'

Knowing fully well that a court case would take years, SEWA decided to use some political pressure and printed leaflets to lobby legislators in the Assembly. The press picked up the story, taking a critical view of the government's stand. The night before SEWA women were scheduled to leaflet the legislators en masse, the government released a press report stating that they had reinstated the minimum wage—but *not* the *daily* wage. This time the Labour Minister astutely pushed through the piece-rate—satisfying both the home-based workers and the garment manufacturers.

Through these struggles, SEWA understood the importance of lobbying and showing strength of numbers at critical periods of policy-making. Each concrete gain the garment stitchers have achieved can be directly traced to their display of political will. To get the new laws enforced, SEWA is now organizing home-based garment stitchers across the state. Rahima described their strategy.

'We want to create strength for home-based workers, and short-cut the victimization and shifting out that we often face in trying to get our legal rights. Now the law is in place, our next step is to get enforcement. We want to sit on a board with the contractors and labour officials, to make sure we get our rights.'

Working with Officials

Getting workers to sit on labour monitoring boards is a step SEWA sees as critical to achieving any long-term and widespread changes in work conditions. As the garment workers' dilemma showed, the government's stand toward workers is complex and sometimes contradictory. While the government promotes development programmes and offers services to workers, to lower and backward castes and tribes, to women, and to 'below poverty line' groups in one of the most pro-poor policy stands of any country in the world, their focus on developing industry can directly work against the intentions of these programmes. SEWA is lobbying for both workers' and women's presence in monitoring positions to balance these trends.

In order for SEWA to succeed in its demands, it needs the cooperation of the labour, justice, and welfare departments. SEWA often comes into contact with officers in the labour department who are corrupted by the employers themselves and will not legitimately pursue the workers' grievances. Judges sometimes do not understand the issues that women workers face, and many officials cling to the perceptions that women do not work, and that home-based work is not work. These perceptions are reinforced by attitudes of discrimination against lower class and lower caste trade groups. This means that a great deal of SEWA's union work revolves around educating officials about women's work: that home-based workers *do* exist; and that these are not women doing jobs in their 'leisure' time for spare pocket money. Most of this is done through meetings, but SEWA also publishes a biannual journal in English, *We, The Self-Employed,* aimed directly at policy makers and activists.

Another problem for SEWA is the sluggishness of the court system. Cases often remain unresolved for years, in which time span daily wage earners have no resources to fall back on. SEWA organizers and lawyers weigh the relative advantages of other actions with legal action. They find which court level can most efficiently decide a particular kind of case. When one of their cases is coming up for admission to court, they remain alert for the sitting of a pro-labour judge, and push to have the case admitted for that judge's hearing.

While changing attitudes and perceptions is a slow process, getting behind the intricacies of corrupt systems can be excruciating. For example, if a labour enforcement official enters into an alliance with the contractors for a certain share of the benefit, he will overlook transgressions of record keeping. In one area, organizers found that while the wages of all the bidi workers were being deducted for the provident fund, none of them were issued receipts, and the contractors were only recording and paying 20 per cent of what they collected. They could perpetrate this because the labour officials helped them get around the law.[4]

Even in the case of honest inspectors, the physical constraints they face make enforcement almost impossible. In one ward of Ahmedabad, 15 inspectors are responsible for 147,000 establishments, i.e., one inspector for nearly 10,000 establishments. Moveover, their quotas for promotions are based on how many complaints they register, not on how many prosecutions result, and these inspectors are transferred every year.[5] These realities shed light on why it takes years of struggle by the same women to effect change—they often have to re-explain the same problem and re-convince a different group of officials of the same issue. It becomes apparent why SEWA women demand that a separate labour department be established for self-employed trades, that their own representatives sit on labour monitoring boards, and that women be appointed as labour inspectors for home-based workers.

The issues of bidi workers and garment stitchers are common to most home-based producers who engage in piece-work. Agarbatti (incense) rollers, papad (lentil wafer) producers, spice grinders, weavers, chikan embroiderers and block printers are other trades which seek protections similar to those which these two trade groups have won: piece-rate minimum wages which amount to a daily liveable wage; social security services such as child care, scholarship funds, and health benefits; and participation in policy formulation and enforcement.

Social Organizing

For most union members there is an increasing awareness that their economic problems are not unrelated to their social problems. Rahima is just one example of women's growing determination to affect the entire equation. A decade ago she could not leave home without her father's permission. In 1989, she was spending three months touring every town and village of the state to survey garment workers and organize them into the union. Although she was once reticent to join the union, she now relates the usefulness of coming together to the other major difficulty she sees in Muslim women's lives.

In 1986, the Muslim Women's Protection Bill withdrew the right of Muslim women to appeal for maintenance after divorce under the common Indian criminal code and relegated them solely to the jurisdiction of the Muslim Personal Law. During SEWA's protest of the Bill, Rahima organized divorced Muslim women who concluded that they should have the same protection that

Hindu women enjoy after divorce. This led to their drafting of a memorandum to the then Prime Minister Rajiv Gandhi, demanding withdrawal of the Bill.

There are 300 women in the Tallakshuda Mahila Sangh, which has three major objectives: to provide legal aid to divorced Muslim women, to help them solve their housing problem, and to help support their children's education. They actively lobby the community leaders to condemn the practices which victimize women, such as the social sanction for men to marry four times. If a man wants a divorce, the Mahila Sangh maintains, he should be required to wait at least three months from the first public declaration of 'talak,' unless the woman is also in agreement. After divorce, the husband should be required to support both the woman and the children he has abandoned.

'My brothers are trying to intimidate me in this,' Rahima said. 'They say I might destroy the community, erasing these old customs, and then they will blame me. But I answer, these things are destroying our women! We are firm in these demands. Our practices are relics of times when our men were being killed in wars. Then a man would take more than one wife to protect a woman and her children whose man had died. Now they discard a woman and her children as they get tired of her.'

HAWKERS AND VENDORS

Policy and perception problems exist in every trade for self-employed women. After the vegetable vendors had reclaimed their spaces in Manek Chowk through their *satyagraha*, Kartikeya Sarabhai and the Nehru Foundation for Development organized the first meeting to bring together the police, the municipality, SEWA, and the vendors. They agreed on a compromise that harassment would stop and they would push for closing the market to vehicles, making it a pedestrian zone. Though the police agreed, the residents who lived above the shops subsequently refused.

In the meantime SEWA women demarcated their spaces with chalk lines and the authorities informally recognized these spaces. Later that year, however, when the Janata government was voted out of power and the Congress government came in, the police department was shuffled and the old cycle of harassment began all over again.

During this time SEWA received a letter from Justice Bhagwati, who chaired the All India Legal Aid Committee, inviting voluntary organizations to a workshop to discuss making new laws or amending old ones. Bhatt responded by asking what was the use of such a workshop when the existing laws were anti-poor? She cited SEWA's experience with laws which work against the poor, particularly those not allowing them into workplaces. The Justice requested her letter to be turned into a petition to the court. Bhatt declined, saying that if he wanted a petition, they would enter a proper one.

'Unfortunately, we could not find any lawyer at that time in Gujarat who would help us,' Ela recalled. 'Any one we asked said, "Oh you mean those vendors who cheat people?" or "Those women who make so much congestion?" We knew if their heart was not in it, they could not do us justice.'

After negative responses at home, SEWA approached the Bombay lawyer, Indira Jaisingh, who had represented Bombay slum-dwellers in the Supreme Court against the demolition of their homes. She agreed to help the Manek Chowk vendors, and drew up a petition representing SEWA, Laxmibehn, Sakribehn, Devibehn and Ela Bhatt against the Municipal Corporation, the Police Commissioner and the State of Gujarat. The petition which was admitted to the Supreme Court claimed that by denying the petitioners licences, the municipality was violating their fundamental right to trade.

The Court ordered that the Municipal Commissioner issue licences to all SEWA members in Manek Chowk and that the police and municipality stay prosecution and work out a compromise solution with SEWA. After many aborted solutions, the parties agreed to situate the vendors on the terrace of the municipal market in front of which the vendors now sat. The vendors' reluctant agreement to this solution stemmed from their fear that customers would not climb the flight of stairs to reach them but instead buy from the more expensive shops located inside the market. Their agreement hinged on the following conditions: that the municipality construct a wider staircase up to the terrace and a roof to protect them from exposure to extreme sun and rain, and that they instal lights and water facilities. If any vendors were allowed in the future to sit in their old spots, SEWA vendors would have the first claim. The management of this new market would be in the hands of a committee comprising equal numbers of vendors and representatives of the municipality. The Court agreed to all the conditions, and passed them as judgement in 1984.

The vendors burst firecrackers in celebration of their Supreme Court victory in front of the same merchants' shops who had lit firecrackers the day SEWA was ousted from the TLA. Till 1990, the municipality had not done anything to improve the terrace. Although this is favourable to the vendors who legally continue to occupy their old, more desirable spaces until the conditions are met, many other grave transgressions against the vendors still continue. Laxmibehn (now about 60 years old) was severely beaten up and hospitalized by a new policeman for refusing to pay him a bribe. Other police officers continued to harass the vendors for encroachment, ignoring the Supreme Court order. SEWA lawyers and legal coordinators frequent the court to get hundreds of fines invalidated every year. They have filed 103 cases of police harassment and obstruction of carrying out business, and have succeeded in getting 45 bribes returned from the police to the vendors.

Many of these legal cases have been pursued through the courts partly due to the efforts of an energized young woman, Meena Patel, who joined SEWA in 1987 specifically to coordinate the legal activities of the union. She has played a key role in organizing workshops which help the trade organizers acquire the skills and logic to turn their issues into legal cases which they can develop and represent themselves. 'Although the organizers are literate and extremely sharp,' she explained, 'they are not used to learning things through books. There is simply no time for reading in their social context. They are well versed in action and issues, but not in legal theory. So we set up case studies of legal issues we are pursuing, and the organizers put their heads together with the lawyers to develop cases.'

Besides prosecuting offenders in court, SEWA is trying to positively change the attitudes and policies which affect vendors. SEWA conducts numerous studies and organizes forums which focus on the vendors' legal problems and on the urban planning processes which affect them. All these have contributed to SEWA's draft of a National Policy on Hawkers and Vendors, which calls for legitimating and planning for them in the modern urban economy.

PROVIDERS OF LABOUR AND SERVICES

Most women who are providers of labour and services have very low skill levels, no tools of trade, and no assets other than their labour to sell or trade. Extremely vulnerable women who have become destitute through whatever circumstances even fall out of the bottom of this work. As World Bank anthropologist Lynn Bennett (1989) said in an interview: 'Many of these women exist at levels of poverty so deep that their nutritional and general health status preclude manual labour, which is the only work they are qualified for.'

Those women who do manage to sustain themselves and their families by labouring for someone else find themselves absorbing all the risks, seasonal lags, work delays, and losses for the contractors they are labouring for. Women in the construction industry are not paid on days when weather precludes their building, when supplies have not arrived on schedule, or between jobs for the same contractor. Contract labourers in industry and contract cleaners for institutions find themselves doing the same work as permanent employees for as low as one-third of the wage and without day-to-day job security, while contractors pocket the profits of their labour. SEWA's studies revealed that almost 60 per cent of the textile mill contract labourers were women, while men held 97.5 per cent of the permanent protected positions.

Cloth Loaders

Headloaders and cartpullers have tried to counter their problems of underpayment or accidents on the job which keep them out of work at their own expense by forming a Cloth Loaders Board. The idea was based on a successful tripartite board in Maharashtra, which registered workers and traders, collected payment, paid wages, and provided welfare services. The Cloth Loaders Board has not been very successful. The crucial problem has been that while SEWA represents most of the women headloaders and cartpullers, the men, who constitute three times more of the labour force, are not organized. Also, several powerful contractors placed themselves in the seats of workers' 'representatives,' thwarting its functioning. In 1988, SEWA succeeded in getting the government to prosecute merchants for failure to register with the Board, and its future is pending the court outcomes of appeals. The Board's success will depend on the government taking a firm stand on requiring and enforcing registration, or on the appropriate organization of the male workers. The outcome will be important for SEWA's pursuit of such boards under their proposed Home-based Workers' Protection Bill which advocates similar boards.

Paper Pickers

Paper pickers are another example of vulnerable women labourers who fill a vital niche in the national economy at their own risk and expense—not only unacknowledged, but often vilified. There are over 20,000 waste pickers in Ahmedabad alone, of which about 1000 are unionized under SEWA. Since it is considered such a degrading occupation, women and their children account for a large proportion of the workforce of waste pickers. Men usually prefer remaining unemployed to withstanding the humiliation inflicted on those engaged in combing every street and garbage heap for recyclable refuse. The 'collective diagnosis' of SEWA's surveys amongst paper picking families reveals one of the most dismal trade realities around which women workers have organized. Although there is no official data, SEWA paper pickers all agree that the number of women engaged in this work has risen dramatically in the last two years due to further closure of the mills and increased migration after the severe three-year drought (1985–88).

Paper picking women work 10–12 hour days collecting, carrying, sorting, and selling to the contractors used paper, glass, plastic, and metal. They begin at 5 o'clock in the morning and walk about 10 kilometres a day, stopping in front of every house, in the alleys behind markets, at collection bins and any other refuse pile, hoisting the bulky 20–30 kg loads to their heads.

They carry their children with them if they are too small to stay alone at home. Children from about one and a half years to 6 years of age stay home alone, the 5 to 6 year olds looking after the toddlers. Their state of health is generally poor, with a high incidence of accidents taking place in their mothers' absence.

Children above 6 years help their mothers collect. More than half of the waste pickers' children do not attend school. Those who go to collect are constantly exposed to infection, hook-worm, toxic chemicals, broken glass, and other sharp objects in the refuse piles.[6] When a woman is injured, she is forced to give up her work and lose income until the wound has sufficiently healed, or until her family's need for income outweighs the immediate considerations of her recovery.

These families have an average of six members, and survive on incomes below Rs. 200 per month. During the monsoons, when they cannot collect paper, their earnings are even worse. The conditions of their work and the victimization they face all point to their humiliation. Babubehn, a 53 year old woman who was retrenched from the mills, characterized many of her sisters' plight when she said, 'When I was in the mill we used to look down on the paper pickers, thinking they are dirty and without shame. Now I am degraded too. When I had to start picking paper, I used to make my *ghungat* (veil) long so no one could see my face.'[7]

Ambabehn Chohan, a 47 year old group leader, recounted many stories of the abuse they receive in the middle class housing colonies. 'Everyone is afraid we will steal something. Sometimes they yell at us to get out. Sometimes they even throw stones, as if we are stray dogs. It's no wonder we feel terrified at times.'

Others expressed their humiliation by saying that before joining SEWA they were too timid to buy even a cup of water or tea on the roadside, for fear of being refused.

Their low incomes do not reflect the value of what they collect. Recycling is a lucrative business in India, reflected in 1989 paper prices which had escalated to four times the cost of western countries at Rs. 20,000 per ton.[8] The lucrative aspect of the business, however, is channelled to the contractors to whom these women sell. They can resell the refuse at up to 10 times the value the collectors receive because they deal in large quantities.

These issues gave SEWA some leverage points from which to start organizing paper pickers in 1975. SEWA's first step, with the help of the TLA, was to secure contracts from the mills for all their low grade waste paper. They wanted to reduce the drudgery and hazards of collecting on the street, and promise them a more steady supply of waste—albeit only for a limited number of collectors. The promise was not realized, however, when the mill employees who privately collected the paper continually thwarted the contracts. The intervention of higher authorities was required on several occasions to get the contracts honoured. They collectively stored paper in a common godown to sell it for higher profits when they had sufficient volume. By increasing women's access to paper and profits, more and more paper pickers came into the union, which was then faced with the difficulty of how to ensure work for all of them. Some of the more powerful women began controlling the godown as their own business. When a large quantity of paper disappeared, internal disputes arose over alleged corruption.

While trying to sort out these problems, the 1981 anti-reservation riots broke out in the city. The violence, which quickly turned into a caste war, was particularly devastating to Harijan women whose work was largely in the streets which were closed by curfew or shadowed with the threat of mobs, stones, and acid bombs. Under the stress of not being able to work for five months of curfew, these women became divided by a more long-term crisis. Due to SEWA's stand on supporting the reservations for Harijans and its consequent expulsion from the TLA, all the paper picking contracts were called into question. The TLA launched a campaign to stop the paper from going to SEWA, and the women were forced to choose their allegiance. Many women's husbands were members of the TLA, and could retain their access to paper if they left SEWA. A majority of SEWA women appreciated the stand SEWA had taken by speaking up for Harijans, and chose to forgo the paper contracts in their loyalty for the union.

SEWA regrouped to secure other channels of access to waste paper. It petitioned the state government to issue a directive to all government offices stating that any D category waste (the lowest quality waste paper) should be given as a priority to women—specifically to SEWA women. The directive received approval from the higher government officials, but the lower level officials, mill employees, and contractors who had been dealing in paper did not want to honour the directive.

Prior to SEWA's reception of the contract, all the D grade paper had been thrown in with higher value waste and contractors bid for it in lots. Bribery often tipped the scales in the contractors' favour, or the waste was undervalued, and the contractor and the government peon split the profit of the excess. Women worked their way through these illicit deals to finally secure a fair delivery of paper, only to have the former contractor file a case against them. The wording of the women's contract stipulated that they were entitled only to paper so low in quality that it had negligible market value. The contractor, however, said he was willing to pay for it, so it *did* have market value, suspending women's right to pick up paper until the sluggish court system could deliver a judgement.

The paper pickers countered the contractor's move by forming a small business cooperative in order to compete with him by his rules. They outbid him for the paper contract, lifting the court stay to again start collecting paper.

Two years and over Rs. 100,000 worth of paper scrap later, however, women discovered that they had only been receiving the D grade paper they were entitled to for free, while the contractor had all the while been collecting the higher quality scrap the SEWA women were paying for. SEWA lodged a complaint with government officials who promised to look into the situation. They closed the government godown for three days—supposedly to the contractor as well as to SEWA—in order to investigate.

Luxmi Parmar, a 30 year old hefty, young group leader, recalled their reaction: 'We were suspicious of this "shutdown," and decided to post a vigil on the godown. In the middle of the night a truck arrived and some men started hauling our paper from the building and loading the truck. We waited till the truck was half full so they could not claim they were innocent. Then we all surrounded them, shouting, "Whose orders are you following?" No one would claim responsibility, but they started trying to bully us, saying, "Show us *your* papers." We refused to be intimidated, though, and went straight to the police.'

The police, however, refused to register a report. The police inspector, the government official who was in charge of the paper contracts, and the contractor appeared to be acting in collusion. These women could find no way to break through.

Shortly thereafter, Doordarshan TV approached SEWA, they wanted to film a story on a trade group struggle. The paper pickers saw this as their opportunity to register their case, and Luxmi insisted on telling the entire story in detail.

'I gave the names and positions of everyone involved, directly onto the camera,' Luxmi recounted. 'Within a week of the tele-cast, we were collecting paper at Gandhinagar and noticed that we were all of a sudden receiving the entire lot of paper! The officials whom I had named threatened me, but within another week, they got transferred.'

Outside of exposing corrupt officials, the paper pickers were the one trade group at SEWA who consistently got an audience with the Chief Minister, Amarsingh Chaudary, whenever they went to his office. When asked why they got admission to see the Chief Minister, Ambabehn responded like it was a naive question: 'The Chief Minister is interested in us at election time because Harijans make a lot of votes. Well, we are interested in him when we want to get paper contracts from the government offices. He sees voters at his door and he lets us in.'

Through their struggles, some paper pickers now earn more consistent incomes, and their occupational hazards and very long hours of work have lessened to some degree. Their projected visions for themselves and their work are the most remarkable changes from their earlier feeling of degradation. They have developed three cooperatives, two production units and one godown which are functioning as a non-exploitative paper market where any paper picker can sell her waste.

Ranjan Desai, the senior organizer who has worked with the paper pickers since they came to SEWA in 1975 speaks slowly, with a sense of humour—an invaluable quality in the face of her trade group's struggles. She admits that the basic fact of most paper picking women's poverty has not been greatly altered. There are limitations beyond limitations, which take a long time to change. 'For some women, a definite economic improvement is there,' she said in an interview. 'But there are too many to fit into the small niches we have carved. Then there are the problems of vested interests which our values will not play against, like for our unit of women who make office files. We have great difficulties acquiring orders for their files. I even have relatives in positions to order lots of files, but they will not order from us because we will not give them the illicit cut which other private traders offer.'

This nexus between government officers and contractors is one of the most difficult links for women to break.

'Then there are the problems of the social structure itself,' Ranjan continued. 'These women only have their lives as their example. All their lives as untouchables, they have been treated poorly by those above them. Their definition, then, of getting ahead, is based on what they have observed by being stepped on. You step on someone else to get ahead. You run faster to the garbage dump, you get the better collection. Unravelling this conditioning cannot only happen from our end. The society which is stepping also has to change.'

To begin changing the negative middle class perceptions about them, the paper pickers participate in an ongoing publicity campaign. They speak on public radio shows and organize photo exhibitions of their work. They also are collaborating with the National Institute of Design to reduce occupational hazards for street collectors. Together they have designed gloves, collecting sticks, and shoulder collection bags which bear the name 'SEWA.'

The paper pickers' cubby in the office is always one of the most crowded. Here they drink tea in friendship, plan strategies of change with people who believe things will change, and find a welcome break from the drudgery and social stigmatization of garbage heaps. The biggest goal of the SEWA waste collectors is to run their own paper reprocessing plant, eliminating the middlemen at every stage. In their daily meetings they develop plans to not only get access to land and machinery, but also to help them network to women all over the city for their daily requirement of 4000 tons of waste paper.

Luxmi articulated her analysis of their work situation in the following words: 'The municipality pays people to sweep the streets each day to remove the dirt. We also clean the streets, along with the garbage piles and dumps too. We bring valuable things back to be used again. Since we are not earning a wage for the service, we should at least be receiving the full price for the goods we are recycling. The only way that will ever happen is if we run the whole process ourselves.'

When one sees the landfill and pollution problems of western countries which recycle very little, one cannot help wondering why these women are disparaged at all. What technology, overconsumption, and lack of political will cannot accomplish, these women manage daily with their labour. They should be hailed as one of India's more sound ecological forces.

Rural Agricultural Labourers

While many urban self-employed women labourers are involved in only one type of income generating activity, albeit often for many different contractors, SEWA has found a different reality amongst its rural members. All poor women in rural areas depend on several occupations to carry them across the different seasons and the yields of those seasons. They combine several of the following occupations, depending on the skill of their community or their level of need: seasonal agricultural employment, construction, or digging work; raising animals for milk, eggs, wool, leather, meat, and for doing agricultural work and transporting of goods; catching and selling fish; practising a skilled craft either as 'own-account' workers, or on a piece-rate for a contractor; and the non-paid family labour involved in providing fuel, food crops, processed grains and pulses, water, cloth, and clothing for household use—all the products which, without women's labour, the family would be compelled to pay for.

This multiple-occupation base and the fact that much of her work is unpaid or traded for subsistence commodities contributes to her invisibility in statistics which largely categorize one occupation, one worker—an industrial, or western service-oriented model. As Anker, Khan and Gupta's 1988 ILO study concluded, 'It is activities where women are active that are not usually considered to be labour force activities. It is almost as if the criteria have been made on the basis of existing knowledge of male and female activity patterns.'[9]

SEWA organizers have learned the need for respecting and reinforcing the interlinkages and dependencies of these occupations when developing an agenda for change. In most villages where they work, they have found that the same people who own the land in the village also own the shops, lend the money, exercise political control, and give employment. A woman's labour is remunerated not only with wages, but also with subsistence goods from large landowner's land—including fuel, fodder, grains, and water. If she asks for a higher wage, it might not only mean the end of her daily wage, but also the loss of her other collection privileges. The threat of losing access to any of these 'privileges,' however limited, makes direct demands for fair wages difficult or impractical.

Caste dynamics also control a woman's ability to demand change, as Renana Jhabvala explained: 'If a woman, or a group of women asks for a higher wage, it is often interpreted as a caste issue—that this caste is asking that caste for something. Then the demand is seen as a threat to the caste structure. Once it is brought up as this kind of an issue—rather than as straightforward wage issue—then her caste members will either support her or not support her on caste principles, depending on what kind of relationship they want to have with that other caste. Also, the other caste people will try to influence her—not by dealing directly with her, but by putting pressure on the other members of her caste to influence her.'

'If we want to do organizing in a village, we have to be very aware of these forces, and what dynamics are linked to our demands. The village is very isolated, so it is easy to do violent acts in a village. You cannot easily get police, or other kinds of protection. When we first began organizing agricultural labourers who wanted minimum wages in Dholka taluk, the women involved were beaten up. They had to go 16 miles to a police station. By the time they could get there, it was just too late for any kind of help.'

SEWA has had to develop less resistant channels than wage demands to initially organize women around in rural areas. Its community health organizing, rural savings groups, and the implementation of government maternity benefits have been non-threatening focal points for women to come together around and develop trust, while laying the foundation for subsequently uniting on more difficult issues of work and wages. Just as SEWA set the precedent by uniting urban women across community barriers, it deserves immense credit for its ability to organize across caste barriers in its rural work. While always honouring a woman's religious convictions and the skills imparted through her caste, SEWA has broken away from the traditional organizational hierarchy of the village. Every caste is represented in the union and cooperative leadership, and the fact of outside organizers and resources has helped reduce rural women's vulnerability and victimization in their struggles to develop. Issues that a poor low caste woman would *never* have broached alone a decade ago, she can now raise. She cannot be beaten up or simply disappear unaccounted for. People outside of the village know about her existence and exert themselves to protect her, thereby changing the old dynamics.

The tobacco processors of Anand taluk, one of Gujarat's most prosperous farming areas, provide an important illustration of how delicate the employment balance is for women dependent only on their labour, and the need for outside support which can help them overcome their victimization.

This district produces 80 per cent of the bidi tobacco for the country. The people who own the fields also own the plants which process the tobacco. There are basically two communities in Chikodera village where SEWA has members—the very large landholders, who wield all the economic, social, and political control, and poor landless labourers who work for them. There is virtually no other work in the immediate area, and men from the landless households often migrate to other areas for more remunerative work. Landless women in the area divide their time between sowing, weeding, and harvesting the tobacco for the landowners, and then working in the landowners' factories processing the tobacco for the other months of the year. The cultivating work is arduous in that women work long hours for low pay, but the processing work is gruelling. For some women it means loading heavy weights into large processing machines for 12 to 16 hour days. For other women it consists of beating the tobacco leaves with a long bamboo pole which they swing all the way back behind themselves, and then beat full force onto the ground in front of themselves, thereby pulverizing the leaves. Women then sift the tobacco through large screens, inevitably breathing large quantities of tobacco dust before packing it into jute bags and carrying headloads of it to a godown.

SEWA came to know about the problems of tobacco workers in Anand through one of its organizers, Indirabehn. She was from Anand and had married a man from Chikodera village when she was 15 years old. She had been sent to work in the factories, but fainted several times from the tobacco fumes, so she could only do field work. She later moved to Ahmedabad with her husband and four living children—four other children had died of accidents or unknown diseases. She began to work as a contract labourer in the mills, where a SEWA paper picker told her that SEWA was seeking applications for organizers. Following her contact with SEWA, she began organizing the other contract labourers in the mills. She later wanted to take up organizing work in her home area.

Jhabvala maintains that SEWA would never have been able to work in that area without an organizer whom the village women considered one of themselves. Even with Indirabehn as the link, the Chikodera women did not want to talk to SEWA for the first three years. Everyone recalls the atmosphere of fear which pervaded their interactions—and which also caused the SEWA organizers to persist.

'The land and factory owners in this area keep the women perpetually intimidated that they will stop their work on the slightest pretext,' Indirabehn related in an interview. 'In 1975 they were paying them as little as Rs. 1.25 a day for this work and acting like the women should be grateful for that. Then the government enacted minimum wages for tobacco workers. Based on their contact with a Labour Inspector, some women tried to get the legal wage.'

In 1982, an inspector questioned women in Chikodera village about what wages they were receiving. He had already inspected the employers' books and seen the women's thumbprints next to amounts detailing Rs. 18.50 per day of labour. This was the legal minimum wage. The women told the inspector that they were actually receiving Rs. 7 a day. He told the women to refuse their wages the next time until he was present, and that they should accept their wages only in his presence. The employer came to know about the plan, so he called all the women on a Sunday to take their wages. With the level of intimidation involved, there was no way the women could refuse their wages.

When the inspector arrived the next day, the owner immediately ushered him up to his office before he could talk to the women. He gave him tea, made small talk, and effectively quelled the inspector's ability to investigate the wages before he sent him out by a side door. All the women who were waiting below to talk to him did not see him leave. When someone came and told them that he had already left, they ran out to the road to tell him what had happened. They stood in the lane in front of the landowner's houses and talked to the inspector, and everything that was said was reported back to the owner. For two months he let them continue working without saying a thing. When the season was over, he simply never called 17 women who were involved in this back to work, despite that some of them had worked there for 30 years.

'This story came up casually when I was conducting a workers' education class, and a couple of the victimized women were present,' explained Indirabehn. 'This was three years after they had lost their jobs, and they had not been able to get work since. This was the only reason they were in the class. We had met with a lot of reticence in organizing here, and suddenly I understood why. That landlord's tactics had effectively quelled any action by other labourers. The reason these women had come was the feeling that they now literally had *nothing* to lose.'

SEWA's lawyer, Rani Advani, who was consulted about the case recounted the difficulty they were up against in representing these workers.

'We really wanted to do something for these women, but we were confronted with the reality of what it meant to represent poor rural women in an industrial dispute. The minimum time this case would take in the Labour Court would be five years. Then it would be appealed. What would these women do for seven years? And how could they come to Ahmedabad every time the case came up? Who would pay for their transport and their lodging?'

'We finally came up with a solution to this dilemma. We helped the women draft a letter to the Chief Justice of the High Court and to the Secretary of the Legal Aid Committee (LAC). The LAC immediately got interested in the case of poor women, and before we knew it, the High Court van was pulling into Chikodera to investigate. The legal costs the women incurred were only those of the postage stamps to the Judge and the LAC.'

At this point, SEWA helped the women enter demands for recovery of minimum wages for all the years they were underpaid and out of work, and for reinstatement. The landlords were so astounded by this turn of events, according to Rani, that they willingly negotiated a settlement out of court. They reinstated the women at the minimum wage, and paid severance to 11 women who were too old to return to work.

Indirabehn said that the ramifications of the court settlement were tremendous. 'What happened next was that all the tobacco employers in the village—not only the one we had taken to court— began to pay all their labourers this wage. What can I say except that SEWA membership suddenly increased dramatically in that area.'

Rani observed an important aspect of representing self-employed women: 'Besides the obvious use of law to help individuals get their rights, I have also seen how the legal process works as a tool for integrating poor women into the flow of society. So far, the only way these women have been getting any rights is by the law of the jungle. For a space to live, or for water, or work—you run, you grab. If you get it, you win. If not, you grin and bear it.'

'Exclusion from the formal legal system is just one of the ways that our society maintains its codes and strata. Introducing poor women into the legal process is one means of empowering them. For the first time, these Chikodera women experienced the qualities of an *ordered society* benefiting them.'

SEWA's union work attests that SEWA is not simply bringing its members into the mainstream as it exists, but reshaping the definitions of what kind of mainstream is acceptable to them as self-employed women. For home-based workers, this means a National Bill which guarantees minimum wages, social services and enforcement. For hawkers and vendors, the minimal legal protection they demand lies in the allocation of licences and space. Labourers continue to collaborate on a system of decentralized tripartite boards which set conditions, make payments and insure benefits.

SEWA women have proved exceptionally resilient and open as they have set long term goals for themselves which they work steadily toward, gaining more recognition each year from working class women, from the government, and from international policy-making bodies. SEWA's ground-breaking work of bringing self-employed women into the flow of an ordered society was expressed by Godavaribehn in another way when she said, 'My life with SEWA has become a lot calmer now. It is not three jobs, daily disaster and repeated starvation. How can I explain this? I still work long days, but they are not *desperate* days. Life is just a lot calmer now.'

END NOTES

1. Krishan Mahajan, R. Jhabvala, and R. Dhawan, *Women Who Roll Bidis: Two Studies of Gujarat*. Ahmedabad: SEWA, 1986, p. 29.
2. This account of organizing Patan bidi workers is drawn from Renana Jhabvala's account, 'Women's Struggles in the Informal Sector: Two Case Studies from SEWA.' A paper prepared for the Indian Association of Women's Studies, 1986.

3. Jhabvala, 1986, *op.cit.*

4. *Shramshakti*, 1988, *op. cit.*, p. xxi.

5. Krishan Mahajan, 'Socio-Legal Study of Home Based Ready Made Garment Workers, Ahmedebad.' Unpublished Report for ILO Study on Home-based Workers, 1987, pp. 29–32.

6. Much of this account of paper pickers draws from Elizabeth Bentley's paper, 'The History of SEWA's Struggle to Organize the Paper Pickers of Ahmedabad,' 1988.

7. Renana Jhabvala, *Closing Doors*. New Delhi: Tej Press, 1983, p. 20.

8. *The Statesman*, 15 April 1989.

9. Richard Anker, M.E. Khan and R.B. Gupta, 'Women Participation in the Labour Force: A Methods Test in India for Improving its Measurement.' ILO Report, 1988.

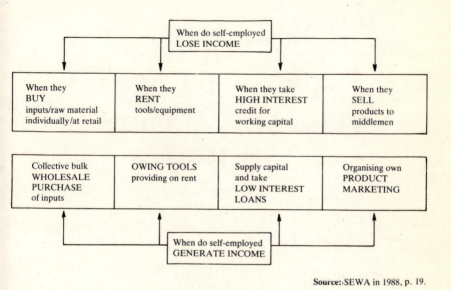

Source: SEWA in 1988, p. 19.

Figure 5.1 From Pressure to Command

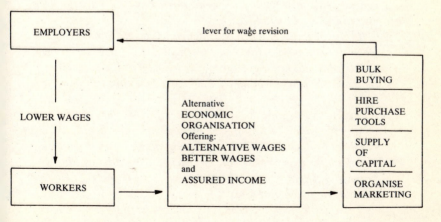

Source: SEWA, 1988, Report, p. 19.

6

Video SEWA: Focusing on Issues

'We go out to the villages and markets and city slum areas where we live to make videos about women. I used to be a vegetable vendor, but I have left that work to my family now, and I work on videos full-time. I do recording, editing, and replays. I am usually the sound person when we shoot. Editing is still the most difficult aspect for me. There is so much equipment, and since I cannot read instructions or write them down, I have to keep everything in my head.'

'In the beginning, when Marthabehn (Martha Stuart) came to teach us, I thought "How can I learn all this?" I have never been to school. I had never even seen television then. But something in me said, "Maybe it will take a little more time, but I should learn it anyway." '

'Learning to shoot the camera was difficult. They would say, "Shoot the room." I would look through the camera and only see one part of the room. How do you shoot the room in parts?'

'I had no experience with electricity, either. I did not even know about light switches, really, much less AC and DC. No one has electricity where I live.'

'I can hardly read Gujarati, and I had to learn how to recognize

English technical words like "Eject", and "Reverse", so that I could operate any kind of video equipment.'

'I think this video work is important because all the poor women who are working are so exploited. They try to work more so they can get more money. They start early in the morning and work till late, but still cannot get enough.'

'We interview these women who tell us how much they are working and for how little pay. Then we show these to women from all the trades, telling them, "See, we should all be together." We also make videos about our protest marches, like when the vegetable vendors marched to the Municipal Corporation to demand licences and space . . . . It helps new women visualize the work SEWA does. It helps them see that others have already done it, that these are not just ideas. It helps them understand that they are workers, exploited workers, because other women like them are talking about their problems. These videos give women confidence in SEWA because they can see for themselves that SEWA takes an interest in their problems and has gone to all the trouble to make a film about them."[1]

'Once we showed the chikan workers (embroiderers) in Lucknow the video of the Ahmedabad bidi workers' street march. They got so excited that they started planning the route for their own procession before the film was even finished . . . .'

'We women are living in a hell. We do not know any other way of living in these slums. No one is bothered about us. We can make complaints for years about these conditions, but no one hears. When we make videos about these problems, though, things happen. They finally see that there really is a problem— like in Shankarbhavan. For years we told the municipal authorities about the filth of the open trenches, but no one came to see. They do not like to walk in such stinky places. Finally they saw how bad it was when we made a video and showed it to them. Then they got worried because we had recorded it on film and said all these things about them ignoring the problem. They are afraid the film will be seen elsewhere and they will be shown lacking, so they took some action to fix the problem.'

'We also use the video for court cases, to show the condition of the women who have brought the case, like the Manek Chowk vendors. We made the film from the vendors' point of view, describing our problems of police harassment. For the first time,

the Police Commissioner understood the problem from our point of view . . . .'

'And it makes us look like a big, serious organization, that we are making films about these things. It always impresses people.'

'Another way we use video is for practising things we have never done before. The bidi workers had to go to court and testify against the biggest manufacturer in Ahmedabad. We set up our own courtroom with a judge and lawyers and practised everything that might happen when they really went to court. Then the women could watch themselves and talk about what was good and what was bad about what they did.'

'We also use them to help women who are setting up new cooperatives. There are many things the sisters do not know about and have to learn them. For the dairy cooperatives, we made a film of an experienced Managing Committee during its monthly meeting. We show that video to women who are new to cooperatives and say, "See, this is how to run a meeting." '

'. . . . More training should be given to uneducated women to make videos. When we make videos, and women like us watch them, we get confidence to try and make changes. When we see women like us who have done something brave and new, then we get the confidence that we can learn something new too. When poor women see other poor women as health workers on the video, they say, "I can also learn about health and help solve these problems in my neighbourhood." When other self-employed women see me, a vegetable vendor, making these films, they also have the confidence that they can do things which at first seem impossible.'

Lila Datania is a steady, serious woman whose strong jawline makes her look intensely determined. When not filming, she moves methodically about her work in the small storage closets allocated to their production and viewing rooms. She and Jyoti Jumani, the video coordinator, form the full-time core team of SEWA's video work, though each trade group and department of SEWA is represented by an organizer or a member who has been trained in video productions and replays. These videos not only give voice to SEWA women's issues but also reach thousands of other members every year as a tool for teaching, organizing, and inspiring. There is an increasing demand for such videos as other voluntary organizations solicit the SEWA video crew's services to make films on their organizations and issues.

Through videos, Lilabehn also shares the wide range of SEWA's work with the many daily visitors—from other self-employed women, to activists from other unions and voluntary agencies, to government officials and international delegations. Lila has participated in filming and teaching workshops across India through SEWA's membership in a global network called the Village Video Network (VVN). The VVN is sponsored by the United Nations University in Tokyo, and Martha Stuart Communications of New York who have provided training and equipment to SEWA.

Martha Stuart's work with non-literate people led to the production in the early eighties of her video series entitled 'Are You Listening?' which featured not 'experts,' but individuals who were personally affected by the issues. She extended this concept through the VVN to actually provide video equipment and producing skills to the villagers (or non-literate urban dwellers) in India, Mali, Indonesia, China and Jamaica, so they 'would not fall prey to the distortions built into the use of conventional media.'[2]

Both the women learning to produce videos at SEWA and those viewing them display infectious excitement at the immediacy of the technology and its result in seeing women like themselves organizing and demonstrating their empowerment. Video SEWA provides the most concrete testimony to SEWA's assertions that illiteracy is not a bar to technology use if creative training methods are developed. The legitimacy role such technology lends to the organization, to women, and to their defined issues has been enormous. Most heartening to note is the appropriateness of a media like video in the hands of women who depend on their verbal skills of bargaining, agreement, and face-to-face interaction as their means of doing business in the world. With cameras and televisions in their hands, that world has expanded dramatically.

END NOTES

1. For more extensive discussion of the benefits of video for self-employed women, see Jyoti Jumani's account, 'Getting An Opportunity,' SEWA Report, 1988; and her 'Coordinating Video SEWA: A Personal Account,' SEWA, 1985.
2. Mina Krishnan, 'Listen to Martha Stuart', *SPAN Magazine*, December 1984, pp. 14–17.

1. SEWA organizing begins with a survey of workers' conditions. Here, surveying bidi workers in Ahmedabad (see chapter 4).

2. Cartpullers were the first trade group to join SEWA. Now they have formed a tripartite board to oversee their payment of wages and benefits.
Credit: Rajesh Bhatt.

3. Waste paper collectors sorting the day's collection. They need common areas to sort and store what they collect.

4. Smiths recycling tins and old roofing material into inexpensive stoves.

5. From early on, girls contribute to the family income. They require schools with flexible schedules and creches for their younger siblings so that they can both earn and study, practise traditional skills and learn new skills. Here, girls participate in the incense trade. Credit: SEWA.

6. Ela Bhatt (head uncovered) strategizing with vegetable vendor members.
   Credit: Rajesh Bhatt.

7. Laxmi Tetabhai Patni, Vice-President of the Union, appeals to her sister vendors to fight the authorities for their legal rights to vend (chapter 2).
Credit: SEWA.

8. Ela Bhatt and Shankarlal Banker, trade union leader with Mahatma Gandhi, inaugurate SEWA's newsletter *Anasuya*, 1981.
Credit: SEWA.

9. Tarabehn Marthak, mobile savings organizer, counting the money from a SEWA television bank on a doorstep. 'The Bank is open!'

10. Santokbehn Pritviraj, carpenter and member of Video SEWA team. Credit: Rajesh Bhatt.

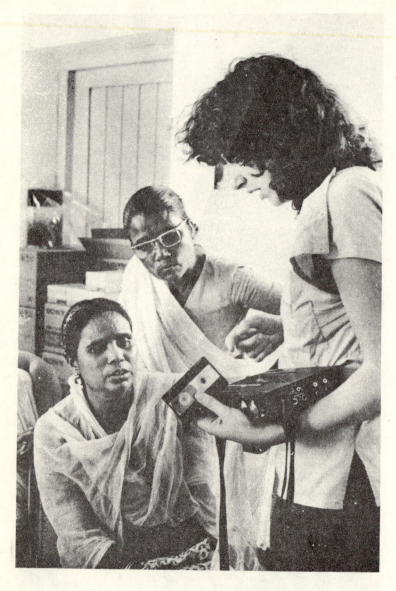

11. Medina, shopkeeper, left, and Leelabehn Datania, vegetable vendor,
centre (chapter 5), learn video sound recording from an instructor
from Martha Stuart Communications, New York.
Credit: Rajesh Bhatt.

12. SEWA members celebrate the Supreme Court Order recognizing street vending as a Fundamental Right under the Constitution of India. Ela Bhatt (uplifted at centre), with Renana Jhabvala directly to her right. Lalita Krishnaswami is behind.
Credit: Shukdev Bhacheh.

13. Child care for self-employed women is high on SEWA's advocacy list. Thirty per cent of self-employed are the sole supporters of their families. Many of these do daily wage labour, carrying their children and cradles with them. This girl is returning from a 44 degree day alongside a road construction crew where her mother works.
Credit: Kalima Rose.

14. 22 June 1987 :The vendors march in protest against police atrocities and in demand of a just licensing policy.

15. Samubehn and Ramubehn, Secretary and President of Devdholera's Dairy Cooperative, tell over 1000 SEWA members from 40 villages, that they need to be organized for strength, 1989.

Credit: Kalima Rose.

16. 1000 women at an Ahmedabad district rural sammelan showing their affirmation, January 1989 (see chapter 7).
Credit: Kalima Rose.

17. Led by Ela Bhatt, SEWA organizers and support staff jumped up from an annual office meeting to march to the Municipal Commissioner's office in protest against vendor harassment, despite a High Court stay on prosecution.
Credit: SEWA.

18. They stormed the Commissioner's office and used their subtle persuasion to insist he make the necessary phone calls immediately.
Credit: SEWA.

7

The SEWA Bank: 'This Bank is Like Our Mother's Place'

It is no joke, building a bank for illiterate women. How do we illiterate women do things? With our hands. By walking. By carrying loads on our heads. By talking to each other. This kind of work makes us strong. This is how we built this bank. By walking all over this city, talking and talking to our sisters, carrying small amounts of cash from so many women until we had one big amount. We have built a strong bank from this work, and this bank has made us stronger too.
Anandinibehn Budhabhai, Savings mobilizer and former vendor

Why do SEWA women say 'the bank is like our mother's place?' At their mother's place, the doors are always open for the daughters. It's the place she can cry out her problems and diffi- culties, her dreams and aspirations. There are many secrets a woman cannot tell the outside world which she can tell her mother. Her mother takes her seriously and helps her mediate problems.

Then, the atmosphere is always informal at her mother's place. She can laugh, play, cry, whatever—and foolish behaviour is taken for granted. They do all kinds of foolish things in the bank: because the practice has been that you always deposit something when you come to the bank, whenever they want to withdraw Rs. 15, they deposit Rs. 5 and then withdraw Rs. 20.

And from the beginning we have maintained an informal atmosphere. Women never are in a hurry to have their name called, because they enjoy meeting their other sisters here. In the early days at the TLA they used to sit and smoke bidi and talk, and they marked their places in the queue by their ash piles . . . .

In those days, we were on the same floor of the TLA as their office bearers. The toilet was right across from the President's office. SEWA women would all wait in the hall for their turn at the bank, and one by one would go to the toilet. There was a big mirror and they enjoyed combing their hair. But they made it so dirty—I was exasperated—and everyone in the TLA was complaining. So we had to teach them how to use the flush, and how to keep it clean. So literally, it is a mother's place . . . .

Also, after marriage, women go home to their mother's place to deliver their children. One day while many women were waiting in the TLA hall for their turn at the bank, one woman suddenly gave birth to a child. Four of us jumped up and held our saris around her as a wall, and one midwife helped her deliver her child . . . .

Then, like a mother would, the bank goes to explain for a woman. For example, one of our members was married to a policeman. They had not been speaking to each other for several years, but lived together in a sort of quiet hostility. She cooked for him, and he gave her money to run the family. She wanted to buy a used sewing machine, and earn her own money. Her husband used to be a tailor and had a machine in the house, but how could she negotiate with him? So the bank went to his office and negotiated the price for him to sell it to her. What other bank would do this? Yet without this kind of support, a woman like her may never get her own assets.

In other cases, when desperation has set in for a woman, and she may be on the verge of suicide, the bank helps her find constructive solutions. In 1975 when the bank was not taking many risks, a vegetable vendor came who was under such economic pressure that she was absolutely desperate. Her husband was an unemployed textile worker, and he would somehow roam about and fill his belly each day, but it was a very difficult situation for her and her children. The bank decided to extend her a loan of Rs. 50, and someone went with her to buy green masalas like coriander, mint, ginger, garlic, and chillies. That day SEWA cared for her children, who were sick and hungry. She earned Rs. 6 profit selling the masalas that day, and took home food that night. She continued building her business day by day, and the next week she repaid Rs. 51. It was hardly any risk for the bank, and it literally meant life or death for that woman. After that we started extending those Rs. 50 loans to many women . . . .

Then, it is the oldest association a woman has, with her mother. We built SEWA around this bank. Now women are dealing with courts and the government, but this relationship with the bank is the oldest association of all these new relationships.

And also, mothers are generally wise people. And I think starting our own bank was the wisest thing we ever did. We have our own financial resources, immediately, whenever we need them. Because of this, we can set our own rules, and do things at our own pace . . . .

Ela Bhatt, May 1988 interview

It is no coincidence that the most obvious central entrance to SEWA is the open doors of its bank. It is one of the few such doors which explicitly opens the formal, institutionalized world of money to poor, illiterate women. While the bank grew out of women's immediate need for working capital at lower rates of interest and loans to buy their own tools of trade, the understanding and working and offerings of the bank have expanded exponentially since the conception of those initial projects. Through delving deeper and deeper into the root of women's financial crises, SEWA has built one of the most progressive savings and lending institutions in the country.

SEWA Bank has received international acclaim for its innovations in extending credit to poor women, but through the course of this credit extension the organizers have also learned that women's need for savings is even greater than their need for credit if they are to gain control of their income. It is in times of emergency or obligation that they borrow heavily, beginning the downward spiral which high interest rates or mortgages initiate. If they can plan for these times by saving, they can avoid resorting to severe indebtedness at the hands of private lenders.

This of course raises the question of how women so desperately poor and underpaid can save. Women often approach the bank in a state of high indebtedness to private money-lenders, contractors, wholesalers, or to the landlords of the fields where they labour. This kind of indebtedness leads to a kind of perpetual crisis, a vice-like grip which rarely releases its hold on a woman. It may begin with any sort of emergency, or a social obligation like the marriage of a child. If the woman of a half-starved family finds work, she may take it up against an advance from the employer, to hold the family over until the first wages are collected. This creates the climate for a kind of bondedness to that lender, who is in a position to dictate all the terms. These terms usually translate into extremely low piece-rate or daily wages; high rents for any tools of trade; high interest on wholesale advances; or, if the woman borrows against assets like jewellery or family land, the extremely high interest rates usually result in loss of the asset forever.

The first step for SEWA Bank, then, is to extend credit to such women so that they can release themselves from these high interest (or high toll) debts. The woman then moves from being indebted at high interest rates (most commonly 10 per cent per day to 10 per cent per month) from private sources to being indebted at lower interest rates (12 per cent–16.5 per cent annually) to the bank. Once she is free from the exorbitant interest rates which consume her monthly surplus without even denting the capital, she gets an opportunity for bargaining power. While used-garments traders take vessels on credit from a merchant, he can set both the price of the vessels and the rate of the interest high—take it or leave it. If, however, a used-garments trader has her working capital in hand, she stands in the position of saying, 'If you want my business, then what price will you offer?' The glint of cash in her hand evokes a different response than the extended thumb signing on credit.

The second step is for the woman to use her new credit productively so that she generates more income, which she can use to repay the loan and build up her own working capital, which can provide her future investments in her work, or cover the times of family emergency or need. Before borrowing, while repaying, and after repayment of the loan—during all the stages of her indebtedness or prosperity—SEWA encourages its members to save.

This may not sound like such a novel idea on the face of it, but imagine it: How does a poor woman who does not have easy access to a bank save? She lives in a slum on the outskirts of the city. She earns an extra Re. 1 to Rs. 5 above her consumption needs on some days when she has good sales, or has found good waste on her collection route. It is too small an amount for her to take precious time off from her work, or to spend the bus fare to get to the bank and deposit it. Even if she could sustain the lost time and expense, she still faces the problem of her illiteracy, and the bank formalities which she will have to depend on the sometimes impatient or even hostile bank staff to complete for her. Such small change in the house is easily spent—a toffee for each child, tea or hooch for the husband or elder sons. These occasional daily surpluses amount to nothing, and there is nothing, therefore, when a woman leaves the house in the morning to buy her daily stock of vegetables, or when an emergency arises, or it is time to marry a son or daughter, and the recurring cycle of debt continues.

THE MOBILE BANK

Tarabehn Marthak, 40, is SEWA Bank's main urban savings mobilizer. With her motto: 'I will bring every woman in Ahmedabad into SEWA Bank,' she provides one answer to how poor women can save. She is a good natured woman with an ability to change her personality expression in a split second in her dealings with hundreds of women every day. She speaks sternly to those who need to be admonished to save more, laughs loudly with women who want to pass a little time joking in her company, answers softly when commiserating about a family illness, or encouragingly to women who are managing to save a little extra—all the while filling receipts, signing pass-books, and counting small change.

She was educated up to the seventh class, and then married into a family of *agarbatti* (incense stick) rollers. She began conducting surveys for SEWA of agarbatti workers, got drawn into bank work, and has collected savings for over 10 years. She visits women all over the city at their homes or workplaces so that they can easily deposit their savings. She knows thousands of women's work schedules, and weaves her visits into the hours and the part of the city when they will have their cash in hand and be free enough to deposit it.

She says that none of her collection days are really 'typical.' They depend on which trade groups she will be collecting from, and what their work schedules are like. 'I try to reach bidi workers in the mornings, since they receive their wages in the morning when they go to collect that day's supply of raw material. Collecting from vegetable or fish vendors, on the other hand, is most lucrative in the evenings, after their peak hours in the market. For all the carpenters, smiths, used-garments dealers and headloaders, I go to the Sunday Market, and collect from them when they are all taking in money from their week's work.'

One collection day in March 1989, began at 11:30 in the morning, leaving SEWA Bank with a car, a driver, and one helper, heading towards the busy neighbourhoods squeezed behind the markets of Relief Road. After stopping in front of a mosque to collect from women water vendors, she headed toward a neighbourhood of paper pickers. Many of the women had returned from their first collection of the day and were busy sorting out their goods in the streets. They have asked her to come once a week, so that what they have earned will not slip out of their hands. It is startling to see some of these women proffering up to Rs. 50 or Rs. 100 for deposit. One waste picking family in Gheekanta offered three pass-books, and each woman explained that she liked keeping her own accounts so that she could control her own income. They attested that they were also startled to see how quickly their savings grew into a substantial amount. After two and a half years of saving, each woman had between Rs. 1370 and Rs. 2320. They said before they used to keep the money in a small clay bank which their husbands (or sons) broke any time they wanted money, hence they did not have any incentive to save. 'Now I keep the money on me until Tarabehn shows up,' the younger one related, withdrawing her cash from a small pocket in her petticoat and slapping Tarabehn's hand in jest at their successful collusion.

As Tarabehn passes workers' houses, she yells out that she has come, or she sends children with messages to other streets, as she finds a small shady corner of the neighbourhood to sit. Soon women and children will be clustered around her clutching their pass-books and small amounts of cash. These women on her daily rounds almost unanimously testify that before they began these weekly or monthly deposits with the mobile bank, they did not have any savings. And while it might sound commendable that they are saving Rs. 25–Rs. 50 every week or every month, to witness *how* these women save is the most heartening and sobering.

A 68 year old, somewhat enfeebled woman, Parvatibehn Murilal, dressed in a tattered sari, brought a small handkerchief with coins enfolded in it. She counted them slowly, before relating that she is a widow with no living children, residing alone in a rented house. She had saved between 50 paise and Rs. 2 per day from her daily income of Rs. 6 which she earned by stitching buttons onto ready-made garments. Tarabehn recorded Rs. 15 into her pass-book, which was two weeks of savings. She is saving for the days when she cannot work any longer. In March 1989, she had saved Rs. 417 (US $24) toward that eventuality—enough to cover eight months of her rent.

From there Tarabehn moved on to Bapunagar, a very poor area where women are engaged in home-based activities like bidi and incense stick rolling, cement bag repair, and chindi stitching. Between two to three dozen women, most looking dishevelled from overwork, appeared in Tara's shady corner with small SEWA television savings banks in hand. Tarabehn comes to Bapunagar once a month, with the only key to open the savings boxes, which she empties, counts, and records the deposits of. Most of these banks are filled with 20 paise or 50 paise or Re.1 coins, and some tightly folded Rs. 2 notes. Only an occasional Rs. 5 or Rs. 10 note tumbles out with all the small change. The women look on expectantly, and on several occasions when their savings total Rs. 23.70 or Rs. 18.20, or some other odd amount, they would send their daughters running back home to try and secure the extra rupee or two to make the month's deposit a round number. One woman apologetically took back Rs. 10 of her deposited change to buy medicine for herself, and Tarabehn assured her it was all right. 'That is what savings are for—to fall back on when you need them.'

During a lull in depositors, Tarabehn explained how she goes to new areas repeatedly, even for only one depositor in the beginning. 'I just have to get women used to seeing me coming back. They have been cheated enough times in their lives, they are often suspicious that I will simply disappear with all their money.' The other factors which lend credibility to Tarabehn's repeated appearance are the simultaneous work of the other parts of the organization. Many organizers reiterate that the union would never have been able to survive without the bank, nor the bank without the union. Zubeida Mansuri is one of Tarabehn's regular depositors in Bapunagar who, without the dedicated work of the union, would never have been in the position to deposit anything with SEWA Bank.

Her past is a chain of disasters and deprivations which intensified with her mother-in-law's death. Her brothers-in-law manipulated her, her husband, and children out of the family home. They could not afford to pay Rs. 50 a month as rent of the small room they moved to, so they began to occupy a hut on the river-bank. Zubeida has been pregnant eight times, but only has four living daughters. Three of her pregnancies resulted in miscarriages, and one in still-birth which led the doctor to recommend her to go to SEWA.

The union subsequently took up many struggles for Zubeida, which the bank complemented with financial support. The union first filed a case and helped her negotiate with her brothers-in-law for a settlement on their house. With that Rs. 1500 she bought a small plot in Bapunagar. Then the union struggled for years to help her acquire a kerosene vending licence, despite officials who did not believe women should be vendors. During this time her hut was destroyed by a flood, and she borrowed Rs. 500 from the bank to repair it. This house was subsequently burned to the ground during the 1985 riots, as Bapunagar was one of the worst affected areas, and Zubeida and her family had to stay four months in the demoralizing relief camps. During the relief work, SEWA entered Zubeida's name in the list of victims, and helped her acquire a kerosene hand-cart and Rs. 700 for her destroyed hut. With the cart as an asset from which to rebuild her family's life after the destruction, she took a loan of Rs. 1000 from SEWA Bank to buy kerosene for her business. She began to vend kerosene in Bapunagar, door to door, regularly repaying her loan, and saving. Her husband, who had previously been sickly and had abandoned his bidi rolling for Rs. 4 or Rs. 5 per day, began to take an interest in Zubeida's new business acumen, and started helping her in the work. She then took another loan (Rs. 2000) from SEWA Bank to buy another kerosene cart, so that they could both vend, doubling their monthly income. In 1989, with that loan repaid, she took another, with which she has finally built her family a permanent house.[1]

Events like these do not go unnoticed in communities like Bapunagar. The women who were collected to deposit their savings all knew Zubeida's history, and related the stories of her success and transformation proudly, as though it represented their own personal victory. The small savings boxes, their pass-books, the ability to *save*, represented likewise, for them, that ability to change their lives through a small daily action.

After leaving Bapunagar, Tarabehn stopped to collect deposits from a slum where women who were out working as domestic servants had left their pass-books and deposits with their daughters or neighbours. Then she collected from a woman who had a small shop selling provisions, a typist, and finally from all the women vending fish in the fish market. In almost every location, new women would approach her and ask to open an account. For those who could sign their name, she did so on the spot. For those who could not sign, she told them the next date she would be back, and that they should have two small photographs of themselves by then.

The money which Tarabehn collected was to be deposited in regular savings accounts, recurring deposit accounts and as fixed deposits. By the time Tarabehn returned to the bank at 6 o'clock in the evening, her small canvas collection bag emitted smells of incense, tobacco, cement dust and fish. The pungent collection embodied plans for old age, for independent bank accounts for young daughters, for children's marriages, for expanding businesses with new machine tools, or larger stocks for trading, or raw materials in bulk. One woman was saving for the birth of her next child. Many would use their savings in emergencies like illness. Some saved for additions to their houses, to increase work or storage space beyond the one small room they now had, while others who lived in *kaccha* settlements saved for the house itself. Also, 5000 of those who save are covered under a group life insurance plan, with Rs. 6 per year deducted from their interest.

CONSTRAINTS OF THE FORMAL SYSTEM

It is worth mentioning that 24,000 self-employed women's savings accounts are not simply the result of Tarabehn's and other union organizers' admonitions and encouragements to save. They are, more than anything else, the proof that the combined services and support of the union and cooperatives can work to change women's economic situations. Poor women's pooling of their own money to provide themselves fair credit has radically shifted control in their lives. Though the nationalized banks are required to lend to the poor, they are not effective at lending or recovering from the poor and continue to marginalize poor women because of the women's lack of collateral.

Jayshree Vyas, SEWA Bank's Managing Director, began her career with a nationalized bank, and has an insider's understanding of the problems poor women encounter in those formal institutions. 'Unfortunately, many of the loans sanctioned to the poor are just for political vote catching,' she explained in an interview. 'No one is concerned how the money is used, or in the other supports which make it productive money. Then no one makes sincere efforts to recover the loans, and the majority of them end up being written off. One real problem is that the nationalized banks hire well-educated personnel at high salaries. These employees do not have any experience dealing with the poor. They cannot or do not want to find their way through the slums to collect from those who are defaulting. When one bank complained to us that some of our members were defaulting with them, we offered to send our organizers with the officials to talk to the women, but they quickly refused, saying they did not want to go there.'

'Then the problems in the rural areas are even more severe. If you want to get a promotion in the nationalized banks, you have to go and work in a rural bank for two years. I myself was guilty of not wanting to do that duty. Most employees spend that two year time using all of their accumulated sick leave, personal leave, and vacation, so that they are in effect only there for one year. It is not their fault—it is just no one's idea of banking. We did not learn *this* kind of banking in school.'

'The other thing that compounds the problem for women in the middle class banking world is the pervasive assumption that women are bad credit risks because they do things like have babies, and get their children married, and tend the sick—which might make them default.'

Women's roles, then, both as the providers of all the welfare services to their extended families and as the providers of income to pay the bills cause them to be discriminated against in the formal banking world. While formal industry provides benefits to employees to cover these services, recognizing them as necessary and socially valuable, women in the informal sector who provide these services are denied credit based on these roles.

'On top of that,' Jayshree continued, 'they do not have their own assets as security, which makes them the biggest risk.'

The way SEWA Bank has countered all these trends to set up a serious bank for self-employed women has been by pooling their own money, setting their own terms for sanctioning loans, putting themselves on the Board of Directors, hiring their field workers from amongst themselves, and using the services of the greater SEWA body to support women's other needs. Since it is their own money they are lending to their sisters, no one is about to write any loan off, as it would mean writing off their own savings, and ultimately, their bank. One rural organizer, Savita, characterized the essential difference in SEWA's approach to lending to poor women:

'The way the nationalized banks lend is kind of like the way the government subsidizes fertilizers. People all accept the fertilizer as long as it is free or heavily subsidized. It definitely increases their crop output for that year, and everyone likes it. It just does not replenish the soil like compost made from dung and wheat or paddy straw. So when they have to pay for it, they think about it longer, they think about what to put in and what will come out . . . .'

'Likewise, people accept the government loans which are heavily subsidized, and they also temporarily increase their assets. Without all the other supportive services, though, these loans do not usually really improve a woman's life—she gets a cow, but no way to feed it, or no vet services, and it dies, or it does not give milk. Also, no one takes the loan that seriously because everyone knows that they are vote-gifts, and can be written off.'

'Self-employed women pooling their own money, on the other

hand, feels like well-balanced fields. What they take out, they put back in, looking seriously after their field and their crops, as they mean not only this year's survival, but also their long-term ability to generate a living for their family.'

RELEVANT SUPPORT THROUGH CREDIT

SEWA Bank oversees their finances beginning with the Board of Directors, which comprises 10 long-standing trade leaders from different self-employed occupations, four organizers with professional training, and one cooperative manager. They take the major decisions about the bank, and sanction all the loans. The trade leaders have an insight into both the financial and psychological workings of the self-employed, while the professionals have the skills and literacy to link the trade leaders' insight with banking economics and the formal guidelines and cooperative regulations of the Reserve Bank of India, from which the bank receives its authority. The Board does not hire well-educated personnel to help in loan recovery. It seeks the help of the union organizers and group leaders, and it hires women well experienced in self-employment, who live in the neighbourhoods of the borrowers themselves, who speak in the same dialects and wear the same clothes, and most importantly, who understand the constraints and unpredictability of the trades and lives of the self-employed. Armed with this understanding and sensitivity, and supported by the other services of SEWA, they have shown self-employed women to be excellent credit risks.

How to extend credit to poor women raises more complex issues than how to extend savings programmes. If a woman has the information and the will to enter an ordinary state bank and persevere through procedures she is unfamiliar with, she can open a savings account, however small. This is not even remotely true, however, for her similar desire for fair institutionalized credit. The nationalized banks want security in the form of assets which poor self-employed women virtually never possess.

The majority of SEWA loans, by contrast, are unsecured. In 1987, 79 per cent of the loans SEWA Bank extended were unsecured loans, amounting to 48 per cent of the advanced funds.[2] The majority of the secured loans are secured against a woman's jewellery—often the only property considered a woman's own—which nationalized banks do not recognize as adequate collateral.

All the organizers involved with the bank attest that their major accomplishment as an institution has been learning how to lend to and recover from the poor. The building up of assets in a woman's own name is encouraged by every aspect of the organization from day one. Women in the union and cooperatives are all encouraged to own their own tools of trade, to have savings accounts in their own name, to have their house or land in their own name or at least be jointly named with their husband. These objectives are most easily met in the case of the self-employed women through the extension of fair credit, but the obstacles to acquiring this credit are numerous.

Informal interviews with women who were new to SEWA Bank, and applying for their first loans revealed their initial reluctance to approach a bank. Many women said that they had heard they could get credit here, but they did not know *how*. They all expressed fear about approaching a bank and exposing their ignorance about procedures, or their illiteracy. Many women who had approached nationalized banks for loans reported incidents which caused them to leave frustrated: A woman stood in the bank for two hours and no one asked her why she had come. Bank employees got impatient and spoke harshly with women over the extra work involved in filling forms for them because they were illiterate. Women were laughed out of banks when they had to answer 'no' to every question concerning security, fixed salary and employer, assets in their own names, credit guarantors, etc. Other women who got past all these obstacles complained of the number of times they had had to go to the nationalized banks for application formalities— sometimes seven or eight times over a long period—and were still denied the loan. Even if they got the loan, the loss of work time and the delay in acquiring the money when they needed it made it a much less productive loan than they had anticipated.

One carpenter who was receiving her second loan at SEWA Bank described her experience:

'A money-lender in our neighbourhood used to lend to us, but we had to pay 10 per cent interest per month. It was convenient, but it just was not profitable for this kind of business (making inexpensive stools and tables). So we first tried to get a loan from the State Bank, but we did not have any one who could sign for us as a guarantee, so they refused. When we came here, they asked for people who knew us, who would speak for us. That's how our world works—knowing people and speaking for them. Plenty of my sisters who do this work come to SEWA. Two of them came to speak for me. Then a behn came from the bank to my house to see what I was making. I showed her my work. She thought I was a good carpenter, and she told the bank to give me the loan.'

'And another thing—look at me (displaying her dress). I come here on my rounds of buying junk wood. But does anyone say, "Oh how dirty you are?" No! They ask, "How is business? How have you come?" It is a feeling of friendship. And friends trust each other....Now every carpenter who sits in the Sunday Market knows where to come to get a loan for her work.'

Women who have just received the payment of their first loan are easily identifiable in the SEWA Bank. Their expressions often reveal a mixture of incredulity, excitement, and relief. Sometimes they laugh, or shout, or jump up and down. They unanimously attest that there is no other bank where they could get a loan so quickly or so simply. Most of them only have to make two visits: the day of application, and the day of collecting the sanctioned loan.

SEWA Bank does not advertise or encourage loans, but waits for the woman to approach the bank of her own initiative. Some hear about it through the field workers, others through another part of the organization, some through other women in their trade who are SEWA members, some through friends. Many domestic servants reported learning about SEWA from their employers.

Kinds of Loans

The bank provides three-year term loans for women for what they call *productive* purposes: buying tools of trade, for working capital, for capital investment like a house or storage or work space. In 1988, an average of five women received loans from SEWA Bank every day, the loans varied from Rs. 500 to Rs. 20,000. The majority of applicants ask for unsecured loans. They usually come with a reference person, someone whom SEWA Bank already knows, and if it is a woman's first time to the bank, she will also be accompanied by some other family member or a friend. A long queue of women and children waiting for their turn to apply usually snakes out of the small loan application room, through the corridor, and into the large central bank room. Chandrikabehn, the veteran loan officer, fills out the loan application after conducting an oral interview with the woman who wants the loan. She asks the woman the purpose for which she wants the loan, the amount of loan, what her other debts amount to and to whom, who else earns income in her family and how much. Chandrikabehn asks many questions about the investment and expenditure of the woman's trade. From this conversation, she gauges the extent of the woman's knowledge of the trade she is taking a loan against and gets an idea of whether the woman is making a genuine business request. She asks her how much she will repay each month. Chandrikabehn also assesses the woman's ability to repay, and bargains with the woman on the amount of the loan, based on this ability. When everyone is agreed, the woman attaches a photograph of herself with the loan application, and puts a thumbprint or her signature on the form.

If the woman asks for an unsecured loan, she will be told when to come back, after the meeting of the loan committee—usually two to five days later. During that time the bank will check their referee ledger, to see how the other clients recommended by the same reference person are doing with repayment. (Apparently, the referees enjoy elevated social status if they can help friends get loans, and if their friends maintain reputable repayment records.) If some clients fall behind, the bank uses this time to leverage the referee into following up on the tardy clients. Then the bank takes the help of the field workers or the union organizers to check on the applicant, and collect all the information they can. This often means an organizer going to the applicant's neighbourhood, and seeing her at work and meeting her neighbours, or enquiring about her from other SEWA women in her trade. Sometimes the bank also has to investigate the economics of the trade if the woman requests a loan for a business the bank is not yet conversant with.

Within a week, with all the information and approval by the loan committee, the woman returns to the bank to collect the loan. She is then required to buy 5 per cent of the loan amount in bank shares and open a savings account if she does not yet have one. In 1989, when SEWA Bank was 15 years old, it had over 11,000 share-holders, and had extended over 6000 loans to the members. On the rare occasions that the bank denies a loan, it is usually due to: the client being completely unknown to anyone who knows the bank and can speak for her; a previous bad record with the bank; or if the bank believes the woman is not requesting the money for herself or for a genuine business.

Secured Loans

A woman can get a secured loan immediately. If she has some jewellery to offer as security, or less commonly, a fixed deposit or a mortgage, she can receive the loan on the same day she applies for it. Once a week a goldsmith sets up his scale in the back room of SEWA Bank. After moving through the application process, each woman proceeds to the smith, who weighs and values what-ever ornaments she wants to offer as collateral. She can get 60 per cent of the value of her jewellery in cash. It is not uncommon to see a woman progressively stripping herself of her ornaments, until she can get the desired amount. Her ornaments are then locked in a safe deposit box until the loan is fully repaid.

Receiving loans against jewellery is an extension of a traditional way women get credit from private money-lenders, by pawning their jewellery with them. Jewellery is often the only asset a woman owns, usually gifted to her at the time of her marriage. SEWA learned early on that the high interest loans women are extended privately often cause them to forfeit their jewellery forever. The problem first came to SEWA's notice when Hatibehn Kaluji, a Marwari domestic servant was brought by her employer to SEWA Bank. She reported that she had pawned her silver ornaments with her previous employer, one piece at a time, taking small loans, until all her jewellery was gone. She had borrowed a total of Rs. 325 from him. She had tried to pay him Rs. 100 the year before she came to SEWA Bank, to get one piece of jewellery released, but he refused. He told her to bring Rs. 800, and take all her jewellery at once. The next year her daughter was getting married, so she took Rs. 150, and again asked for one piece to give for the wedding. This time he told her she owed him Rs. 1200 now, and again refused.

SEWA decided to send their bank manager with Rs. 1000 and a government money-lending inspector to the old employer's house to settle the account for Hatibehn's jewellery. After stalling them for hours, the employer finally settled the account for Rs. 600. They took the jewellery to be assessed the next day, and found that its current market value was Rs. 10,000.

Breaking Debt Bonds and Recovering Mortgages

This inability to recover assets is characteristic of women indebted to private lenders. Whether they borrow against jewellery, mortgages, labour wages, or even take unsecured loans from known parties, the usual condition is that the entire lump sum must be repaid in one instalment. Even if the debtor wanted to repay in small amounts, she is required to pay interest on the entire amount until the loan is entirely repaid, giving her no incentive to do so.

After recovering Hatibehn's jewellery, an account of it appeared in the TLA newspaper, which led to many women approaching SEWA for help in recovering their lost ornaments. This made bank workers realize that besides extending fair interest credit against jewellery, women also needed help recovering their jewellery. SEWA then began this as a regular part of its banking programme.

This revealed a similar need for women who were highly indebted to private lenders against their mortgages, or against high interest rates. While the board members of the bank wanted to maintain the policy of loans for productive purposes, they also acknowledged the reality for women who could not free themselves from their previous high interest debts—if they were not helped out of these, they would never be in a position to change their economic relationships. Thus, SEWA began interacting with an increasing number of private lenders. To release a woman from her old debts, they never put cash directly into her hand, but call the lender to the bank to ensure that the money reaches him and releases the woman entirely from the debt. If he refuses to come, someone from the bank will then go to his place to negotiate and pay off the debt.

One of the most traumatic realities SEWA encounters with its members is the increasing loss of land for poor rural families through the process of indebtedness. If there is a drought, or some emergency in the family, or several accumulated small debts, they often take a loan to cover these from a money-lender in the village—against the mortgage of their small landholdings. Zabubehn Mir, the Secretary of the Baldana SEWA Women's Milk Cooperative, related how she almost lost her land to mortgage: 'When our daughter was 19 years old, we did not have any savings—in fact we were already indebted Rs. 2000. We could not wait any longer to get her married. There were many conflicts in my husband's family, so none of the family members were willing to lend to us. Neither of us had regular work then, so we decided to mortgage our land for Rs. 5000, pay our old debts, and marry our daughter. We had to pay Rs. 500 per month as interest on the land. I was interested to take this job as Secretary so that I could pay the interest regularly. That's how much I earn each month—Rs. 500. In one year, my entire income of Rs. 6000 went for the interest, but we did not have one *paise* saved to pay on the original Rs. 5000. We were on the path to starvation. What should we do—keep paying the interest and losing Rs. 6000 each year, and may be never get the land back anyway? Or just quit paying and let the land go?'

'I see many families in this situation here (in Baldana village). Sometimes the men mortgage the land without telling anyone in the family, and women do not have any say in the matter. If they no longer have the land, then they have to do daily labour on someone else's farm to feed the family. If they make Rs. 6–Rs. 10 per day, where is the repayment to come from? Like that, the value of their loan doubles every year, and the land never comes back to the family's hands.'

'Our land would have been gone, if SEWA Bank had not helped us at that point. They went and negotiated with the money-lender in our village. It took time to work out through everyone's different interpretations of the agreement. Finally, the bank handed over Rs. 5000 to him. Now we pay the bank Rs. 175 per month. Like this, slowly, we can manage. At the end of three years, this debt will be repaid, but in the meantime, we can work and also earn from our own land.'

Not only through its rural work did SEWA recognize the magnitude of the situation, but also through numerous self-employed women in Ahmedabad itself, who reported migrating to the city in search of work after they had lost their land to indebtedness. In 1988, SEWA conducted surveys in 60 villages of Ahmedabad district to learn more about the problem. It was seen that 80 per cent of the people in these villages were indebted, largely to relatives, money-lenders, landlords, and the *sarpanch* (local political leader) at high interest rates. SEWA's real chance for offsetting this trend came in 1988 when the Reserve Bank of India agreed to extend the bank's jurisdiction to the whole of Ahmedabad district. This is the first urban cooperative bank in the country to receive this rural authority.

RURAL BANKING

Jayshree, who has been their Managing Director since 1986, explained how rural banking differs from their urban programme: 'Since 1977 when SEWA began working in rural areas, we were painfully aware of women's poverty, their lack of assets, and their mortgaged land. We realized that they needed a credit facility, but we did not want to just start extending loans from an outside financial institution which they did not know the meaning of. We wanted them to be strong, to learn how to save, to know how to handle money. From there, credit could be extended. In the city, women are more accustomed to handling cash. In most rural families, men still control the money, while women are bartering work for foodgrains. Therefore, women first of all needed a real sense about cash—that was the first objective.'

'Second, we wanted to use this as another way to get women organized. We had seen from the beginning of SEWA, that women organize easily around money. So we decided to start rural savings groups. There was such a need—such an overwhelming demand—in one year we have already organized more than 40 villages.'

These rural savings groups comprise a team of four women who perform the kind of work Tarabehn carries out in Ahmedabad. They approach a village where SEWA is already working in some other capacity, and the women have expressed an interest, and they call a meeting. If they are trying to organize in a rural area where SEWA has not worked before, they go in the cold and begin

establishing contacts. The women who want to start saving set all
the terms: they decide how much money they want to deposit each
month, and how long a time period they will fix the deposit for
before any member can withdraw the funds. Most of the groups
agree on a period of a one year fixed deposit, and deposit between
Rs. 10–Rs. 50 per month. They decide on a fixed monthly amount
for each group, so that no large depositors can dominate the
group. Usually one illiterate woman and one literate woman,
representing different communities act as the savings group leaders.
All the members of the group learn enough numeracy to be able to
corroborate their own accounts. They deposit the monthly amount
with their group leaders, who issue receipts and record it in their
pass-books. Then the SEWA rural savings team visits once or twice
a month to collect the deposit and meet the entire group of women
to work out any difficulties that have arisen.

Kokilabehn, a wiry, aging group leader from the Thakur community of Pasunj village recounted some of the difficulties they
overcame in their first year of savings: 'The first problem that
came up was getting all the women in our group to trust us. The
other women think, "Who are you Kokilabehn, all of a sudden,
that I should be giving my money to you?" So for the first few
months, everyone would hold onto the money until the SEWA
Bank team showed up, and then they would rush to put it in their
hands. They refused to take it, though, and said, you have to work
this out with your group leaders. So slowly, they began giving their
money to us, and we built trust.'

'Then our second problem came up. Sometimes it happened
that one month a woman could not make her deposit. Then the
next month she wanted to deposit double the amount. But for the
last month there was no interest. Then everyone's accounts would
have different amounts. We finally decided, if we miss one payment, the next month we have to deposit the payment plus the
interest, to keep everyone's balance equal.'

'The biggest thing is making decisions together. Sometimes we
shout all at once, trying to decide something. We never did this
before, and money makes all of us excited . . . .'

After a year of saving together, most of the initial problems
have been solved, and women have travelled a long way in understanding banking. Then SEWA Bank approaches the group to ask
how the women would like to use their assets. Some opt for

collectively purchasing seeds or fertilizers at wholesale to reduce their costs. Others do not want to spend, and want to fix their deposits for another year to let their savings grow. Many groups opt for taking loans against the fixed deposits, and collectively decide which women in the group should be extended credit. This is the most common place for women with mortgaged land to make an appeal to the group that they get a loan to recover their land.

This, then, is the turning-point which marks a quiet but radical change in what Ela Bhatt calls 'a very Gandhian way.' When SEWA Bank makes an extension of the savings scheme to provide credit, it naturally insists on dealing with the women who are known to the bank. When a rural woman wants credit to recover her land, SEWA Bank workers tell her, 'Certainly, but the land must be listed in *your* name, since it is you we know, and it is your fixed deposit against which we are lending money.' Whether the men of the household appreciate the idea or not, they recognize that this is probably their only chance to recover their land, and agree to the transfer of title.

In one village, Pardhol of Dehgam block, most of the women were initially stunned when the workers told them this condition of the loan. They had simply never considered that such a thing was possible. While many women echoed that their men would never agree, their group leader, Santokbehn, who is an agricultural labourer, got visibly excited following this progression of ideas through with them.

'We come from our family's house to live in our husband's house. If we mention *our* name in this house (husband's), they say, "Oh, that is *another* family." Yet when it comes to working, they say, "What you earn is ours, because you are in *this* family's house," or "because you are working on *this* family's land".'

'Let the land be registered in our (women's) names, so that we will not always feel like we are in someone else's family!'

Women in other villages are sometimes quicker to acknowledge the benefit of listing the land in their names, if the land was mortgaged without their knowledge or consent. Some women who have recovered their land through SEWA Bank even claimed that their husbands approved of the arrangement, because not having the land in men's names 'put a check on their irrational impulses.'

So far, SEWA Bank has negotiated 139 landholdings back into

family possession by extending loans and titles to women. In a few cases, the bank has managed to recover a portion of the land if the debt is too large to recover the entire property.

Both the rural and the urban loan extension system is based on creating a sort of 'character network' where people are known to each other and responsible to one another. In the urban areas it is to the reference persons, the trade organizers, and the bank; in the rural areas, to the savings group members and to the bank. By extending loans based on responsibility rather than security, SEWA has reached women who otherwise would not have had access to institutional credit.

USE OF LOANS

The variety of loans sanctioned is an interesting study in itself. Working capital loans cover a multitude of purchases. For instance, Dhangauribehn Chhotalal, who previously stitched cheap garments cut by someone else on a piece-rate basis for a contractor, used her loan to buy her own satin and gold shiny cloth and trim. Now all the grown-up members of her family are engaged in stitching fancy skirts and tops for girls, which she and her husband cut. They have made such profits ever since they started their own business, that the rented 8' × 8' room where the whole family previously lived and worked is now their workshop, and they have built a new two-room house of their own with their profits.

A carpenter, who used to make only stools and bats for washing clothes, used her loan to buy machine tools like electric saws and drills, and more expensive raw materials. She now produces desks and cupboards for a more middle class market. Likewise, a smith bought a machine to mechanically ream chemical barrels to get better raw material for her metal work.

Besides extending loans, SEWA arranged to take its carpenter and smith members to the Industrial Training Institute. Seeing the different types of machinery and its uses, the women realized the possibilities of how to expand their work horizons.

Other purposes of loans for vendors included fishing nets for a Vaghari woman whose family vends fish. She took a loan to buy new nets so that her sons could work in two other areas and add to the family income. Another Vaghari woman who previously sold vegetables from a head-basket took a loan of Rs. 4000 to purchase one large truckload of water-melons, which she piled on the road-side and sat beside for a month, until they were all sold. Vendors often take loans for small hand-carts, or for the construction of a small stall, or for a storage shed so that larger lots can be purchased at one time, saving on time, transport, and wholesale prices.

Mirabehn Kakubai is one urban vendor whose business acumen has blossomed with the support of SEWA Bank. Her family lives in one of Ahmedabad's largest slums, Shankarbhavan, built on the eastern bank of the river Sabarmati. It is the place through which the entire eastern city drains during the monsoons, and is exposed to flooding and severe sewage and sanitation problems. Mira has been constantly taking loans from SEWA Bank since 1977. The first two loans were small amounts which the bank extended to her to tide over her family's health problems. The third loan marked the beginning of her commercial use of the money. Though her family usually sells vegetables and fruits, this credit (Rs. 1200) allowed them to diversify into a large purchase of religious threads known as *rakhis* which people use during the festival. With the profits from this they paid off an old debt. The next loan they took to buy another hand-cart for another member of the family to sell from. Then a larger loan helped her set up a small stall in a fixed market, from which they could triple their daily sales. Each time successfully repaying her loan, she built her savings, expanded her business, and took another larger loan. Now she has taken a loan of Rs. 15,000 and is building a new house outside Shankarbhavan for her family.

SEWA is one of the only cooperative banks in the country which lends to lower income groups for housing purposes. And while the government has many schemes for low income subsidized housing, the beneficiaries of these schemes are still largely government employees with permanent jobs, who have access to the formal channels to receive the benefits. In 1987–88, 40 per cent of SEWA's loan funds were given for housing.[3] Half of them were for women like Mirabehn, to build a new house. The other loans were for upgrading the existing house. Upgrading can mean laying a floor in a house which has only a dirt floor, like one woman did who runs a nursery school in her house for the children of self-employed women. It can mean replacing *kaccha* walls with brick walls and window frames, or constructing a permanent roof on the house. This kind of lending—for upgrading the house gradually—is suitable to both self-employed families and the bank. It is affordable for people with low income, and it is less risk for the bank. All the densely populated working class neighbourhoods of Ahmedabad reflect this kind of evolution. *Kaccha* houses stand next to semi-*pucca*, next to *pucca* houses—some owned, some rented, some encroaching on public land. Once people have upgraded from *kaccha* structures to *pucca* ones, they often feel the need for more space, and take a loan to expand the one room to two, enlarging their work space. Many of the loans are taken for building a toilet, or installing water taps in the house. Again these housing loans are sanctioned for titles in women's names—if they are legally titled houses or land—and the bank considers this not only a personal asset, but also a capital investment, because it renders her work space more efficient and protected. This is the most common loan sought by a home-based worker. SEWA Bank's commitment to the needs of poor women is reflected in its loans to upgrade *kaccha* houses even on rented or encroached land. If the woman has the ability to repay, SEWA considers her reality and need for housing as the primary objective.

NURTURING REPAYMENT

Out of approximately 3000 loans extended in March, 1989, nearly 300 women faced difficulty in repayment every month. Checking the bank's area-wise ledger of who is falling behind in repayment, the bank contacts the friends who gave their 'promise' about the client, or the organizer who works with that particular trade group. If the referees or organizers cannnot help the bank, they assign the case to one of the four women who, along with other duties, constitute the loan recovery team.

Another Niru, whom everyone addresses as 'Naniniru' because she is much younger and smaller than 'Police Commissioner' Niru-behn, is one of the loan recovery agents. When she first began to work at SEWA, she would clean the office and serve water. She took up this work when the bank needed another worker. Unlike Tarabehn, Naniniru does not carry anything with her when she goes out. She travels by bus to the workers' neighbourhoods, and visits women from that particular area who may be behind in their instalments. She asks politely, in their language, what problems they are facing, and why they are behind in repayment. If they pay her something, she tucks it into her sari blouse for later deposit in the bank.

'I never harass a woman,' she explained about her approach to the problem of recovery. 'I understand what it is like to be poor. I go like I am her friend who has gotten news that she is in trouble, to see if I can help. Sometimes the biggest help is just that I have come. May be she has sick people in her family, and just cannot get to the bank. Or may be she is in trouble with money. Then I sit with her and try to work out a way to help her repay. Sometimes women ask me if I can come everyday, and they will give me a few rupees each day. Some ask me to come once a week on their pay-day from their merchant. I agree to whatever they ask. If they need some help from the union, if their employer is harassing them, or if they are having health problems, I ask that part of SEWA to visit them. Then it usually happens that they begin catching up with their payments, and they tell me to stop coming, that they will come to the bank themselves.'

The kinds of difficulties women experience in repayment have not changed much over the decade and a half that SEWA Bank has been in operation, since its membership is steadily growing with women who face the same social and economic constraints. Repayment problems usually revolve around her family, her health, or some occupational fluctuations. If anyone in her family falls sick, it is her responsibility to care for them. If her husband beats her or appropriates her money or loses his work, she has little recourse except to work harder to recover the loss. If her health is poor, or she has to bear the burden of frequent pregnancies, her work time and stamina are sacrificed. Her profit margin is low even when work is progressing smoothly. If there is loss of work, or a change in the market or raw material supply, or she faces extreme police harassment, she may simply not have the ability to repay for a while. When Naniniru, or someone else from SEWA learns of her constraints, they try to help her solve the cause of the problem, and not merely treat the symptom of her defaulting.

'It is this close, personal contact, at every stage of the banking process, which makes the bank successful,' Jayshree related. 'We don't just get involved with a woman's money, but with all the aspects of her life . . . . We also realize that it is not education which makes successful bank workers, but experience and sensitivity. Which middle class well educated bank worker wants to go out in 43 degrees heat to the slums to meet women and collect small change against their loans?'

The biggest problems in repayment that SEWA has faced since its early difficulties in 1975, usually centre around times of crises. Following the prolonged riots of 1985–86, a curfew was imposed on the city indefinitely, and many women fell behind in repayment. It was not only a question of losing work, many women also lost their homes, and all their tools of trade. They had to be compensated for these losses before any small instalments could again trickle in. The severe drought from 1984 to 1987 also adversely affected many women's ability to repay. Weavers who had taken loans on looms, suddenly saw cotton disappear from the market at any affordable price, and their work stopped until the rain and a good crop could come in. Also, in 1988 when several mills simultaneously closed their doors indefinitely, families lost their major source of income. During these crises a woman can do without harassment from another source, however she needs creative support and planning to help her stay on her feet and meet her obligations.

SEWA has learned that by providing support at these times— rather than harassment—strengthens its image as a friend of the poor, and results in better repayment than legal recourse or threats could do. SEWA Bank is flexible in helping a woman reschedule her instalments when these crises occur. Jayshree explained that 'here we do not see defaulters as defaulters. The reality is that sometimes women fall behind by a payment or two. Sometimes they are paying regular monthly instalments, but are paying less than the originally agreed amount due to unforeseen circumstances. Nevertheless, they have full intention of repaying all of their loan.'

A study conducted by Seetharaman and Shingi (1986) the year after the communal disturbances corroborated this view: They found 47 per cent of the SEWA borrowers overdue, but only 12 per cent of the total loan amount was overdue. Instead of issuing another loan to cover the first one, or labelling her a defaulter, or writing a loan off, or taking legal action to recover the loan,

SEWA kept encouraging the women to repay as and when they could. Within a year, 93 per cent of those falling behind in repayment had regained current status. In this way, a woman does not become a defaulter, but a responsible creditor who can slowly, with perseverance, build up her assets.

POLICY ADVOCACY

Ela Bhatt is one of the most nationally and internationally outspoken proponents for women having assets in their own name. 'We should encourage women to build up their assets for two reasons,' she said in an interview at the end of her nationwide study for the Commission on Self-Employed Women. 'Because women's income is used mostly for *roti*, *capra*, and *makaan* (bread, clothes, and house), the more cash income which goes into her hands, the faster the family's quality of life goes up.'

'And secondly there is an increasing number of women headed households, and in times of crises, assets are the only things which help them.'

Internationally, she has been involved in helping channel assets to women through both her and SEWA's interaction with the Women's World Banking, a global organization based in New York which Ela says is 'perhaps the most concrete result of the Women's Decade.'

The inspiration for the WWB came from a group of women from diverse cultures brainstorming at the 1975 Mexico City Conference launching the UN Decade for Women. These women resolved to create a global support network for women who have entrepreneurial skills but lack the capital, management skills, and confidence to build viable businesses. One of these women, Michela Walsh, a US investment broker, actively carried that inspiration to establish the WWB in 1980 to provide loan guarantees to banks for women who had not previously had access to formal banking institutions. In July 1990, the WWB had a capital base of $7 million to provide guarantees. There are affiliates known as Friends of WWB in 40 countries.

In 1990, WWB's new President Nancy Barry credited SEWA

Bank for serving as a model for the entire WWB global network, which extends similar integrated services along with credit. SEWA has worked closely with the WWB since its inception, and Bhatt has been Chairperson of its Board of Directors since 1988 and has worked to channel increasing WWB funds to poor women worldwide. SEWA Bank houses Friends of WWB, India, which extends banking services to rural women and women in other districts of Gujarat which fall outside the jurisdiction of SEWA Bank.

Bhatt is well-known in Gujarat for her litany: 'Every district should have a women's bank.' Pushing this recommendation at the national level through the National Commission's *Shramshakti* Report, the issue was first raised in Parliament in February 1989. Though Members expressed doubts about the expenditure involved in such a venture, SEWA's experience shows that overhead costs need not be higher in lending and recovering small amounts, and that the constraints both poor women and the nationalized banks have faced can be better overcome by an institution catering specifically to these women's needs.

SEWA's conviction in this regard stems from its interaction with the Reserve Bank of India (RBI), from whom it gets its authority to operate. Each time SEWA Bank wants to expand its field of activities, it must take the permission of the RBI. It often faces resistance because, for the first 14 years it did not meet the banks' 'viability norms'—which are set up for commercial banks—despite SEWA's unusually high recovery rate on loans (93 per cent) and the profits it is earning on both loans and deposits. It took SEWA many years of lobbying before the RBI agreed to grant it rural jurisdiction.

On the basis of the resistance it met, SEWA Bank petitioned the Union Minister for Banking and Economic Affairs to segregate 'development banks' from commercial banks when establishing viability norms.[4] He was asked to recognize the needs for supportive services for the poor, which increase the functions of women's banks, but which commercial banking clientele do not need. It pointed out that providing banking services to large numbers of people who have not previously had access to banks should be considered equally important to mobilizing large amounts of money. In the midst of SEWA's lobbying, the bank actually met the norms for the first time in its decade and a half of existence, emphasizing the *process* of economic integration.

Besides petitioning for the RBI's priorities and standards of viability to be changed to enable other cooperative banks for women to be established, SEWA has furthered its demand for district level women's banks by asking for a separate women's forum at the national level comprising all the organizations who extend banking to the poor. SEWA's experience reinforces its belief that women need their own space to voice their concerns and problems in order to become competent and confident in their dealings in the formal economy.

As Usha Jumani put it: 'If you know how to handle money, you are a free agent. If you don't, you are dependent and vulnerable.'

Their own forum gives self-employed women the place to demystify the formal world and its procedures at their own pace and in their own terms of understanding. Chandabehn articulated it well when she said, 'This bank has been like a village well for us. Sisters from all castes and communities gather here not just for our "water", but to exchange news . . . . When we are drinking tea out front, we teach each other about this bank . . . . One sister talks about money like grains of wheat—if they are scattered, you don't know how much you have. If they are in a bag, you can lift it and feel the weight . . . . Another explains about savings and loans and interest like this—if you plant a tree to feed your cow, that is your savings account. If you cut the tree down, your cow gets full one day but starves the next. If you cut a little bit at a time, your cow and your tree grow slowly. If you have more than one account, it's like more than one tree. If you can leave one without touching it for a few years, you get a really big tree. This is like a fixed deposit. If your sister has some nice big trees, you can also ask her if you can borrow leaves to feed your cow until your trees grow big....Other women explain in other ways, but we all learn like this.'

The early members and builders of SEWA Bank are extremely proud of this bank today. No one had conceived in those days the magnitude of what they were initiating. Every year an annual meeting of all the shareholders is held to discuss how the bank is doing. Large charts are prepared to graphically show the thousands of women present their profits and investments. These meetings are electrified where women feel the power that their collectivity gives them as they talk about their one and a half crore (15 million) rupees working capital.

SEWA Bank has operated from this all-women's space for 15 years now, supporting its members from their position of no control over their income, to their current bargaining power not only with their contractors or wholesalers, but also with their families. They have moved from being assetless to holding assets as wide ranging as identity cards, work sheds, spinning wheels, camel carts, machine tools, land titles, and authority in the family business. SEWA Bank is working toward bridging another gap for women, that is, their need for formal financial management training. Women want to invest their credit and gradually growing capital wisely so that they can plan for the future, buffer themselves against emergencies, develop business plans, and save for housing.

'We are determined to refute by our own examples the relic assumption that "women are bad credit risks," ' Jayshree Vyas emphasized in 1989.

When the Reserve Bank of India announced its decision in 1990 that it would adopt *Shramshakti*'s recommendation to permit the establishment of women's banks in each of the country's more than 500 development districts, it appeared that they had made their point.

END NOTES

1. This account is compiled from oral interviews, and from Usha Jumani's profile of Zubeida in 'The Informal Sector as People's Economy,' *op. cit.*, 1988, pp. 26–33.
2. S.P. Seetharaman and P.M. Shingi, 'Reaching the Poor: A Case Study of SEWA Bank,' Paper prepared for Indo-German Pilot Project on Poverty Alleviation, p. 21.
3. Meera Mehta and Dinesh Mehta, 'Housing Finance Systems in Metropolitan Areas of India,' Second Progress Report to USAID, March 1989, pp. 3–6.
4. See SEWA's 1988 Decade Report for further discussion of these policy issues.

8

Women's Cooperatives: A Lever for Change

Organizing Song

We are poor women in a hostile land
With no foodgrains in our vessels
Droughts come often and
unemployment is rife.
We have neither land, nor work
Our houses are small as our hands
And our needs are many.

We are women, illiterate women
Coming together in Nalkantha villages
We are women, poor women
Coming together to make a union.

We started spinning thread
to earn some grains for our families.
We then wove cloth
to bring cash into our palms
We defied the drought with our thousand trees
And began milking our cattle together.

We are illiterate, but so what?
We challenge everyone with our strength:
the landlords who paid us so little
the men who would not let us out.

We have come together to fill
the village pond with milk
We have contained it with the
strength of our union.

Composed in Gujarati by Anila Dholakia

As one traverses the small road from the main highway at Bavla into the scattered villages of Dholka taluk, the landscape presents harsh scenery. It is a drought-prone, saline, thorny scrubbed land. It was at its worst perhaps during the three years of no rain from 1986 to 1988. The animal carcasses littering the road margins served just one reminder of the absence of food and water. Teams of women and men dug pits along this roadway as government drought relief work for daily wages and grains. Fallow, baked fields stretched out behind them. On some days the temperatures rose to as high as 46 degrees. Women desperately struggled for haphazard patches of shade for their infants and small children who had to accompany them to the work site, several miles walk from the village.

Both the landed and the landless laboured at these sites, breaking the baked earth with picks and headloading it out of the carefully measured pits—a task which had no purpose beyond measuring labour to pay wages. Families with animals lamented the most. Although some families with land were forced to mortgage to cover their debts, a majority would still have their land once the rains came. Those with herds, however, had to send their animals out to other parts of the state to find grazing land. Many died due to diseases in the cattle camps. Others starved at home.

In the height of the third year, one woman Samubehn said, 'We do not know if we should come and dig to feed the family while the cattle starve, or if we should spend the days collecting fodder for them while we starve. While the drought is on, the only way to feed ourselves is by this digging. Once some rain comes, the only way to feed ourselves will be if our cattle survive. Which do we choose?'

Equally sobering were the poorest landless labourers who reported that, unforgiving as the work was, they had earned more consistent income this drought year by digging labour pits on government relief than they could earn in productive years working on others' farms. They informed that even during years with adequate rainfall there were always five to six months a year when no work was available.

The morning of 10 January 1989 reveals a beautiful, soft contrast to those scenes along this road. Grasses grow along the road margins and some standing crops are seen in the fields. This year's monsoon has relieved some of the burden of the people.

The soft winter light deepens the vibrant colours worn by the hundreds of women who traverse the road in the tractor trailers, open freight trucks, small buses, or on foot. More than 1000 women from 40 villages are gathering for a *sammelan* (rally) of rural SEWA members. They are coming together to affirm their solidarity and agree on an agenda for employment which would help them avert a repeat of those last three years. They want to develop local ways to stave off the devastation of droughts, and they want year-round employment which would override the meaningless labour of relief work as their most remunerative option.

They all converge on the village of Devdholera, crowding into the spacious grounds of SEWA's rural headquarters. The large building which houses training equipment and bamboo supplies is open but quiet. Milk and antiseptic smells emanate from the dairy cooperative. The plantation of four-year old fodder trees which feed landless women's cattle casts a partial shade over the tightly assembled women, forming a lush contrast to the barren landscape beyond.

Elabehn inaugurates the meeting with her belief that this is a sacred spot, as whatever women have started in this village has flourished. She attributes this success to their solidarity, encouraging all the women present to draw strength from one another. She asks them to speak about their work and to continue finding common direction together. As woman after woman rises to meet her encouragement, the experiences they relate draw an important picture of rural women's reality.

RURAL WOMEN'S WORK

Women are engaged in many occupations through different seasons of the year, depending on each one's skills and assets. Their occupations are mostly traditional and revolve around livestock, land, and artisan work. The remuneration for their work spans a continuum which includes unpaid subsistence work, bartering of goods or services, paid wage work for an employer, and self-employment.

Women's family subsistence labour includes tending animals, raising and processing food crops, collecting fuel wood from distances as far as 10 kilometres, preparing fuel cakes of dung, raising children, feeding the family, and caring for the sick. All these services for the family would have to be paid for if women were not performing them for the household.

Wage earners include landless, poor, and low caste women who tend animals, work in the fields, and do domestic duties for other households; artisans who work on piece-rate for a contractor; or women who migrate for several months every year in search of agricultural or construction wage work.

Self-employed women raise and sell crops from their own land or from sharecropping of others' land; they sell or barter their artisan work; they raise animals to produce milk, clarified butter, meat, eggs, and wool which they sell; and they hire out animals for transport or ploughing. Poor women often render services in exchange for goods: they clean cattle sheds in exchange for grains; care for cattle in exchange for their calves; and trade home produced pottery, cloth, grain winnowers, rope or tools in exchange for foodgrains or other goods.

As each woman rises from the crowd to come to the microphone and address the gathered women, the vulnerabilities which plague their work and livelihoods become obvious. Several talk about the uncertainties of the rains and the toll of their unemployment. Another complains about the loss of fuel and fodder from anywhere near the village, and asks 'Why don't we spend the hours we use everyday to collect these things to grow them ourselves near the village?'

Many women refer to their increasing debt burdens, problems

of landlessness, and persistent social problems in the village. Two landless women approach the microphone and lament the underemployment crisis even during years of sufficient rains, and protest the low wages they receive when they do find work.

The testimonies are not all bleak, however. Agricultural labourers who have become SEWA organizers stand and narrate their stories of acquiring literacy and administrative skills, and how they have helped develop fodder and water resources in their villages. SEWA cooperative members report increased incomes and describe important initiatives: they now have access to tools which were formerly controlled by men—looms, money, potter's wheel, livestock breeding tools and irrigation equipment. They exercise some degree of control over resources which previously were outside the realm of their decision-making—water, wood, bamboo, wool, cash, land, animals, and the managing committees of their organizations.

Balubehn, Lakhubehn and Mannibehn convey the importance of the training in weaving they have received through SEWA. They verbally reconstruct the bridges they have built to credit for their own looms, to markets, and to material supplies.

Samubehn talks about their dairy cooperative, now 10 years old, run and membered by all women. When asked about the history of their cooperative, she gives a half-toothless, knowing smile. 'What have not we fought to keep this cooperative going?' she asks in response. 'Illiteracy, men dominating our accounts,' she counts them off on her fingers, 'extortion, droughts, the tactics of milk traders to lure members out, government refusal to registering women's cooperatives. But even during the last three years with no rain,' she says with defiance, 'we made one and a half to two lakh rupees every year.'

The usefulness of SEWA's central strategy—the *joint action of union and cooperatives*—is particularly apparent in this rural environment. In urban areas, women of one trade are extremely concentrated and tend to be engaged in only one income generating occupation. This makes collective bargaining and negotiations of union work more feasible in the urban context. In the case of women assembled from 40 disparate villages at this rural sammelan—an event they can accomplish only once a year—the number of women from each occupation apart from agriculture is relatively small and scattered. Landless rural women are un-employed for up to six months in a year, extremely limiting their bargaining power. They perform numerous jobs and services for several individuals, with many dependencies beyond wages built into the work relations.

Takhubehn, a Harijan woman from Baldana who works as a labourer in the fields of large landowners, explained the inter-dependence of her livelihood with one of the farmers who employs her, making wage demands impractical: 'I take the waste from his paddy harvest for animal fodder. Sometimes I collect the dung animals have dropped on his fields to make fuel with, or wood from a few of the trees that border his field. I also get water from his well in summer if the other village wells and pond go dry. Sometimes they feed me, or send home extra food for my family. They are small things. Not much. But when I do not have work for two months running, each small thing *matters*.'

Takhu does not want to challenge the below minimum wage rate he pays her. She knows that such demands have provoked violent responses in the past. Neither is she prepared to sacrifice the work or the subsistence resources she depends upon, nor to incur the potential caste conflict such a demand might elicit.

Takhu's situation is just one of the many kinds of situations SEWA encounters in every village it takes up work in: impoverished women struggling under the combined burden of underemploy-ment, underpayment and intricate social relationships which render them dependent and vulnerable. As land degrades and droughts intensify, women who solely depend upon agricultural wages become extremely vulnerable when agriculture fails, as it did for three years in Gujarat. With the breakdown of the traditional social security systems under changing economies, and markets altering beyond the comprehension of many rural artisans, poor families cannot individually muster the resources to fight all these conditions.

Such women who work with SEWA find cooperatives to be a tool which provides the first leverage they have ever wielded in work relations. Cooperatives offer better opportunities for self-employment by improving women's skills through training and providing market links which result in increased income. Their dependence on landlords, traders, and money-lenders is reduced, and they are in a stronger position to negotiate on issues related to agricultural wages and credit. With the increased options cooperatives provide for year-round employment, and women become less desperate to accept exploitative work arrangements.

Somee, the teenaged daughter of a member of the Devdholera weaving cooperative, is the first female of her family ever to sit on the loom. Her mother spins the wool which her father weaves into traditional coarse wool blankets on his pit loom. Somee weaves handloom cotton dress material on her modern upright pedal loom.

'I used to go to shell cotton pods in this season for Rs. 4 a day,' she related to women gathered at the sammelan. 'I also worked for Rs. 5–Rs. 7 a day in others' fields. Now I don't usually do any job for less than Rs. 10 per day because I can earn more through the cooperative from my weaving. If someone offers me Rs. 10, I will go, and save the weaving for a day when no one offers work. If they offer less, I will sit and weave, and leave that work. It used to be the other way around. We earned so little from our blankets, that we would leave them to work in the fields for whatever we were offered.'

Likewise, when Takhubehn joined the Baldana dairy cooperative, she found the milk revenue stabilized her income through the months when no farm work was available.

There was a great deal of resistance to women's attempts to improve their situation through membership in a cooperative. The larger union provides significant help to the small cooperatives by backing their agenda, extending supportive services and making linkages which a small fledgling cooperative cannot achieve on its own. SEWA sets up a savings group in a village, between one to three women's cooperatives representing different trades and services, and a small village union of women emerges, creating cohesion across occupations. Each cooperative pays membership to the larger union, the union bolsters the cooperative's local efforts, and the relationship continues to build and strengthen.

KINDS OF COOPERATIVES

SEWA's cooperatives span diverse trades and services. Besides building the highly successful cooperative bank—which inspired

SEWA to pursue organizing more cooperatives—women have formed artisan cooperatives, vendors cooperatives, dairy cooperatives, land cooperatives, and labour and service cooperatives.

Urban members belong to only one occupational cooperative: (*a*) artisan cooperatives include chindi stitchers, weavers, and cloth block printers; (*b*) service cooperatives include child care or health care services provided by the self-employed women for the member community; (*c*) vendors' cooperatives include kerosene vending, fish vending, vegetable supply service to government hospitals, schools, and jails; and (*d*) labour cooperatives provide industrial cleaning services to large institutions on a contract basis, and collect recyclable waste materials from government institutions.

In rural areas, women are engaged in diverse seasonal occupations and often they are members of more than one cooperative. Simultaneous membership in land-based, artisan, and/or dairy cooperatives can provide the necessary resources to keep women employed throughout the year.

Although there are now almost 40 SEWA cooperatives, these cooperatives have to pass through a long process of evolution to become viable. At the local level women have to overcome caste barriers, cheating and competition within the cooperatives, men's resistance to putting assets in women's control, old feuds within the community, space constraints for production and equipment, and the problems working class women face when trying to develop the necessary links with businessmen. In the larger scheme, viable cooperatives have to overcome women's low skill levels; low literacy levels; government policies which allocate the resources they need to large industry; and cumbersome bureaucratic hurdles which prevent cooperative registration or credit being allocated to women.

DAIRY

In 1978 SEWA recognized an anomaly: the National Dairy Development Board's (NDDB) programme to create a market economy for the rural poor through milk targeted men, though women did most of the dairy work. SEWA approached the NDDB (whose headquarters are in Gujarat) to forward the idea of giving training to women to form cooperatives. After some initial reluctance, the NDDB did extend training, and 12 cooperatives were formed. The ensuing six years marked protracted, tumultuous struggles to shift the control of women's occupations from men to women, and to shift profits from middlemen to the actual producers.

Before women's cooperatives were organized, families were often indebted to the milk trader, resulting in low rates for their milk. The existing cooperatives were male cooperatives controlled by the dominant caste or village political leaders. Since women were not members of these cooperatives, they rarely received any income from their dairy work. Even if a woman did belong to a male dominated cooperative, she rarely attended meetings or spoke up in them.

Since the advent of the NDDB's 'Operation Flood' and its widespread introduction of high yielding cross-bred cattle, dairying shifted from being a largely subsistence activity to becoming the most lucrative commercial enterprise after agriculture in many of the Dholka villages. Milk, unlike crops, kept income flowing to the village almost year-round. The milk traders and male political leaders of the 12 villages where SEWA first organized dairy co-operatives did not condone women channelling so much of the village finances. Only four of the original 12 SEWA cooperatives survived their retaliation.

After those initial losses, SEWA succeeded in setting up 18 women's dairy cooperatives with 50–400 members in each of two districts of the state and revived 35 defunct men's cooperatives in Banaskantha district into women's or mixed cooperatives. SEWA's all-women's cooperatives represent women's first significant economic and decision-making participation in the dairy movement. Like the union, these cooperatives provide important models of modern organizational forms which defy old gender, class, or caste power hierarchies by including women from many communities.

When forming new dairy cooperatives, SEWA organizes all village women who want to participate, but they cater especially to the poor landless and small landholding women by creating and making accessible an integrated package of training and supportive services. The package includes linkages to obtain a loan, a good quality animal, cattle life insurance, and training in animal husbandry, dairying, and veterinary skills. The women's dairy movement in India has expanded during the eighties through the Andhra Pradesh and Bihar State Dairy Federations and through other NGOs, there are now over 500 all-women's cooperatives. SEWA has proved to be most effective at integrating poor women into cooperatives because of this service package it nurtures so carefully.

Credit

Until 1988, SEWA Bank did not have rural jurisdiction, limiting its ability to extend credit to its rural members. Nationalized banks, though under government pressure to lend to the rural poor, were reticent to extend any loans to assetless women when SEWA applied to them. Stalling, refusals, and offers only to extend loans in the husbands' names went on for months. SEWA was compelled to make a fixed deposit of Rs. 50,000 with a nationalized bank in order to get the loans extended in women's names. Even then loans were delayed, women lost out to other buyers, or the selling cost had gone up, exceeding the sanctioned loan amount. Loan sanction dates and repayment rates did not match milk production cycles. With loans covering only one animal, women found themselves extremely stressed to pay instalments during the animal's dry period in the lactation cycle when it was not generating income.

Exacerbating credit problems were cooperative laws, which hinged membership on individuals selling milk to the cooperative for 90 days to qualify for membership. Women without cattle obviously could not meet this condition, yet their ability to get a loan sanctioned relied on their having the legitimacy of cooperative membership. SEWA channelled international aid money into revolving loan funds to help members purchase cattle, and got the cooperative bye-laws amended to allow future cattle owners membership. SEWA also fought to get members access to the subsidized government loans offered under the Integrated Rural Development Programme (IRDP), and to change IRDP loan policies to cover two animals with alternating lactation cycles so that women could continue to meet repayment schedules even if one animal was not producing.

Vying with Vested Interests

Attempts to register the various cooperatives summoned other formidable obstacles: SEWA's paperwork circulated endlessly through a maze of bureaucratic red tape. Milk traders wielding political power pressured officials to reject SEWA's applications over petty objections to the wording. Since only one cooperative per trade may be registered in each village, local men did not want women's cooperatives to assume control of the heavy subsidies allocated to cooperatives. Social prejudice against women caused registrars to reject applications on the basis that women were illiterate, or that they were not workers. SEWA repeatedly had to call on higher political authorities to intervene and exert pressure on the registrars to get the cooperatives registered.

Once their first milk cooperatives were actually registered and women began selling milk through them, the traders and Sarpanches launched an attack. The women's cooperatives were easily destabilized because of management problems. No lower caste literate women could be found to fill the position of Secretary in the cooperative, so the jobs were filled by either high caste women (often those whose husbands exercised political and economic control in the village) or by men themselves. In some cases, the previous trader or village Sarpanch simply nominated himself to the position. Though such men met no resistance from the village women, SEWA organizers should have been more wary.

These vested interests found many ways to add fuel to the fire: sanctioning cooperative loans to family members who did not belong to the cooperative; issuing false receipts for loan instalments while pilfering the women's money; and simply extorting profits by under-reporting and underpaying milk collection and underpaying members.

The private traders who did not work themselves into the cooperative retaliated from outside: they temporarily offered higher milk rates and immediate loans for any purpose—a service, women could not get through the cooperative. If these tactics did not lure women out of fold of the cooperatives, they resorted to more overt means: hijacking milk cans on the way to the dairy, and spreading malicious rumours about women who were in leadership positions in the cooperative, which resulted in divisiveness and distrust.

For a few years difficulties continued to plague the cooperatives until SEWA developed a strong relationship with the district dairy and National Dairy Development Board. Till then, the Sardar Dairy in Ahmedabad had been buying milk from both the cooperatives and private traders in the same village, giving traders the leverage to play against the cooperatives. SEWA pressed the NDDB on its commitment to bring higher returns to producers and help cooperatives survive as democratic units. With the NDDB's alliance, SEWA successfully lobbied the Sardar Dairy to mandate that they would buy milk only from legitimately registered cooperatives. As only one cooperative per village may be registered, this radically altered SEWA's position. The formerly intractable traders suddenly came to the organizers' feet, begging the cooperatives to purchase their milk.

Gender Resistance

Although the problems with traders were mostly solved with the Dairy's mandate and enforcement, and the cooperatives began pulling in profits, other problems with male domination continued. In Baldana, at the villagers' request, SEWA had helped convert a male-run cooperative operating at a loss to a women's cooperative. The women's cooperative made profits exceeding Rs. 18,000 by their second year of operation. The men then insisted on repossessing the lucrative cooperative, slandered the widow who was the Secretary, and got the women to acquiesce.

Within the first two months of the cooperative's repossession by the men of the village, it incurred a loss of Rs. 5000 because of corruption on the part of the new office holders. The cooperative then became defunct for a year and a half before the women again approached SEWA for assistance in reviving their cooperative. In the interim they had been reduced to selling again to traders for about half the amount the dairy paid through the cooperative. Control issues were clear to them now: this time the women were insistent on running their own cooperative.

Leadership Goals

To overcome the various manifestations of the same difficulties all the cooperatives were experiencing, SEWA focused its attention on developing strong female leadership. It organized intensive training for two levels of dairy organizers through the Sabarmati Ashram Gaushala Project: Six SEWA organizers and an accountant from outside the villages received training for Secretary from the Dairy, and local women leaders from each village were trained in milkfat-testing, as payment is made on the basis of milk quality. The trained SEWA organizers played an interim role of Secretary. They helped stem the corruptive use of cooperative benefits by vested interests in the village until they could pass on the skills either to local women Secretaries, or to a literate woman the cooperative hired from outside the village. SEWA found that outside women were less susceptible to power brokering by vested interests because they did not have the dependency relationships of many local women.

By 1990, despite losing eight cooperatives in the early years, SEWA has successfully supported 18 women's dairy cooperatives in Ahmedabad and Mehsana districts. Credit constraints and problems with male dominance have been worked out. All members receive training in animal husbandry which includes how to care for cross-bred cattle. One or two women from each village have become para-vets. All members have cattle life-insurance, which is crucial for poor women if they are not to become irretrievably indebted if an animal under loan dies. SEWA continues to extend and reinforce training, even in cooperatives which have been functioning for as long as eight years. SEWA can now extend loans from its own bank for cattle, and identifies beneficiaries for the IRDP subsidized loans. SEWA's positive experience of having cooperative members identify women who should get loans reinforces its policy demand through the *Shramshakti* Report that local women's organizations be vested with the responsibility for deciding development priorities and for identifying beneficiaries.

Savitabehn Patel, the main field organizer for the SEWA milk cooperatives, said that most milk cooperatives, if working with experienced organizers and dairy personnel, are capable of standing on their own feet by the end of two years, with an organizer occasionally checking in to help solve problems.

'Before, when vested interests put pressure on the cooperatives, we did not know how to respond,' she explained. 'They would see us wavering and push further. Now we know exactly what to do. When they see our confidence, they back off.'

SEWA perceives the dairy cooperatives as one of the best strategies to organize poor rural women. The marketing problems faced by the other cooperatives are not a problem for dairy cooperatives because of the NDDB network which can sell all the milk it receives. Women are conversant with animal care already, and through the cooperative they can acquire the business skills.

'Once we had worked out so many problems,' Savita said, 'the system seemed set to bring in a lot more women. We went to the dairy and asked to see their maps. Wherever we saw a village where there wasn't yet a cooperative, we went there to see what interest we could generate among the women.'

The kinds of transformations the cooperatives elicit in members were particularly apparent after observing the workings of a new cooperative in Degham block of Ahmedabad district. Many of the women members collecting their second payment from the cooperative were so unfamiliar with money that they had to ask others the value of each note they received. Most were quite incredulous at the amounts they received. They had never been paid so much before—the average being around Rs. 100 for a two-week collection cycle.

The older cooperatives, by contrast, are a routine progression of women pouring hundreds of litres of milk, testing fat, checking accounts, issuing payments, deducting loan instalments, discussing fodder options, sanitizing vessels, and solving weekly problems.

The Importance of Exposure and Training

An important training bridge that SEWA cooperatives create for their members is through their 'Exposure Programme.' The programme exposes women to all the physical steps involved in the production from their village to the central market, or conversely, from the origin of resource supply to its arrival in their village. Women who rarely or never had left their village and were previously selling milk to traders against advance credit had no idea that their milk could command four times the price outside. They had no clue as to how it was transported, processed or distributed. Trips to the large district dairy processing plants were eye-openers for them. They saw their milk join the *lakhs* of litres of milk being processed into pasteurized milk, cheese, milk powder, butter and clarified butter, and moving out along distribution routes to booths and shops in urban centres and towns.

Similarly, all SEWA women in Banaskantha district visit the pipeline head-waters of the regional water supply scheme to understand and be able to participate in managing the technology which, since 1988, pipes drinking water into their villages. Similarly, women weavers undertake nationwide weaving study tours, not only to be exposed to various weaving techniques, but also to experience other social and cultural milieus.

'Until women have extensive exposure to new ideas and technologies, their desire and ability to assume responsibility are big constraints to making our cooperatives successful,' said Lalita Krishnaswami, SEWA's veteran cooperative organizer. 'At first we focused on training them only in the specific skills of their occupation, like finer weaving, or block printing, or veterinary care. Women had to struggle to learn administrative and management skills each time a problem came up. Now we have an entire human resource development training programme for women in cooperatives. It includes training in cooperative management, legal issues, functional literacy, marketing, and communications. It includes repeated exposure to both new places and new knowledge. It is a systematic way for them to learn cooperative and business skills as well as the trade skills.'

SEWA has organized skill training for its members through numerous channels: government extension, the Labour Department, voluntary agencies, vocational schools, village council training institutes, universities and industrial boards, cooperative unions, handicraft boards, and their own skilled artisans.

Usha Jumani, SEWA's Management Consultant, believes self-employed women have very specific needs for training: 'It has to directly relate to their daily problems of work and survival,' she said, 'or they will not be interested. They have to be compensated financially during training for the work they are missing or they will not be able to afford to come. Development of interesting training material is essential, like audio-visual, because most women who undergo training are illiterate . . . . Also, we have seen that the best training, if possible, is outside of the village for three to five days. The break gives such a relief from domestic duties that women become more open to new ideas.'

LAND ISSUES

Lack of Land Titles

While SEWA developed artisan and dairy cooperatives to help women supplement their agricultural labour income, organizers also focused specifically on agricultural issues concerning women. According to the 1981 Census, 79.4 per cent of female workers are engaged in agricultural work, mainly as labourers. While women are engaged in the most laborious manual tasks, very few do the more skilled jobs in agriculture. Though SEWA members might bargain for higher wages and possess other marketable skills, they were not moving into any greater control of land or crops or equipment. The National Sample Survey data does show an increasing number of female cultivators because of men's movement into salaried jobs, but women are still not granted land titles. The two major disadvantages for women not holding land titles in their own names are that they do not receive training from the agricultural extension services which systematically goes to the landholders, and they remain ineligible for agricultural credit.

Many SEWA women reported that because they did not hold land titles, their husbands mortgaged the family land without their consent. Widowed women reported that not holding title to their husband's land led to their being forcibly evicted from it by his relatives after his death. Chen (1988) found that even for women who did claim their husband's land, their ability to make the land productive was dependent on access to assets such as bullocks, plough, and irrigation facilities. That access was dependent on the in-laws' discretion, putting these women again at a disadvantage for cultivating the land or reaching a good sharecropping tenancy agreement, since tenants rely on such access. Chen's data also revealed that households headed by women in Devdholera have recorded the highest percentage of sale and mortgaging transactions in the village,[1] indicating that they experience more difficulty in holding on to their asset.

Shortage of Resources

SEWA's involvement in the burgeoning dairy movement raised other issues related to land for women. While the dairy movement promised fair remuneration for essentially as much milk as the cooperatives could produce, it also increased pressure on the drought-prone and already degraded common lands as village herds increased. SEWA's major goal of helping stabilize year-round income with milk production was hampered in the case of landless women who could not grow their own fodder. For them, fodder collection meant travelling long distances to collect from common lands, or sacrificing part of their coveted daily labour wages in exchange for green fodder from the landlord for whom they laboured.

The problems of rural women's fuel crises came to SEWA's attention when it took up a massive *chula* (cooking stove) building project at the behest of the Forest Department in 1985. Organizers trained women who built 15,000 smokeless stoves in Ahmedabad, Junagadh, and Mehsana districts. A major incentive for SEWA was its interest in reducing health hazards to women constantly exposed to wood smoke. Many women who used the new stoves said they liked breathing less smoke, but what they *really* needed was wood. 'Why don't you help us get wood near the village?' was the repeated challenge. With forests receding and common lands increasingly degraded, landless women commonly walk up to 10 kilometres to fetch between 20–40 kilograms of wood.

While most rural women collect fuel for their own use, 'head-loading' jungle wood can also be an income generating activity for women. In Junagadh district, SEWA has 700 Baravali members who sold the firewood they collected from the Girnar forest for their livelihood. Collection is an extremely arduous job which takes about eight hours, demanding a daily round-trip walk of 10–20 kilometres, climbing over 2000 feet of trailless, steep, slippery slopes. These women carry between 20–35 kilograms a day to a contractor who pays them Rs. 10–Rs. 20 per load. Because most of these women are the sole supporters of their families and their earnings are low, they must collect even during rains or when they fall ill—or else go without food that day.

In 1983, with the forest under extreme deforestation pressure, the Forest Department limited entry to the forest for firewood cutting, though a large part of the problem was due to the large timber contractors and mining erosion. This led to a severe conflict between the forest officials and firewood cutters who depended on this occupation for their survival. After long negotiations, SEWA succeeded in getting its members licences to cut one headload of wood per day, but it also saw the long-term need of orienting members toward other income earning activities.

With women in dairying lamenting the need for fodder access; with poor landless labourers clamouring for land access; and with the need to regenerate fuel resources, SEWA recognized that if rural women's situation was to change on a long term, sustainable basis, it could not be achieved in isolation from land access. The urban programme could work out economics through union activities, but the rural programme could not significantly improve independent of ecological regeneration. Rural women depended on the land; the land was in danger of degradation; women were in crises. If women could have access to land, and training in generating the resources they needed on a sustainable basis, they could avert some of the accumulating crises: they could solve their fodder problem, their fuel problem, their wage labour problem, and their exclusion from skills problem.[2]

Agenda for Land Access

SEWA launched several experiments to help women deal with their land constraints. First, women developed their own fodder plantations in two villages where SEWA had bought land for cooperative centres. The landless members of the dairy cooperatives cultivated subabul trees and had first access to their leaves for fodder.

Second, SEWA lobbied the Forest Department to extend training to women members for running nurseries. The Baravali women headloaders were the first to be trained by the Forest Department. They started a nursery on the Gujarat Agricultural University land, raising seedlings to sell to the Forest Department for its reforestation of the Gir. These women appreciated the nursery work. They got regular income from working with trees, and were not subject to harassment by the forest guards or bad weather.

The nurseries were limited in approach, however. They were dependent on yearly project funds, uncertain short-term land lease, and they dealt only with the saplings—not the entire sustainable process. While SEWA supported similar tree growing cooperatives in Ahmedabad and Mehsana districts, it sought out more holistic, long-term solutions.

As the majority of SEWA members are landless, cooperative acquisition of land for women seemed the logical goal. SEWA cooperatives operate on the principle that members can pool resources in the form of share capital and acquire assets which they could not get as individuals. In 1986 SEWA undertook a large survey of all existing wastelands (degraded common lands) in the areas it was working, and petitioned for land leases to be extended to women's cooperatives by whichever governing body controlled the land—village, panchayat or state. Chen, who studied common property resources (CPR) in the Dholka village of Devdholera where SEWA's rural headquarters are located, found that benefits are tapped from CPRs by women as a buffer against seasonal shortages. CPRs contributed to rural equity for the landless because the physical products of fuel, fodder, fruits, and honey derived from those lands supplemented their income and employment.[3]

Chen's research documented that when the commons were vegetated and well managed, the general community enjoyed benefits like effective drainage and recharging of the ground water. As they degraded, erosion, salinity, lowering water-tables and droughts became problems for all.

With most commons facing increasing degradation, SEWA wanted to develop models for women to regenerate both subsistence and income resources on wastelands as a way to reverse environmental degradation and women's poverty. Wasteland regeneration requires substantial capital investment, which the landless who use the commons cannot generate themselves. SEWA's efforts to acquire wastelands for women and channel capital and development support from state, central, and international programmes make an important case study of women's roles in both ecological and social change.

One Wasteland Experiment

When SEWA began petitioning in 1986 for 600 acres of revenue wasteland in three villages of Dholka taluka, the drought was only a year old. No one had envisioned at that time the extremes it would reach before it abated, or the number of years it would take to actually acquire the sought after land. The landless and marginal landholding SEWA women who were meeting in Metaal village were encouraged by the National Wastelands Development Board (NWDB). The NWDB is a centrally appointed board which promotes the development of state and local wastelands—sometimes a problematic equation since the land the NWDB is interested in is under autonomous jurisdiction.

The women who came together to acquire the wasteland experienced this problem when they had to spend two and a half years meeting the talati, the Sarpanch, taluka officials, the Collector, state officials, and finally the Chief Minister—all of whom offered obstacles and resistance. Once land acquisition looked like a reality, the district officials insisted that the women be registered as a cooperative before the land would be granted.

Initially SEWA resisted registering the cooperative. It had a decade of experience which reinforced the need for a pre-cooperative stage wherein women could receive training, and begin the work process while learning about the responsibilities and utility of a cooperative. Experience showed that if the cooperative was initiated prematurely, the members depended upon SEWA to function as an employer or as a mediator in the face of every crisis. To promote self-sufficiency, SEWA tries to move at a pace conducive to women assuming control and initiating the cooperative as their own organization. The only way women could get possession of the land, however, was if the cooperative was registered first.

SEWA called together all the landless and small landholders, from which 20 women came forward to participate in the wasteland cooperative. Each woman eked out Rs. 25 share capital required to register the cooperative from her drought relief digging wages.

After pooling their resources, it took another five months for the registration to go through—almost three years from the date of their initial efforts to acquire the wasteland.

Once the cooperative began to work on the land SEWA found that one of the most difficult processes for the women was learning to assert their opinion and take decisions after a lifetime of working for others. Before the cooperative was formed, Ramubehn, a member, was engaged in agricultural labour for only three to five months in a year. The other months she survived by making *indhonis*, the woven reed rings on which water vessels are balanced, earning about Rs. 2 per day. She told Usha Jumani in a case history:

'We have always had to live by the bounty of the farmers and the people in this village—if they have money, we get something. If they don't, we get nothing. There is a lot of untouchability practised here. Our caste is considered the lowest. We try to live peacefully in the village, because we are dependent on people here. We have never had land or cattle, and have always lived by our manual labour. When there is no work we sometimes borrow small amounts of Rs. 10 or Rs. 20, which we later repay with labour. If no one helps, we have to go and beg at upper caste homes for food.'[4]

For Ramubehn, living peacefully means trying to avert violence from herself or her caste members by not making waves. Yet when poor women acquired land, it called the old rules into question. Their desire to stabilize their income challenges the old power relationships which kept these women desperate to the point of dependency. As she and the other women in her cooperative developed their skills to make productive use of their 20-year lease of 218 acres of dry, stony, saline, ravine-cut land, they worked under the shadow of the fear of repercussions.

Dealing with Resistance

Ramubehn and the other Metaal land cooperative members had begun to contour the land and dig rain catchment ponds, when their first major local conflict surfaced. The Bharwads (shepherds) of the village who had been driving their cattle and sheep over this open land for decades filed a case in the district court against the

SEWA cooperative. Though the case was resolved in SEWA's favour, it bounced between three other courts in appeal, each time halting work through the court stay orders and evoking fear amongst the members that extra-legal actions might also be carried out against them.

SEWA called for a compromise with the Bharwads, who are an economically strong force in the area, but they refused to negotiate. The Bharwads instead tried to destabilize other SEWA cooperatives so that they would withdraw their land pursuit. They tried pressuring dairy officers, telling them to keep their dairy cooperatives, but leave the land alone. Because the Bharwads are not traditionally a landholding community, many of them still depend on common property to sustain their herds. By March 1989, when SEWA had not acquiesced, the Bharwads called an inter-village meeting of their clan to discuss their worries over SEWA members' claims to 600 acres of wasteland in three villages.

Rumours began floating that the Bharwads were going to disrupt the Devdholera dairy cooperative's profit distribution ceremony. SEWA organizers called a meeting of the cooperative members and asked them their stand on the issue. The Ahmedabad organizers asserted that they would not intervene at the time of such a disruption, and that the local organizers and members themselves should decide the course of action.

The Bharwad women went home from this meeting and requested their men not to disrupt the workings of their dairy cooperative. They cited SEWA's fodder relief work during the drought which saved their herds, and the greater profit they were earning through the milk cooperatives compared to their previous business with the local traders. A week later the Devdholera ceremony proceeded without any untoward incident.

Two weeks later the same event took place in Baldana village and everyone waited to see if there would be any incident. The only incident was the presence of the old Bharwad milk traders of Baldana who sat taunting the women as they carried home the numerous steel vessels and cash bonuses they had opted for from their profit. One Bharwad woman turned heel and retorted, 'Sure, make fun of all these vessels. Did we ever even see so much as a teaspoon from you all those years?'

These incidents marked important milestones. Women showed solidarity first as women and co-workers regardless of caste lines, and thereby overcame a major obstacle to collectivity. They offered strong rural testimony that modern organizational forms *could* integrate a community of women who could in turn influence the broader community.[5] Equally impressive was that after years of work, women were clearly becoming strong enough to resist male domination to which the cooperatives were initially so vulnerable.

A few months after these incidents the District Collector called on the Bharwads to compromise with SEWA. At length they agreed that SEWA would only bring half of the 218 acres under cultivation, and the Bharwads could graze the other half. The women then proceeded to plant fuel, fodder, fruit trees and legumes on their land. The cooperative workers continue to receive daily wages through the NWDB programme for the first two years of the programme, until the land generates income for them. Land cooperatives give SEWA its first opportunity to develop models which will *reverse* the environmental degradation that increasingly affects rural women. All observers are monitoring events here and in the other two nearby villages where SEWA has acquired land to see if the peace the women have struck will hold.

A Process of Reassessing

As they rehabilitate the land, Metaal women are trying to adapt their initial conceptions of a land cooperative with the realities they have found on the ground. Some of the founding members of the cooperative, who were included because of landlessness, showed their unwillingness to do labour on the land because of other employment which seemed more immediately stable in the face of the village conflict. On the other hand, women who were not included as founding members on account of their being land-holders, have been working daily on the land.

Manju Raju, the organizer developing these wasteland cooperatives, explained: 'Though some of the landholding women appeared better-off on paper, in reality they weren't. Some who own land are so indebted that they have not held their own mortgage in more than six years. Others, who are small landholders, have land which is unfit to cultivate for various reasons—no water, too saline, etc. This was one reason why we wanted the pre-cooperative stage first, so these wrinkles could be worked out before the actual membership of the cooperative was determined. As outsiders, we do not understand all the complexities of each woman's situation. As insiders who have never been in a cooperative before, the women members need experience to judge what role they want to play in the cooperative.'

PRE-COOPERATIVE POLICIES

The one to three year pre-cooperative phase has developed into one of SEWA's major policy focal points. There are several issues which necessitate this.

First of all, women need the legitimacy of cooperative affiliation in order to be granted assets like land, or loans to purchase assets like equipment or animals. The existing cooperative guidelines which require production or equipment ownership as prerequisites simply exclude poor women. A recognized pre-cooperative stage can serve a legitimacy role which qualifies women for credit, training, assets, and later membership.

Second, when developing cooperatives intended to give control to the poorer women of the village, it is extremely rare to find such women who already have the literacy, accounting, administrative, and democracy-oriented organizational skills to perform the necessary cooperative jobs. Although SEWA believes that the cooperatives are the best form for imparting these skills, they are cumbersome and bureaucratic. A pre-cooperative stage allows a necessary time frame to train women in all these skills.

Third, because women are excluded from many of the skilled technologies of artisan work, the time frame in which their products can become competitive on the market is also longer than for men's cooperatives. SEWA tries to upgrade the skills women already know and practise, to both reduce the viability lag and to allow women to assess the risks of the business ventures their cooperative enters into. If they develop a skill for which they have no experience of its raw material supplies, market vagaries, etc., they are dependent on SEWA organizers—who may also be inexperienced—for all decisions about what directions to proceed in.

Pre-cooperative stages can give women the necessary experience to work out the major production constraints they are likely to face.

Fourth, if all the cooperative women have the opportunity to develop the range of necessary skills to make a viable business of their cooperative, the chances of corruption, vested interest domination, or even the domination of one powerful woman from within the cooperative are greatly reduced. In Banaskantha district, for example, SEWA found a women's embroidery cooperative into which women had been enlisted by the Registrar so that they would meet the minimum membership quota. Most of the women members had no idea of what a cooperative entailed three years after its formation. The woman appointed as Secretary, managed the cooperative like a contractor, only distributing work to the 12 of the 50 members who were her friends. SEWA helped dissolve that structure, and ensured that all the members received minimal literacy, numeracy, and cooperative training so that one powerful and literate figurehead could no longer usurp work and control.

Fifth, the pre-cooperative stage helps develop the solidarity necessary to overcome the powerful pull of old power structures, old feuds, and social pressure against women's control.

And finally, when women are first entering cooperatives from the vulnerable position of extreme underemployment and dependency on their employers, they often express little interest in the responsibilities of the cooperative: their primary concern is *wage*. The pre-cooperative stage is one in which interests in other areas of responsibility and control can be nurtured and developed.

Cooperatives' Importance in Multiple Occupations

SEWA sees cooperatives as an important organizational form which can support complementary multiple occupations, rather than imposing the one person/one occupation trend which most industrialized countries adopt—a trend which SEWA perceives as counter-productive to the realities of rural life.

'As we have developed cooperatives we have seen the importance of recognizing the interdependence of resources and occupations,' Bhatt commented in an interview. 'Crop residues support livestock.

Crop and animal products provide artisan work in the off seasons of agriculture, and families traditionally barter their artisan goods for grains. This means there are very close links between home-based manufacture and agriculture.'

'We have to be aware of how agricultural policies and new technologies affect other rural occupations. For example, a certain weedicide used on crops kills the plants which women make rope from, displacing an entire occupation. We need to strike a balance between subsistence needs and commercial needs. A purely commercialized economy does not insure subsistence for all.'

SEWA encourages a range of cooperatives to cover multiple occupations in order to provide employment year-round while using the local environment in a sound way. Displacing women's occupations without offering any alternatives is the equation which results in poverty according to SEWA.

'When we commit all the quotas and price subsidies for raw materials to industrial plants, it displaces artisans who can no longer get or afford raw materials,' Bhatt said. 'Artisans should have priority over industry for raw materials and rural women should be included in planning the development of new technologies.'

The union of SEWA cooperatives which cover many occupations provides a platform for addressing the present economic values which displace women's occupations. 'Women cannot be "policy invisible" and succeed,' said Bhatt, 'because there is such a demand for resources that "invisible" is negative and translates into *no access*. There has to be an explicit allocation of resources if we are to get any.'

Women's cooperatives are a useful strategy for poor women's development because they receive financial and policy support from the government. Weavers' cooperatives, for instance, qualify for equipment subsidies, loans, and certain quotas of raw materials, for rebates to customers on finished goods, and for administrative costs for the initial years of the cooperatives' operation.

Redressing Technology Exclusion

SEWA has attempted to redress women's exclusion from technology in every trade it has worked with. In rural areas, SEWA began with traditional occupations by helping women develop the skills which had previously been under men's control. They trained women who were previously involved in the weaving preparation work (like carding and spinning) to sit at the loom. Women who dug and prepared clay and fired the vessels got training in use of the potter's wheel. Women who cared for cattle learned how to cross-breed their animals for higher productivity using artificial insemination. Women who performed agricultural tasks like sowing, transplanting, weeding, harvesting, and threshing learned how to run modern irrigation equipment, graft fruit trees, use high yielding varieties of seed, and make cropping decisions based on the knowledge of modern agricultural techniques.

One unique solution to the problems of firewood headloaders in the Girnar forest was to use women's knowledge of different types and qualities of wood by training them in carpentry. Young women headloaders were most inclined to learn this non-traditional skill, and now have a lucrative furniture cooperative in Junagadh.

ARTISANS

Weavers

Balubehn Palabhai Vaghela, the Chairwoman of the Devdholera weaving cooperative, is an inspired weaver, who when not dealing with the cooperative business can be found at her loom 12 hours a day. Her family's movement out of the extreme poverty of a one-room hut furnished only with a few aluminium vessels and a rustic pit loom can be directly traced to her training in weaving and her determination to make their cooperative work—which has been no small feat. She now works from the large covered verandah of her two-room house which protects the two large pedal looms she and her husband weave shawls and dress material on. She explained the difficulties the cooperative has faced:

'It took us 10 years to get where we are today. All of us (women) were participating in weaving work, but mostly in spinning. No one gave it any importance. Our whole community made wool blankets on these pit looms. We traded them to the shepherds. It was exercise in labour, nothing else. What we spent on materials, we earned back—no more. We barely survived by our agricultural labour wages.'

'SEWA helped us get *khadi* spinning work, which helped financially, but I became most interested when they suggested weaving training at the National Institute of Design (NID) in Ahmedabad. I had always wanted to sit at the loom, there was just no chance—it was considered men's work. I barely went to school as a child, but for 6 months I went everyday to the National Institute of Design in Ahmedabad. I left the village at 6 a.m. and returned around 8 p.m.'

'We decided to weave shawls first, because we were familiar with wool, and we could use the designs from our blankets. After the training, we started a production unit. The first year I earned up to Rs. 1200 a month—after never earning more than Rs. 200 previously! But the second year we over-produced and could not sell all our shawls, so we suffered a loss. Those were our initial dealings in city markets and we had to learn everything from scratch. It has taken eight years.'

'Now we are starting to turn the corner as a cooperative. Just now we are understanding what colours people like in cotton, or in wool. Now we see what sells in summer and in winter. What did we know about these things? We wear the same clothes year-round. Now we know how to deal with customers at our big exhibitions. At first we thought whatever SEWA offered was just a chance to get some money. Now our entire way of life has changed, and we have started feeling like it has because of this cooperative. It took us many years to understand it is our own work, our own effort that changes our life.'

Not all of the cooperative members share her sense of responsibility. Many still want to depend on SEWA to get them more work, and have trouble perceiving themselves as other than production workers. The cooperative training SEWA began in 1989 is helping shift consciousness and responsibility, but Balubehn admits it is a very long, slow process.

Shifting Dynamics

Placing the entire process in women's hands has changed the power relationships for many categories of artisans SEWA has organized and linked to training and cooperatives. For example, women block printers had been working on a piece-rate basis for a trader doing only the one step of the process they knew—the actual stamping of the dye onto the cloth, for very low rates. Once they were trained in how to make dyes, design blocks, prepare the cloth, and make more sophisticated designs and garments, they broke their relationship with the contractor, controlling the entire process and selling through the cooperative.

Women such as weavers or basket-makers who participated in the crucial steps of the process but had no control over the income from that process (because their husbands sold or bartered the product themselves) have acquired some control of the family income through their cooperative membership.

Many artisan women had taken cash advances from a trader and were indebted to him. Others were bound to a trader's terms because he owned the equipment they worked on. SEWA has used the artisan cooperatives specifically to break these relationships by helping women get loans to purchase their own equipment, or to release them from old debts so they could earn higher profits through their cooperatives.

Material Constraints to Participation

Although these are encouraging signs, the impact of SEWA cooperatives has not been as widespread as that of union initiatives. Of the seven artisan cooperatives, only 142 of the 472 members (30 per cent) are active members in the cooperatives. Managers usually blame raw material shortages, and lack of sufficient markets, but much has to do with the skill levels unable to command larger markets. By contrast, in the pre-cooperative stages of the new artisan cooperatives in Banaskantha district the participation rates are 100 per cent. This can be explained in terms of the existing high skill levels of embroiderers there which can command a broad market. The District Rural Development Agency provided funds to SEWA to open a retail shop in downtown Ahmedabad, and they have garnered large international orders, allowing their production unit to command markets employing 400 women within the first two years.

Lalita Krishnaswami, the main organizer of SEWA cooperatives defended the importance of organizing any number of women to begin the process of change, even if initial participation rates are not high.

'One of the most important aspects of organizing even a very small group,' she said, 'is that we get first hand knowledge of the policy constraints which affect all the artisans of that trade. That experience gives us a place to start working on interventions which will change the dynamics and eventually affect large numbers of women.'

This stand is corroborated by the experience of the bamboo cooperative. Until 1988, the regular full-time participants of the cooperative were only 16 women who had benefited by the Government Resolution (GR) which SEWA and other women's groups lobbied the state to pass in 1978. The GR mandates that goods will be purchased first from women's groups. It gave 16 of the bamboo cooperative members a steady market for brooms and waste baskets which they supplied to government offices.

The other 75 women members who had undergone training to learn fancier bamboo work such as furniture and paper trays, had found only intermittent work, however, largely due to shortages of reasonably priced raw materials. Bamboo has been allocated to the paper pulp industry which in Maharashtra pays 26 paise per bamboo while the informal sector bamboo workers in Ahmedabad pay a retail price of Rs. 12–Rs. 15. SEWA had to organize bamboo supply from as far as Assam and West Bengal until 1989, when the Gujarat government finally agreed to allot the SEWA cooperative a regular quota at wholesale prices of Rs. 2.50 each. The cooperative membership immediately increased by 30 per cent, and the majority of members became active with their new access to regularly supplied, cheap bamboo.

Rima Nanavati (who turned down an Indian Administrative Service post to stay with SEWA) is the organizer who oversees the entire district development plan of Banaskantha district. She articulated the dilemma of raw material shortages for cooperative management:

'I do not feel comfortable in encouraging any cooperative to form whose raw materials are not available on a regular basis. Yet what are artisans to do? We have to make the cooperative in order to press for access to materials, but it becomes demoralizing for the members who have great hopes that the cooperative will solve their problems if they cannot get an adequate supply of their raw materials.'

Balubehn confirmed this problem in the Devdholera weavers' cooperative. 'We do not get enough supply of cotton to keep all 51 of us working. This creates problems of how to divide the work. Even when we have good markets (through their shop, orders, and the SEWA exhibitions organized in big cities) we still have to struggle for the materials. There is supposed to be an allocation for handloom thread, but we often go to the mills to get that quota and they just tell us they do not have it. Then, with the last three years of drought, the price of yarn went up. The price of the cloth does not go up accordingly. So I watched my sisters trudge off to dig on the drought relief sites. I will not feel happy until each sister in this cooperative has as much work as she wants. This raw material problem is one of our biggest struggles.' Bhatt's solution: 'First priority for raw materials should go not to industry, but to individual producers and producers' cooperatives.'

The Fallout of Industrial Policies

Renana Jhabvala articulated some of SEWA's concerns regarding industrialization policies: 'The reason we talk about industrialization a lot is not because we are pro-industrialization or anti-industrialization. The question is *what* does industrialization do to the employment of millions of workers? We are worried that it is cutting employment. How can it be called "development" if it is disemploying, or semi-employing, or making part-time, or taking away the assets of so many millions of people?'

'When the forces of industrialization which disemploy women come in, how do we deal with them? Oppose them? Try to lessen the effects? We think the basic criterion for whether industrialization is a good thing or a bad thing should be *employment*. The reason we support artisan production is because it *is* giving employment, and what else do artisans have to do? We want to protect what they have, and we want to increase what they have—their bargaining power and their skill levels. But artisan production cannot be maintained unless you change policy—it is impossible.'

'Which cooperatives are going well and which aren't very directly reflects the economy: Trade earns. Service earns, but less. Milk production is earning because of the whole NDDB–Amul dairy movement. Artisan cooperatives do not earn well because the economy is against it. If industry gets subsidies, incentives, raw material priorities, etc. and individual artisans get nothing, how can they compete? How our economies do reflect the larger economy. But this is why artisans' cooperatives are important as spearheads for change. When weavers whose livelihoods depend upon yarn say, "We want cheaper yarn," and keep at it, with force, it carries political effect.'

From Individual Constraints to District Development

The tactics which SEWA pursued in Ahmedabad, Kheda, and Mehsana districts to bring rural women into the mainstream of the development process evolved in a somewhat piecemeal fashion as specific responses to individual situations, constraints, and trades in each village where it took up work. From 1979 to 1988, SEWA was organized as a union, a bank, and two 'wings', the Economic Wing, which oversaw cooperatives, and the Rural Wing, which oversaw village projects. While the Rural Wing oversaw the dairy and tree growing cooperatives, the Economic Wing was also working in the same villages with the weaving and bamboo cooperatives, resulting in less clarity through the cooperatives than the union had. This was due to the varied interests of the organizers in charge of each wing, and the more sound experience of the organization in union work than cooperative work.

These wings were basically abandoned in the reshuffling of the late eighties when a new conceptualization of the organization emerged as a union, cooperatives, services and bank. Under this new framework, and with greater cooperative organizing experience, there is more coherence in the rural activities. SEWA's major emphasis in rural areas is to enhance combinations of agriculture, artisan, livestock, and ecological regeneration occupations, with the appropriate branch of the organization making its contribution to that process.

When SEWA was invited to coordinate a District Development

Plan in Banaskantha in 1988, it had the chance to utilize this integrated model right from the start, with women as the focus of an entire district's development.

The project was launched in 1986 when the Gujarat Water Supply Board and the Dutch government constructed a massive pipeline to bring potable water to every village. The district administration then solicited voluntary agencies to develop a district plan, which SEWA agreed to do in collaboration with the rural people. The plan focused on reversing the drought-migration syndrome of the arid district.

First, SEWA began by insuring that women became functionaries on the *pani panchayats* (water committees). Then they turned to rain-water resources to supplement their new year-round piped drinking water. Banaskantha women continue digging and lining ponds and developing drip irrigation systems across the district. They have started seven nurseries and plan to reforest a green belt using their water harvests in an attempt to arrest the encroaching sands which turn large tracts of land to desert each year. They intend to rehabilitate the wasteland to prevent people from forced migration each year. SEWA contends that using local labour for local resource development will actually reverse the conditions which cause outmigration each year when people have to search water and fodder for their herds, and labour wages for themselves.

SEWA revived 35 dairy cooperatives in the district which became defunct during the last drought, and has converted half of them into women's or mixed cooperatives. It has also initiated pre-cooperative income generating embroidery projects, in which over 400 women are involved on a full-time basis. The highly skilled embroiderers from this district who work in bold colours with chips of mirror were commanding large markets from Delhi to Tokyo by their second year of organizing. In Banaskantha, rather than developing an entire parallel system for women, SEWA has focused more on linking the members to government agencies and programmes and ensuring that those agencies are accountable to women. The District Rural Development Agency and local Sarpanches work *with* SEWA, creating mainstream development changes where women's concerns are central.

SEWA is adamant about using people's skills for local development and not reverting to relief wages. It struggled on the same premise throughout the previous drought years to reorient the government position on drought relief work sites. SEWA lobbied the state to let each community decide priorities for community development—especially drought prevention measures—and use their relief labour toward executing those priorities. They were not successful, however, and most villagers simply dug pits along roadsides, earning daily wages but no long-term project gains. The only assistance SEWA could provide was effective lobbying for more relief sites so that a larger number of villagers could get wages, and constant monitoring of the sites so that there was no corruption in wage payment.

LABOUR AND SERVICE NICHES

While SEWA attempts to reorient policies and priorities of development to support decentralized occupations and to support local labour for local improvements, it has not been slow to fill any new niches which the changes in economies and industrialization have created. It is interested in employment, and in having women in employment at all levels. The labour and service cooperatives which are the most recent cooperative forms have struck innovative chords in women's organization.

Industrial Cleaning and Recycling

SEWA's unionized urban paper pickers organized alternatives to street scavenging through two kinds of labour cooperatives: Pethapur Cooperative collects waste paper from government offices and mills on contract. Saundarya Safai Co-op takes on contracts to clean industrial complexes. The majority of Saundarya's 200 members work on a part-time basis, filling the gaps and hours when the regular employees of each particular institution do not work.

Ratanbehn, the 50 year old Chairwoman of the cooperative, explained why the cooperative had been so important for them. 'All of us were paper picking because we were desperate to feed our families. We could not get out of the problem—no work so you have to pick paper, pick paper and who will give you work? They think you are dirty. Picking paper had never been a choice. It was survival. With SEWA's help, because our cooperative was an official group, we got contracts to clean big institutes. We actually got *jobs* after years of not having jobs. It is something fixed, regular . . . . We know for a year at a time that we *will* earn each month whether it rains or does not rain, whether people throw away glass and paper, or they don't . . . . It is part-time work, which suits us, because we can still manage things at home. Before we could spend all day walking the streets and get practically nothing. Now, at least, we know we can eat lentils and bread each day from our labour.'

Cooperative membership has lessened the occupational health hazards of cleaning work because all members are provided with gloves, masks, and long handled equipment. The cooperative has purchased mechanical cleaning equipment such as industrial vacuums in order to secure contracts with large complexes and increase the skill and sophistication levels of members' work. The cooperative acts like a kind of employment exchange, providing members with domestic cleaning work and catering jobs for parties. Some contracts bring better remuneration than others, which is equalized between all the working members depending on the amount of time they spend working. They appoint supervisors from among themselves to coordinate between the institution, the work, and the cooperative. One of the biggest challenges facing the members has been learning how to estimate workloads.

As organizer Lalita Krishnaswami commented, 'They could not come from their slums and immediately know how to estimate vacuuming work in the Space Research Institute.'

SEWA organizers still help in negotiating contracts, but that too is being gradually taken over by Manjulabehn, a cleaning member in the cooperative who has now become Manager.

Problems from the Formal Sector

The problems Ratan and Manjula are facing in their cooperative have arisen from the formal sector trade unions. At the National Institute of Design (NID), several SEWA women did weekend duty and cleaning jobs which the employees union there had negotiated not to do. After the SEWA cooperative women had worked there two years, the NID employees union took the NID to court, suing for permanent employee status for the SEWA workers under the Class IV labour law, which requires permanent worker status for workers who work more than 120 days a year. The court ruled in the NID union's favour, which outraged the SEWA cooperative—they had not been made a party to the case, though it dealt with their members.

The repercussions of the case for the SEWA cooperative was that some other institutions where they had contracts became reticent to renew them out of fear that they would likewise be sued to make the women permanent employees. One demanded that SEWA get a contractor's licence, which then would hold SEWA responsible for legal obligations and protect the institutions who use the cooperative's services. SEWA declined, pursuing further negotiations with the institution.

'The point of this cooperative is not that SEWA be an employer,' said Nisreen Ebrahim, SEWA's cooperative coordinator. 'The cooperative takes responsibility for each of its members and makes each contract in good faith. The idea of SEWA taking a contractor's licence negates the validity of a labour cooperative by reintroducing the old power structures we are trying to overcome.'

SEWA sees this struggle as a typical process in trying to get their new models accepted, and continues to negotiate 'in good faith' for contracts while contemplating appealing the court ruling on the basis that they were not included as a party in the case.

'Our ultimate aim is to establish the validity of labour cooperatives,' said Jhabvala. 'They fill a crucial role for our members, by giving them a legitimate organization to enter the labour market with.'

In 1989, out of 581 members of the three service cooperatives, 485 members (80 per cent) were actively working in them, though organizers assert there is an unlimited pool of women waiting to join as more contracts are negotiated. Ratanbehn acknowledged the obstacles they are facing, but did not appear daunted. 'This is so much better work than what we had to do for years that we *will* work out a way to keep getting more contracts.' Her determination mirrors a trend in SEWA cooperatives: those managed by working class women have been the most successful.

Vendors' Services

The vending cooperatives fulfil the function of the service cooperatives. One supplies government institutions daily with vegetables, another provides consumers with kerosene at their homes, and the third provides fresh fish, both to the markets and neighbourhoods. Of 98 members, only 10 of the kerosene vendors are active (10 per cent) due to licensing problems, the expense of vending carts, and feuds within the membership. The vegetable supply and fish vendors have recorded 98 per cent participation of their 66 members.

Health and Child Care Services

The other unique service cooperative niches SEWA has pioneered are the child care and health workers cooperatives. Trade unions in the organized sector usually lobby with the employer to provide such services or benefits. Since no employer–employee relationship exists for the self-employed, and their child care and health needs are equally if not more pressing, SEWA developed such services by training low income women and developing the skills they needed to deliver these services to themselves.

Women from all the trade groups have learned how to run child care centres and be responsible community health workers in their respective villages or neighbourhoods. In order to develop their skills and generate resources to run their programmes collectively, they have formed cooperatives of the women who deliver these services. These groups mark the most recent cooperative forms where women from several communities, castes, and trade groups have come together collectively to do business and serve their community.

The child care programme provides a valuable example of the usefulness of cooperatives for women's empowerment. In many of the rural areas where women were initially reticent to participate in union activities, SEWA opened creches for agricultural labourers' children. SEWA later extended the service to urban women whose children were either left alone while their mothers were out working, or brought along and exposed to unhealthy environments.

This brought women into the organization in a non-threatening way, provided one or two women in each trade group a new occupation as child care provider, safeguarded the children from accidents, and linked them to health care services.

SEWA originally supported these child care centres through contributions from international donors and from the mothers using the service. Later SEWA lobbied the Integrated Childhood Development Scheme to fund its centres, but was refused because of the smaller than standard size groups (being in slum homes which could not accommodate more children), and the care providers' lack of educational qualification (ICDS requires 10th standard minimum). SEWA protested this refusal, pointing out that small centres were more responsive to the work hours of each individual trade, and that their care providers with less education had been doing a commendable job for years. The ICDS eventually relented in 1988, and included the SEWA centres in its programme.

ISSUES OF COLLECTIVITY

SEWA now has crossed the hump in organizing cooperatives successfully and coordinating the services and linkages to make them viable, though they have not yet impacted large numbers of women. As members become increasingly responsible in their organizations and their skill levels increase to make them more financially lucrative, they face critical issues of what exactly should be collective.

In dairy cooperatives, for example, purchasing feed supplements or fodder collectively could help reduce costs for individual members, but wealthy women in the cooperatives may not need these. Will all members agree to spend collective money for them then? Milk rates which vary are already a bone of contention for many members. They are calculated on the basis of the fat content and the rates for members of the same cooperative may vary widely in a somewhat complicated system. The system supports paying higher rates for better milk which is usually produced by higher quality cattle that are fed higher quality feed.

The weaving cooperatives work on different standards, though. Women are paid from the cooperative by the metre or by the piece for the type of work. The same type of cloth will be bought by the cooperative for the same price even if its quality varies from skilled weaver to novice. If they shift to a system similar to the dairy system, finer quality cloth would command a higher price. Yet who would determine quality? Would variable rates encourage members to strive for better quality, or would they result in favouritism or alienation between certain members and the quality judge?

For the cleaners, they all earn based on the hours they work, regardless of the contract which is negotiated for their particular job. Some new, more highly negotiated contracts subsidize older, lower paying contracts. Does this have any bearing on the quality of the work? As time goes on, will some women develop particular skills that others do not have, and will members continue to agree that they should be remunerated equally?

So far in most cooperatives, the assets have been taken individually—cows, looms, and kerosene vending carts—but there are also substantial collective holdings. The cleaning cooperative has purchased the cleaning tools, vegetable vendors' cooperative owns hand-carts, and the land cooperative holds the asset of land collectively and purchases inputs collectively, though women earn income based on the amount of work they put in, i.e., hourly or daily wage, and then that percentage from the harvest profit.

SEWA members and organizers are discussing socialist strategies for cooperatives which draw greater profits—like the service cooperatives and the vending cooperative. Will they agree to pool surpluses above some minimum level to create a social security fund that will benefit general membership? Through such a system, the members would be insuring themselves access to health services, child care, maternity benefits, life insurance—all of which they would still pay a small user fee for, but being guaranteed that the service will be available and fulfil their need. This is another of SEWA's long term debates: do women develop a responsive parallel model, or do they invest more energy in demanding an appropriate response from the government? As these debates and ideas develop, SEWA will test important limits on the extent of solidarity and collectivity appropriate to the members it serves.

Health Workers and Drought Relief

On the day of the Devdholera rural sammelan, women health
workers from Ahmedabad district circulated through the assembled
crowd, speaking to women they had met the previous summer at
the digging sites on the drought relief projects. The women and
children whom they had treated on their weekly visits to the sites
recalled the miserable irony of their malaria epidemics during such
a severe drought. Members expressed appreciation to the health
workers for the health care they had provided. These recollections
opened the lid on reiterations of drought grief. Women began to
recall the stories of their distress and of their organizing efforts.
Though many of the cooperatives were not producing because of
lack of materials and a collapsed market, they still provided the
organized forum to rally efforts to avert the mounting drought
crises. The women speaking that day were most proud and appre-
ciative of SEWA's support for organizing fodder and trucks to
save their livestock.

Savita Patel, the 37 year old dairy organizer who was among
the women, began recalling their desperation to find truck drivers
to bring the green sugar cane up to their cooperatives. 'We went
down to South Gujarat. We were two women strangers in this
male world of truck drivers and sugar cane farmers. No one
could believe we were *working*, especially not for other *women*
dairy producers. Each time we approached a driver, he would
laugh and make some joke about "What do *you* want a truck for?
To move house?"'

'After two days without success, we were so desperate we started
flagging down empty trucks on the highway. We finally found two
drivers to take up our work. At first they were hesitant, but I told
them, 'If you help in relief work, God will bless you.'

'They came with us to the cane fields and saw the *kaccha*,
narrow roads full of pot holes. They did not want to take their
trucks over them. They thought they would get stuck. But I
reassured them. "Brothers," I said, "you are doing this work for
us. If you get stuck, I will bring as many women as you need to get
these trucks out!" They could not refuse such an offer . . . .'

'We moved more than 500,000 kilos of sugar cane, more than

242   Where Women Are Leaders

40,000 kilos of feed, and truck-loads of green fodder for more than eight months. It saved the cattle of these eight villages, and it saved our cooperatives . . . .'

Her story was interrupted by the 1000-plus women, hands upstretched in clinched fists, concluding their meeting in unison: 'We are one! We are one!' '. . . and,' Savita interjected, 'none of their trucks got stuck.'

END NOTES

1. Marty Chen, 'Women and Household Livelihood Systems.' Harvard Institute for International Development. Paper presented at the Fourth National Conference on Women's Studies, Waltair, Andhra Pradesh, December 1988, p. 15.
2. See Sri Madhava Ashish's article in *The Economic and Political Weekly*, Vol. XXIV, No. 17, 29 April 1989, for discussion of the need to regenerate both non-cash and cash generating natural resources while enhancing the environment.
3. *Ibid.*, pp. 17–18.
4. Usha Jumani, 'The Informal Sector as "People's Economy": Seven Individual Views from Women of Ahmedabad.' Unpublished Paper, 30 July 1988, pp. 12–17.
5. The milk cooperatives, the bank, child care, and community health workers cooperatives integrate the largest diversity of communities. Artisan and vending cooperatives follow more traditional community lines of occupations.

Some SEWA Strategies: The Joint Action of the Union and Cooperatives Serves to Increase Employment Options and Raise Wages

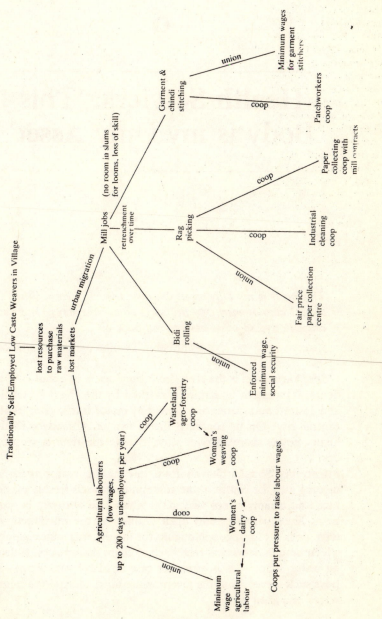

9

Health Services: 'This Body is my Only Asset'

This body is my only asset. On days I work, I earn. When I am sick, I cannot earn. My fire stays cold those days. There is no other body, no other asset to fall back on . . . .'

Kantibehn, Dholka agricultural labourer

Shankarbhavan is the river-front slum home of about 2000 residents. Its western boundary is marked by the river. Its northern and eastern boundaries are formed by major traffic arteries of the central city. On its southern flank, two of Ahmedabad's finest luxury hotels share its river view, though the river is most often dry.

Entering Shankarbhavan from one of the major roads, and moving into the centre of the community reveals freshly plastered huts and cleanly swept verandahs which end abruptly in narrow paths lined with stagnant open drains. At the municipal water taps, pots are arranged in queues for the evening water supply, at which time their owners rush back to claim their places. If there is no water supply—as is often the case in March and April—local boys suck forcefully at the low pressure taps, and spit the captured water into their pots.

Young girls sit at strategic locations throughout the neighbourhood on small *laris*, hawking a meagre selection of toffees or their vendor-mothers' rejected vegetables. Groups of women cluster by sheds where they re-stitch old gunny sack cement bags. At the centre is a community gathering place where a few small tea stalls run by local women and a brightly painted temple are clustered around an open yard. Older boys engage in rowdy play here, while men gamble in one corner.

Following the footpaths down to the river, the huts become increasingly decrepit and haphazardly constructed, and the drainage ditches increasingly difficult to avoid as they cover the entire path. In the monsoons, much of the neighbouring city drains to the river through these channels. The illegal water connections which have been rigged next to the huts are sunk in holes in the ground as deep as 2 metres—the only way residents could tap sufficient pressure. This water is constantly contaminated by leakage from the drainage ditches.

The five women conducting this tour of their community are SEWA Community Health Workers of Shankarbhavan: Shardha, Radha, Palli, Manju, and Lila. They stop to talk to residents who have health problems. They learn about a sick family and they make a detour to visit this family. They are alarmed by the consumed figures of a man and his son suffering from tuberculosis. When asked why they have not sought treatment, the workers learn that they have been denied medicines each time they have gone to the government hospital due to a shortage of supplies. SEWA health workers arrange to get them admitted for treatment that afternoon.

On the way back to their local SEWA health centre, they describe how they have been fighting for two years to get the municipality to provide water and sanitation facilities here. However, the municipality has been refusing on the grounds that these are not legal settlements.

The centre is a small whitewashed room containing a bench, a cupboard of medicines, a table, some water vessels, and some children's toys and cradles used for the daytime SEWA creche which shares the room. These women related the history of their organizing work here.

Palli: 'Before SEWA organizers came to Shankarbhavan, we had seen social workers come and go four times. They always became a nuisance. When SEWA women started coming, the men hired a guard and told him—to keep them out. But Mirabehn (Mirai Chatterjee, SEWA's Health Coordinator) kept coming. She kept meeting Lilabehn and a couple of others . . . .'

Lila: 'We knew if we wanted our children's lives to be any different from ours, we had to do something, trust someone. We told the men to let them come. We took the responsibility on our own head saying, "If any nuisance is created, we will take the blame."'

'Mirabehn arranged a class on health. We talked about why so many of our children get sick and die. We discussed the water and drainage problems here, and what action we could take. There are only two municipal taps for 200 houses. Water supply is available for two hours each day.'

Palli: 'Some families pay municipal workers to come at night and give them illegal water connections at their houses. The municipality says that it is not possible to do anything about our water problem, yet these things seem possible at night by giving bribes . . . .'

Radha: 'Look at these open ditches. They do not drain, but just stay full of garbage and stench. There are flies everywhere . . . . You ask a woman to keep the flies off her baby, she may shout at you. She knows it is filthy, but what can she do? The ditch is one foot from her door . . . .'

'In the classes we discuss these problems and the problems we have with doctors. When we go to the government hospital, we are not treated well. There are too many in the queues and we lose hours from our work. We are spoken to rudely, and the doctors there push us to adopt family planning . . . . Even if we take a child there as the patient, they press us on this matter. While we worry that this child should survive. a doctor may only worry that no more children should be born.'

Palli: 'So we go to a private doctor who does not harass us and we can be attended to quickly. But he will charge us a half a week's wages, and even then we may not get well . . . .'

Lila: 'After the first class we came forward to learn more about how to work on the health problems in Shankarbhavan. Six of us took training for three or four days every month. After two years we became Community Health Workers. Now we treat people in this clinic, do community health organizing, and give training to other SEWA women.'

'In the training we teach how to become health workers, and we conduct classes for SEWA members to learn more about their own health. We talk a lot about the health problems of poor women—anaemia and nutrition, diarrhoea and oral rehydration therapy, TB, why *our* children are the ones who die from measles and malaria, family planning . . . .'

Manju: 'This was the first SEWA health centre, but now there are six. About 15 people use this clinic every day. In Bapunagar we started another centre where at least 40 patients come every day, because there are no other clinics in their neighbourhood. We only open in the evening because we work at other jobs during the day, and it is also easier for people to come after their work. We usually work in teams—one sister who can write records with one sister who does not know reading or writing. One team stays here and the others go around the neighbourhood checking on families and sick people.'

Palli: 'At first no one trusted us. "You are just pretending to be a nurse, you are really just like a buffalo," they would say. Most of us re-stitch old cement bags. We do not see people in this neighbourhood move up. We just keep on. So trust came slowly with everyone watching us . . . .'

'I came to understand things through the training. Like about the flies. I started throwing my garbage away from the house. Pretty soon I noticed that my neighbours also began carrying their trash away. They stopped dumping it in the ditch. Like this people slowly began trusting us and trying out new ideas.'

Sharda: 'I think that most people who come here are satisfied with what they get. The most common problems in Shankarbhavan are skin diseases, diarrhoea, cough, TB, and colds. If you go to a private doctor for diarrhoea, you may be told to buy five medicines—one for worms, one for amoebas, one for giardia, one for bacteria, tonic for weakness—like that. You take them all, and chances are one of them will work. But it is very expensive. And when people are very sick and weak, this "shotgun" therapy makes them more sick because too much medicine is too strong.'

Palli: 'From training and experience we can say *which* thing is causing the diarrhoea. We give only one medicine. If we are unsure, we call the patient to the clinic the day the doctor comes. She visits each clinic once or twice a week and helps us with people who are really sick, or attends to cases we do not recognize . . . .'

Radha: 'We also help people get treatment at the government hospitals. Our access has become better through SEWA. The doctors at the TB Hospital know us and always admit our patients now. Earlier, if someone from Shankarbhavan went on their own, he would be turned away because there was no space or no medicine. Now they recognize us among all those pressing to get in . . . .

'Learning about health was very difficult for us, like learning a new language. After three years we are confident, though many still say: "These women cannot do anything." But we feel proud about what we have learned and what we are teaching. We like teaching the village behns. They live far from adequate medical facilities. Through this training they are acquiring many new skills which they use in their villages.'

Palli: 'What changes have taken place due to this clinic? It is like I said about flies. Slowly neighbours began throwing their garbage out in the field. Like that, slowly people understand they do not have to pay one week's wages for the doctor and another week's wages for the medicines. Understanding these things gives us a kind of strength we did not have before. Earlier we knew nothing. We held out our money and hoped the doctor would listen to our problem. We did not question anything she or he would tell us. Now we also understand about our bodies. It is not only special information for the priest . . . .'

'Once a little power comes to us, we understand we *can* do something. We do not have to believe that our mothers lived with this filth and so it is here to stay. Hardly a day passes that we do not go to the Municipal Corporation with our demands for sanitation facilities. Before we would never go. We thought, "They will not listen, why waste time from our work?" Now, they may listen or they may throw us out, but they cannot ignore us. They are afraid of the noise we are making. They know that SEWA gets heard. That is another big change for us.'

ORGANIZING AROUND HEALTH

These women are veteran members of SEWA's Community Health Committee and the first participants in SEWA's Jagruti (Awareness) Community Health Programme. The basic goals of this programme are to increase women's knowledge and control of their bodies, and to organize more women around health issues. Wherever the union has been weak or on new ground, they have found health organizing to be one of the most effective, non-threatening entry points for bringing new women into SEWA. In Kheda district, for example, where agricultural workers had previously tried to unionize and faced violence, women workers were terrified to talk to the organizers. They anxiously attended meetings on health issues, however, and as their relationship with SEWA strengthened, they subsequently gained trust to take up work issues. Where the union was already strong, SEWA found that health care was the most urgent need after economic issues that the women wanted to organize around.

The Community Health Programme has been developed and is administered by a health team of 12 women, including two part-time doctors and a pharmacist. Women of varying ages, backgrounds, and diverse skills comprise the team. Sumabehn Dataniya and Chandabehn Jhagaria, both vendors and veteran SEWA members, contribute their organizing experience to encourage women to learn about health issues. Roshan, the team's youngest member at age 18, came to SEWA after dropping out of school. She carries out health work with infectious enthusiasm. Shamsad, an older SEWA member who used to sew patchwork quilts wanted to leave stitching to work on the health issues of other members. Madhubehn and Shantabehn are new, more educated members of the team. All team members spend the week in slums or villages, training health workers, supervising the clinics, organizing health education meetings and helping health workers with referral services.

So far 44 women have been trained as Community Health Workers. They work in 16 villages and four urban centres. These women have formed a cooperative of health service workers which they use to collaborate on their programme and develop agenda for financial self-sufficiency.

While the health activities of SEWA's first decade developed mainly along the maternity protection benefits and the 'Know Your Body' classes, they began to develop a comprehensive programme when Mirai Chatterjee joined as SEWA's full-time Health Coordinator in 1984. Since then, health awareness classes, prenatal and maternity benefit services, a child care programme which includes sick and well child medical care, an increasing number of community health centres and their linkages with government care centres, and an occupational health research team have been linked into one programme.

The health team's first major policy goal was met in 1987 when the maternity benefits which SEWA had supported since 1978 (see chapter 1) were adopted statewide by the Labour Ministry to cover landless agricultural labourers. These labourers constitute 75 per cent of the state's female population, and through the programme they are eligible for antenatal care, four to six weeks of wage compensation, a safe delivery kit, one kilogram of clarified butter, and well baby care for their newborn. The state's adoption of this scheme marked the first shift in the policy balance which historically has been weighted heavily in favour of the urban organized sector. In 1986, only 2.28 per cent of Indian working women were receiving proper maternity benefits.[1]

SEWA was requested by the state to implement the project in Ahmedabad district where they had developed the model and had already organized women in several villages. Though there were some problems with SEWA not recovering their administrative costs from the government, and delayed payments of benefits to pregnant women (hence women had to take loans against their forthcoming benefits), the project was running fairly well a year and a half after it had been launched in the 118 villages covered by SEWA.

In 1989, however, it was announced that the Health and Welfare Ministry was going to take over the scheme. SEWA resisted this shift, as it wanted the scheme to be acknowledged as a labour issue, not a welfare issue. SEWA feared that shifting the programme to the Health Ministry would open another channel for women to be coerced about family planning.

FAMILY PLANNING DEBATES

SEWA's resistance to women being treated as the sole targets of family planning methods which they have no control over has led to some allegations being directed at the organization in recent years that it is 'anti-family planning.' All organizers insisted, however, that this was not true.

When SEWA launched its maternity benefit programme in 1978, it followed the government line of two-children families, and limited the benefit coverage to a woman's first two children. The organizers saw, however, that a woman who did have more than two children was usually at more risk health-wise, and therefore more in need of the benefit. They also observed that child mortality was high, and that poor women had no assurance that their children would live.

'We realized that limiting the scheme to two children came from our own middle class perception,' Ela said in an interview. 'For rural women, children are an economic benefit. By the age of six or seven they are contributing to the family economy. The need for more children will not be removed by pressuring or coercing women to have fewer children, but by helping them eliminate the extreme conditions of poverty in which they live, and giving them the confidence that the children they do bear will survive and live healthily. Information on family planning and services *should* be available to all women, so that they can plan their families and exert personal control over their fertility. But this information should be open and unbiased. Women should be able to come of their own accord, on their terms, and not pressured to accept one particular method over which they have no control, such as permanent sterilization.'

'We are not against family planning. We educate about it in our health classes, and we link women to whatever services they need. We do not provide that one service because it is the only thing which the government does for women in profusion . . . .'

Mirai Chatterjee, speaking from her experience as SEWA's Health Coordinator, said, 'Most women—especially in the slums—do not want to have many children. But they are pressured to have sons. Two sons. That is why as feminists we are opposed to the whole focus on only women. Fertility is rarely in an individual woman's control. Often it is the husbands and mothers-in-law who dictate what size family is necessary.'

In order to spread awareness about issues of women's health, including family planning, SEWA continues to conduct 'Know Your Body' classes for its members and their daughters. Ranjanbehn Desai, who began SEWA's early health work, conducts such training sessions in the villages and poor neighbourhoods of Ahmedabad. Working with local midwives, she has reached hundreds of women, listening to their problems and offering the choices available to them in terms of family planning and other health services.

While SEWA helps women make informed family planning choices, it believes that the issue will be most effectively resolved if the policy obsession on women's reproductive roles becomes as concerted around women's *productive roles*, and the constraints women face economically as well as on the job.

Ela Bhatt is most adamant that family planning is not a single issue subject of contraception. 'All over the world we have seen that economic stability is the major factor in lowering birth rate,' said Bhatt. 'Look at the crores of rupees we (India) have poured into family planning and it has not changed our population situation a bit. We are going about it backwards to appeal to women's situations of poverty as the reason not to have children.'

OCCUPATIONAL HEALTH ISSUES

SEWA's health workers and a team of young women from self-employed trades who have literacy skills have been trained to work together, conducting occupational health studies among their trade groups. They collect in-depth data on occupational hazards which range from *postural problems* for women who do long hours of transplanting paddy or piece-rate production work like bidi and agarbatti rolling; to women's *exposure to noxious substances* like chemical dyes, fumes, tobacco, silicon and chilli dusts, and cleaning chemicals; to *work environment problems* due to lack of lighting and ventilation, a common problem for piece-rate workers at the extreme end of the continuum of poverty. The most obvious hazards they have documented arise from the cycle of extended work hours, low wages, and poor nutrition.[2]

In its own experiments, SEWA has found that women like incense rollers or handblock printers will not use gloves to protect themselves from chemicals because it slows down their work or affects the quality of the product they sell on a piece-rate basis, but that they have been eager to substitute less toxic chemicals for the noxious ones.[3] In Lucknow, SEWA embroiderers saw it as a work advantage to get spectacles and regular check-ups, as most suffer deteriorating vision from years of fine stitching work in poor lighting conditions.

SEWA's lobbying on these issues has resulted in the National Institute of Occupational Health establishing a Women's Cell, and they have worked closely with the National Institute of Design (NID) and the ILO on the postural problems of women workers. Women workers and NID researchers have collaborated on new designs for freight carts with brakes, for sewing machines built to heights corresponding to women's frames, for stools or tables which relieve the back stress of bidi or incense work, and for waste pickers' protective collection equipment.

The community health team members have been vital links to recognizing occupational symptoms of women workers. Clinics and dispensaries specially set up for workers, like the Bidi Welfare Clinics, are chronically understaffed and undersupplied with medicines. Doctors who work there generally have little training or experience in the work related health problems of the self-employed (especially women), and SEWA has found many such clinics stocked with medicines which are on the World Health Organization's list of banned drugs.

SEWA health workers, by contrast, recognize many of the chronic symptoms associated with poor nutrition levels, exposure to hazardous substances, and postural problems of work, and are aware of some useful interventions to alleviate the symptoms and exposures. In addition, their clinics use safe, inexpensive generic drugs on a 'rational' basis, meaning that they discourage 'shotgun' treatment and use of injections, tonics and vitamins which many physicians push as cures at great expense to patients.

SAFE DRUGS AND INFORMED DOCTORS

SEWA is trying to convert the high incidence of over-prescription of expensive drugs into safe drug therapy on a wide scale, while at the same time supporting its community health projects in a sort of win-win situation for poor health consumers. In 1989, SEWA opened a pharmacy in central Ahmedabad near the union head-quarters which sells the generic 'LOCOST' drugs manufactured in

Baroda. For consumers, they are cheaper than name brand pre-scriptions. For SEWA, the profits generated through retail sales go toward support of the local SEWA community health centres and the Health Committee members' monthly salaries.

In addition to the SEWA physician who visits all the clinics on a weekly basis, SEWA has entered into an exchange programme with an Ahmedabad Medical College for their students who require rural internship training. Interns provide curative care at SEWA clinics and child care centres, while the local health workers share their experiences of preventive care, occupational health problems, and village life with the interns. This practice establishes an experiential base for doctors with poor and rural clientele.

A strong aspect of the SEWA Community Health programme is its respect for the positive aspects of traditional belief systems in combination with safe modern medical practices. For example, SEWA supports traditional birth attendants, but makes sure they all receive training in sterile birth practices with periodic refreshers. Since a pregnant woman's family usually provides the birth supplies to the midwife, SEWA issues sterile birth packets to each woman who registers for maternity benefits.

SEWA health workers discuss with neighbours and members the epidemics which frequently break out in their slums, and why their children die from diseases which middle-class families survive. In this way, many communities have concluded that their practices of denying measles-stricken children food or drink or access to a doctor are detrimental. They also concluded that their practices of hanging a neem branch over their doorway to inform neighbours that measles have struck their home, and offering prayers to the Goddess who brings measles are useful along with other appropriate health care.

In other cases, SEWA health workers have defended victims of community discrimination against women. Women are frequently accused of being 'possessed' by evil spirits, a condition which elicits 'exorcism' in the form of being locked in dark rooms without food, being forced to breathe the smoke of burning chillis, beatings, electric shock, etc. SEWA workers rescued one woman from such punishments to learn that her 'possession' was actually symptoms of extreme distress due to the all-male community council decision which had granted custody of her children to her ex-husband. SEWA community health team members have defended women in other equally disturbing situations over which the individual woman had no control.

CHALLENGES

While each action is a welcome step for women gaining greater control over their own bodies, they face enormous challenges in the next half decade. Will they be able to make their health services self-supporting? At present, they charge Re. 1–Rs. 3 per visit, including the necessary medicines—a small fraction of the market value for a physician's visit. SEWA now covers the cost of the health workers' half-time salaries, the buildings, and administration of the project. The plan is to increase the charge to users as women health workers become more skilled health providers and as the community values their service more highly, creating a viable economic occupation for women. While trying to develop its own self-sufficient local model, SEWA is simultaneously lobbying the central government to create a social security fund which would include health insurance for the self-employed workers.

The health team's challenge is compounded because as health workers, their task involves as much preventive health services as curative medicine. They extend education and do advocacy work on nutrition, immunizations, sanitation, occupational hazards and family planning. Their communities are not accustomed to supporting such preventive services. They pay when they are sick, and not when well. Yet many community observers do recognize that health will not come without changes at the local level. They observe the women health providers like Palli, Manju, Lila, Sharda, and Radha, and judge the extent of their knowledge and ability to push authorities into action. •

As SEWA lobbies to reduce occupational hazards faced by members, the bottom line is always women's basic work conditions. If there is no regulation of working hours or minimum wage remuneration, a woman hardly has a chance of improving her precarious health balance. SEWA's largest challenges in the field of women's health lie in collaborative work between the union and the health team in pressing for work legislation to cover self-employed women.

Another issue SEWA faces is how to effect large positive policy changes for women's health status without compromising its values of treating each woman as an individual and helping her solve her problems. One international donor recently offered a large grant to SEWA to conduct research on maternal morbidity. SEWA is currently weighing the trade-offs of the value of such a large data base covering 100,000 women, and the fact of its inability to respond to whatever health problems the surveyed women might report.

'We do not want this to be another case of experts doing research on subjects,' Mirai said. 'If we are going to do it, it will mean training members and organizers to design and carry out the study. And it will mean following through on the conditions women report. So far we have not even been able to cover our own membership sufficiently (30,000 women).'

As SEWA members develop models for social security and health care coverage; for community health centres used and staffed by themselves; for policy focus on job protection and occupational health issues; and for massive water and sanitation programmes on slum land whose title is not clear, they are inevitably conducting important experiments into the process of making unresponsive formal systems more responsive, and shifting some control to the systems designed and run by and for the self-employed.

END NOTES

1. As quoted in Mirai Chatterjee, 'The Fight for Working Mothers' Rights: Maternity Benefits for Agricultural Labourers of Dholka Taluk.' Draft report of SEWA for the Gujarat State Government's Maternity Benefits Scheme, March 1989, p. 3. In Indira Hirway's *Denial of Maternity Benefits to Women Workers of India*, Gandhi Labour Institute Report, Ahmedabad, 1986.
2. For the most extensive published coverage to date on occupational health issues of women in the informal economy, see *Shramshakti, Report of the National Commission on Self-Employed Women*, Government of India, 1988, Chapter 6, pp. 136–72.
3. Mirai Chatterjee, 'Occupational Health of Self-Employed Women: Some Issues and Experiences.' Unpublished paper presented at the Advanced Training Workshop on Occupational Health and Safety, Vadodra, July 1987, p. 3.

10

SEWA Bharat: Reaching Across the Country

The individual orientations of each SEWA in the national federation of SEWA Bharat speak volumes for the various approaches useful for women's development. SEWA Ahmedabad is the most active in union activities, which can be directly traced to its TLA roots and initial support from that large trade union. Others have formed income generating economic units; some have focused on providing social services; one is made up of the producers' cooperatives of bidi workers.

SEWA Mithila in Madhubani, Bihar, concentrates on income generation for women painters and lac workers, and has initiated several small animal projects with agricultural workers. It has around 5000 members who have transferred their traditional skill of painting ceremonial designs on house walls to paper and cloth. Several nationally acclaimed artisans have achieved recognition through SEWA Mithila's market networking of their paintings and calendars, which command a lucrative market as far away as Europe and the US. They also design beautiful saris, pillows, and other garments on locally produced tassar silk. This SEWA is run as an economic unit largely beholden to the painters' dynamic leader, Gauri Mishra. Much of their sales within India are done through their networking with the Dastakari Bazar. Though 10 years ago their work was virtually undiscovered, it is quite usual to see a SEWA painter at every major crafts exhibition in the country today.

Madhubani is an extremely beautiful district surrounded by water and greenery, which makes the destitution of so many women there all the more galling. Most destitute women are victims of a child marriage which resulted in child widowhood. With a custom of marrying children very young, it often happens that the boy may die young and leave behind his wife—still a girl who has never left her parents' house. Such girl-widows are some-how held responsible for the misfortune of their husbands, and turned out from their poverty-stricken parents' or, if older, from their in-laws' houses. Henceforth they are ostracized by society, often without survival options outside of begging or prostitution. SEWA Mithila has been an important alternative for women to shape their own lives outside of this system, and they have organized spirited demonstrations against the dowry system at the 'bride camps,' where fathers go to negotiate their children's marriages.

The other three SEWAs in Bihar, situated in Singhbhum, Bhagalpur and Munger, were women's offshoots of local Gandhian organizations. They now have around 1200, 4200, and 2000 members respectively, who are agricultural workers, weavers, spinners, bamboo and papad workers. There are many tribal members who have been engaged in collecting forest products including tassar silk cocoons, and the SEWAs have integrated them into a more remunerative system for their work, including raising and harvesting cocoons, spinning for fair returns, and weaving. Following the Gandhian tradition, welfare services have been set up for their members.

SEWA Delhi was the first group outside of Gujarat to set up a SEWA in 1980. It began with organizing zari workers—women who do fine fancy gold embroidery work on garments—another home-based, underpaid trade. SEWA Delhi now has eight centres and over 4000 members in the urban metropolis. SEWA has connected 452 of its members who are widows and slum-dwellers to government cooperative housing schemes. Like SEWA Ahmedabad, SEWA Delhi has attracted public attention through its advocacy work for Vaghari hawkers. SEWA Delhi won the women hawkers who sell traditional handicrafts in the central markets the right to licences and space.

SEWA Bhopal is similar in size to SEWA Delhi with 4000 members, though its income generating schemes are on a small scale for bookbinding, file making, garment stitching, and bidi rolling. It has worked to rehabilitate women victims of the Bhopal gas disaster, and it publishes the Hindi edition of *Anasuya*—the monthly newsletter of the SEWA Bharat Federation.

SEWA Indore and SEWA Jabalpur have taken different paths in the process of organizing bidi workers. While SEWA Indore organizes the workers to press for legal rights in union-type activities, the women bidi workers of Jabalpur were too vulnerable to attempt negotiations. Instead, they decided to set up producers' cooperatives which would make and market their own bidis (Boston Bidi). They had to fight for more than two years to get their cooperatives registered, a name approved, and establish themselves in business. The organizer of SEWA Jabalpur spent a few years organizing at SEWA Ahmedabad before moving out to start work in Madhya Pradesh. Women of SEWA Jabalpur had a tough time breaking all the corrupt links in the bidi business. The tendu leaves, for example, which the tobacco is rolled in, were previously supplied to women rollers in lots of 1000 by their contractors. All the rotten or torn leaves were deducted from the wages of a roller. This places the cooperative, however, which does not want to penalize the worker, in a bind. By not deducting the damaged leaves from their wages, the cost must be added to the top of their products, thus making them more expensive in the market. SEWA tried to reject the damaged leaves at the depot where they are purchased, but the depot officials became exasperated and told them that they had to take them all or none at all, bringing home the problems of trying to change only one part of a huge market.

SEWA Lucknow organizes women who do the intricate, delicate embroidery work known as chikan work. They use fine white thread on delicate cottons, silk, and linen. The beauty of the work represents a stark and appalling contrast to the lives and workplaces of the Muslim women who do this work. They live in tiny, dark hovels, and most women over 30 are losing their eyesight from the demanding work they do in poor light. They are subjected to more extreme forms of the problems faced by the home-based bidi workers of Ahmedabad. A contractor distributes work to burkha-clad, home-bound women through a group of sub-contractors, each taking his cut, and leaving the women embroiderers to incomes varying between Re. 0.80 and Rs. 2 per day. Their pittance wage is further deducted if there are stains on the cloth. These women say that even if they receive stained cloth, they cannot refuse it or they will not be given subsequent work.

Runa Banarjee, the General Secretary of SEWA Lucknow, who has organized over 800 women into a production unit, estimates that there are up to 60,000 chikan workers in Lucknow and all the outlying villages of Uttar Pradesh. Banarjee has been unyielding in her demand that women not only are paid a fair wage for their work, but also that the finer stitching techniques—which have been dying due to the mass market piece-rate work that contractors put out—be revived. Older stitchers teach the younger ones the intricate stitches which they are now incorporating into modern designs. In the short time since their inception in 1984, they have gained national acclaim for their exhibitions of the finest commercial chikan work in the country. Because SEWA pays its members higher rates than any other contractor, stitchers have demanded that the UP Export Corporation also pay comparable rates, resulting in a 25 per cent increase in rate in 1986 by the government.

The realities of changing the living and working conditions of SEWA Lucknow members have been daunting, nonetheless. Eyeglasses, lights, toilets, loans, creches, a school for 300 members' children, a building, training in all aspects of the work, including designing, block printing, washing the finished garment, distributing—formerly all men's trades—have been tall orders on the finances of a small voluntary organization.

Positive developments have taken place through SEWA, however, increasing the beauty of the work, the remuneration it brings and the empowerment of the women workers: Iraj Fatrana continues to organize her sisters to give up the burkha (cloak/veil) which extremely limits their work opportunities. Saira Banu has transformed from an extremely ill child with crippled legs to a young woman organizer who rides her specially designed bicycle to work where she trains the new members in finer stitching techniques. Farida Jalee works to expand SEWA's network in the rural areas, determined to unionize the larger population of chikan workers that the production unit cannot employ. She is using the leverage of the recently discovered legal loophole which includes chikan workers in the minimum wage legislation.

Khursheed Baji's story seemed to both say and not say so much about the changes of organizing in women's lives. She is about 50 years old, and was recalcitrant and abrupt when she approached SEWA for work without any skills. Banarjee sent her to the sewing machine and told her to see what she could do. She eventually taught herself sewing, and her demeanour softened with her skill proficiency. When she began earning Rs. 400–Rs. 600 a month, she rented a house in Lucknow and moved in from her village with her six children.

'Harassment is definitely worse now when I go back to my village,' she said. 'People always taunt me and say, "Look, she thinks she is so smart now, going to Delhi, Benares, Calcutta (for exhibitions)." No one says, "Look, she *is* smart now, she can finally feed and educate the six children her husband left her alone with."'

She was not really outraged by this treatment as she narrated her story. She seemed, instead, thrilled by her accomplishments and pleased that her neighbours have noticed her. In a community conditioned to a demeaning view of women, the biggest compliment she can get, at this point, is their 'notice.'

Her accomplishments do raise other questions for her children, however. They attend the SEWA school, which each succeeding year adds another class as the children grow older. The school is up to seventh class, and SEWA is faced with the dilemma of what kind of vocational training should be imparted through the school. For the girls, the answer seems simple enough: they are trained in stitching, printing, and chikan work—skills which can find markets inside or outside of SEWA. In the case of boys, however, there are greater difficulties. Does the SEWA school train them in the traditional male skills of the community—the cutting, stitching and block printing of garments—skills which women have now acquired through SEWA? If the boys are not trained in this, then in what? Will SEWA be creating a situation of displacing men, again placing all the burden of employment upon the girls of the community? While this is a longer term ethical problem for SEWA Lucknow, it is not unrelated to similar concerns of each group organizing women in the informal sector—the impossibility of changing one part of the equation without affecting the others.

The SEWA Bharat Federation was established in 1984 to exchange information, generate strength, and develop a common platform for self-employed workers' issues. Representatives of each SEWA group generally meet annually, and jointly publish

Anasuya. Several of the groups report difficulty in financing their buildings, staff salaries, and the services they provide their members. Each SEWA group provides creche facilities, education or training, and credit or savings schemes.

While several of the SEWA groups assert that they would like to have more interaction and support from their Federation, Bhatt, who is General Secretary of the Federation, feels they are not all prepared to collaborate at this point. 'While each SEWA is an autonomous unit, I think there is fear that because SEWA in Gujarat is so large it will dominate the others in the Federation,' she said. 'I had, and still have, hopes that we could all work together, but so far each time we build the fire, some demons throw something in to pollute it and we have to start again. Each SEWA is doing good work in its respective area. We have all learned a great deal from each others' experiences. Still the day may come when we will be a stronger national force for the self-employed.'

Indeed, when one looks at the work on the national policy, a more unified coalition of voices enforcing the same sentiments from diverse locations in the country is still awaiting to be heard.

11

Moving on: Pushing Policy Outward

Women are poorer than men amongst the poor. They are the worst victims of all socio-economic decay, degradation, and distortions. Yet I envisage poor women as being in the vanguard of development processes and movement . . . .

Ela Bhatt in an interview upon accepting her appointment to the Central Planning Commission, December 1989

SEWA began in 1972 seeking visibility for women as workers and women's control over their own income. In the process of fighting for these rights, SEWA has proved itself a resilient, flexible, and innovative organization. To its credit, it has been able to start wherever women are—psychologically, occupationally, financially, socially, and geographically.

The magnitude of its gains in leadership, in visibility and income control marks the crossing over from the empowerment of particular women or a few organizations to more widespread climate change. Women within the organization have used their perceptions and solutions to move from individual survival issues toward government policy change, helping to shift India's development process more realistically towards people's aspirations and abilities.

SEWA's integrated approach has managed to increase incomes and assets of women, increase their access to services, their range of job skills, and their confidence. By evolving ways to bridge the traditional–informal, and modern–formal systems, SEWA has recovered women's land, acquired access to bank accounts, licences, and worker identification cards. By envisioning the kinds of systems they need to serve them, articulating them, developing the training to learn how to build them, and then employing themselves at delivering the systems, these women have made concrete contributions to development thinking and job creation in India.

Ela Bhatt is the most visible of these women leaders, and one can measure the enormous progress made by the women's development movement by tracing her work. She began speaking for India's poor women in 1972 by demanding visibility and assets for them. Together, they spent almost a decade building the grassroots models to support these demands. After recognizing that local models could not work without national support, they began lobbying for a National Commission to study and document the problems of self-employed women workers. In 1986, the government announced a National Commission on Self-Employed Women and appointed Ela Bhatt as the Chairperson of the Commission. This marked the shift from SEWA being mainly a pressure group on the government to its becoming a major contributor to government policy documents and their implementation.

As Chairperson of the National Commission, Ela Bhatt travelled extensively for two years, meeting self-employed women across the country in cooperatives, unions, voluntary agencies, and local women's organizations. She met educators, researchers, and government agents responsible for development and welfare programmes. She commissioned research, and conducted a broadbased survey on women's economic status.

SHRAMSHAKTI

Shramshakti, the resulting report, distils this nationwide study of self-employed women, their organizations, and the policies they require. *Shramshakti* puts forth recommendations aimed at formalizing legitimate systems for women in the informal sector. It calls for decentralized protective boards on which women workers, employers, and labour officials sit together to enforce a system of registration that establishes the employer–employee relationship, guarantees minimum wages, fair conditions of employment, and social security. It recommends formal incorporation of urban self-employed workers in urban planning: licensed space allotted to vendors in every complex; common work sheds constructed for home-based workers; and sorting grounds for waste pickers.

At the state level, a Development Commissioner for Women is called for to coordinate the various state departments to support women's multiple-occupation reality, and overcome the segregated approach to resource planning and use. In addition to the existing formal sector Labour Commissioner, a separate Labour Commissioner is recommended to oversee unorganized or self-employed workers, with Women's Development Corporations specifically promoting economic development for poor women. In addition, *Shramshakti* recommends half of all programme resources to be directed to women.

Shramshakti specifically promotes women's cooperative membership as a way to shift exploitative production relationships and focus economic development into small industries, non-traditional and environment-regenerating occupations like wasteland rehabilitation and agro-forestry. It calls for extending current cooperative memberships to include both male and female family members who participate in production. *Shramshakti* advocates the need for female extension workers, and reservation of seats for women office bearers in mixed cooperative societies and on governing bodies.

Improvement in women's health depends on better medical facilities, a living wage, a safe workplace, improved work conditions, controlled hours, creches, benefits for health and maternity, pensions, housing and potable water. *Shramshakti* advocates for these changes through training local women (including traditional midwives) to be health workers. Supported by Mahila Mandals (women's organizations), these women can provide both immediate local services and links to government health care services. Organizations of community health workers are able to develop effective health networks: they act as pressure groups to improve work conditions; they can focus institutional research to include issues relevant to women's work; and they can ensure that appropriate occupational health training is included as part of physicians' education.

Child care services must be widely expanded in a way responsive to both women and their daughters who look after their younger siblings. Centres need to provide flexible day-care which is family-based, school-based, women's organization-based, or mobile for migrants. As in SEWA's example, it must be locally managed (by women from each village or neighbourhood), intermediately administered (as SEWA administers 30 centres from its Ahmedabad headquarters), overseen by an autonomous umbrella organization (as the Integrated Childhood Development Scheme). Funding should be shared by the Ministries of Labour, Education, and Women and Child Development, by employers (through a tax), and by parents using the service (or their workers' organizations). Schools must include facilities for young children so that older girls can attend school. Schools and creches must operate on shifts that allow girls to both help their mothers earn and attend school.

To fight the escalating industrial retrenchment of women, the Commission calls for job protection for women in the formal sector through a 'Technology Policy Cell'. This Cell would have the authority to review all plans for technology transfer and auto-mation, assess its impact on women's employment, and assign employers responsibility for redressing that impact.

To enhance a change in attitudes and values toward women, the Commission calls for a Media Monitoring Unit to reorient media to the interests, concerns, and development issues of women working in the informal sector. The Monitoring Unit would insure that realistic images of women as workers are projected; that women produced videos are used for television; that readable regional language publications will inform women of economic schemes and rights; and that relevant radio programmes are broadcast in the evening hours so that working women can listen to these programmes.

PUSHING POLICIES THROUGH

Women leaders at SEWA have skilfully survived political climate changes by remaining unaligned and consistently putting their platform forward to whatever party is in power, citing their rights as citizens to have responsible development policies. They understand the voting base that their communities constitute, and that no party can afford to side-line their issues.

In 1989, with national elections imminent, SEWA selected the politically attractive and relatively less complex demands of *Shramshakti*, published them in a memorandum, and presented them to each of the national parties. They demanded all parties to include in their manifestoes a commitment to total prohibition; cheaper and better public distribution system of food and edible oil; co-ownership of land and property by women; planning and management of village forests and village water resources by women's groups; nursery and day-care centres in each village; administration of health centres and primary schools by women's groups; a woman police officer in each rural police station; a women's cooperative bank in each district; technical schools for girls; social security and legal coverage for home-based workers; and a national policy for hawkers and vendors.

During the pre-election campaigns, the Congress (I), Bharatiya Janata Party, and Janata Dal candidates all referred to the National Commission on Self-Employed Women. They affirmed their interest in forwarding *Shramshakti's* agenda, indicating the attention it had garnered across party lines.

PLANNING COMMISSION

Shortly after the 1989 elections which brought the National Front into power, SEWA was granted a monumental policy achievement: Bhatt was appointed as the first woman member of the central government's Planning Commission. This body generates long-term economic and development plans for the country, initiates new programmes and policies, allocates resources to implement them, monitors implementation, and leverages the state governments' flow of resources through the central funds.

Bhatt's agreement to lend her grassroots experience to the planning process did not go without criticism. Because the Planning Commission, usually staffed by formal economists, is an expert dominated, tradition-bound institution, pre-eminent national economists complained that her experience was only in social work. Planning bureaucrats expressed dismay that the planning process was no longer a professional exercise. 'Next you will find that an illiterate farmer has become a member of the Planning Commission,' one lashed out. Even in the non-governmental sector some criticized her acceptance of the position as evidence of her 'co-option' by the government.

For SEWA, however, it marked an opportunity to influence economic policy to better serve the self-employed and their local economies. When Bhatt was charged to draft the new Five-Year Plan on Employment, she focused on the major need of the poor self-employed: employment with fair incomes. Though the fragile National Front coalition faced dramatic crises during its year in power, Bhatt worked doggedly to shape the Employment, Public Distribution System, and Nutrition chapters of the Plan with a fresh perspective—with self-employed workers as the focus.

Her two decades of organizing, training, and advocating for poor women, the grassroots tactics of SEWA, her, nationwide observations and experience from the National Commission on Self-Employed Women, and her work with international labour organizations took root in her work with the Planning Commission.

'Access to the hard data from all parts of the country feels like sitting on the Himalayas and seeing the country laid out, in all its detail below,' Bhatt commented early in her tenure. 'Yet they are not abstract numbers—I know that data represents the ways that vast numbers of people are struggling for their living.'

One of her major achievements was making full-employment the central focus of the Plan. Until her tenure, industrial growth was the focus of economic development, with employment side-lined. The Planning Commission historically increases the industrial growth rate from the previous Five-Year Plan. Bhatt got the Eighth Plan Commission to change the terms of planning from that of an industrial growth index to a people-focused employment-expansion index, slated to increase at 4 per cent annually. To fulfil the Commission's aim of full-employment by the year 2000, Bhatt helped shape a national data bank to cover all types of employment, including the rural occupations performed by women.

Bhatt based the full-employment strategy she developed on food security, income security, and social security—attempting to shift the old paradigms of social welfare for the poor to employment security for all citizens. Half of the resources which were to be invested were to be allocated to rural development under the Plan, and planning and implementation were to be devolved to local area Panchayats.

Bhatt aggressively promoted labour-intensive manufacturing of mass consumption goods through government support of raw material supplies, credit, and marketing facilities. But the link she drew between employment generation and social services—previously seen as separate issues—was her major contribution based on her years of work on women's economic issues. For women, the continuum between social services and employment has always been evident.

Take the issue of inadequate nutrition, for example. According to Bhatt, the social service programme aimed at bringing nutritional foods to poor families should be an employment-support programme which helps such families engage in the cultivation of vegetables, post-harvest processing, dairying, and animal husbandry. These kinds of employment programmes would bring more products into the market, more income into the hands of poor families, and thus better access to nutritional foods. The nutritional supplement programmes could in turn purchase supplies directly from the producers who are in the employment programmes. Similarly, the Plan she drafted directed the existing training and employment programmes to train people to produce the goods that other social programmes deliver to the poor. She drew these simple but vital linkages out of the strategies SEWA had developed in Gujarat.

Bhatt also introduced dramatic changes in the Public Distribution System (PDS) which previously rationed subsidized food to all citizens. The PDS exerts enormous leverage against inflationary pressures on food supply, and is directly responsible for what the poorest citizens in the country eat. With the Commission's changes, the PDS now caters solely to the poor in both urban and rural areas. It links distribution with employment programmes by drawing on locally produced foodgrains. It links directly with the government nutrition programmes by supplying child care, meal schemes through the regional food supply network.

WOMEN NOW PREPARED

The priorities and stability of the future government will in part determine the fate of these policies. With the fall of V.P. Singh's government in November 1990, the fragile coalitions which have followed, and the changing political and economic structures globally, it is still uncertain which policies will carry to the next government. What is certain, however, is that many women now have working models and the leadership ability to participate in policy planning and ensure that their priorities will not be side-lined. Women have developed the understanding to sit at those tables, and put forward the needs of their occupations, their families, and their communities.

People in the world of development are always asking about what is replicable. Is SEWA replicable? Are models from one part of the country replicable on a national level? Bhatt's imprint on this question can be seen in her insistence that regions and states have to work out their own strategies of employment maximization. She acknowledges there is no simple formula, citing some states with growing agricultural and industrial sectors which show a decline in labour absorption while others show a rise. What she does believe is replicable is that people anywhere can organize, plan, pressure, and act together.

However, SEWA strategies do emphasize that certain principles must extend widely. The government must be committed to national policies to avert damage to the environment and to the resource base of the poor. Likewise, the issues of home-based workers require national and international labour laws.

The SEWA team of leaders, organizers, and members have shared a strength since SEWA's inception, and that is their ability to focus their energy on solutions. The low income women are particularly remarkable in this regard: when confronting the ambitious task of devising social change, they have displayed an admirable ability to project their vision beyond the boundaries of their day-to-day drudgery. Women in debt, facing sick family members, and eviction from their vending spots somehow maintain the ability and willingness to focus on what the Eighth Plan should include to benefit women like themselves across the country. Their ability to survive the daily, immediate pressures with a long-term vision is striking.

AN INDIGENOUS MOVEMENT

SEWA's success at changing women's work and living conditions owes to its grassroots, Indian soil origin, and women's ability to translate their values into working systems. Indian traditions are deeply embedded in women, and SEWA starts from where women are: from their strengths, their needs, and their weaknesses. Indian traditions are built as much on economic systems as on social and cultural ones. SEWA women have managed to recognize and build on the vibrancy and strength of self-employment in the face of the rapidly changing economy and its resulting upheaval of traditional social values.

SEWA women acknowledge that change is valuable to sweep away the oppressive and inequitable structures of the past. They resist, however, the process of change that marginalizes and downgrades the people who are part of the traditional system. They resist the unchallenged growth of the new economy, which encourages factories while driving artisans out of employment. They challenge government subsidies to 'modern', 'progressive' agriculture while 'marginal' and 'traditional' farmers are turned into landless labourers.

SEWA has worked to transform the traditional economy and its people into the modern economy while maintaining the strengths of the traditional systems. SEWA Bank exemplifies this traditional–modern union. Vendors, small artisans and small and marginal farmers are all part of the traditional system, with ways of doing business quite distinct from the modern formal economy. Each of these self-employed trades have a need for credit, which they meet through the traditional system of money-lenders who charge rates of interest up to 120 per cent a year. Though there exists a modern banking sector which charges an interest rate of less than 18 per cent a year, it does not cater to women in the informal sector.

SEWA's task, in recognizing the needs of the self-employed for credit, was to bring the modern bank to illiterate women in a form that could serve their very small credit needs. SEWA Bank, their solution, moves with the rhythm of their economy. It deals person-to-person, with small savings and small loans, using traditional networks to ensure customers' repayment. By combining the traditional qualities of self-employed business and the services of modern banks, SEWA Bank creates a new and vibrant model, which serves women—a claim most banks in the world have difficulty in making.

Similarly, SEWA's model of rural development draws on the economic and ecological traditions of the village. SEWA women assert that they are able to survive economically only if they have a mix of employment from the land, from livestock, and from some artisan or manual production. Impoverishment occurs when they have to rely on one limited source of livelihood.

SEWA's rural development work holds the distinction of putting resources back into the local environments while creating jobs, rather than extracting all available assets. Radhanpur and Santalpur areas of Banaskantha district are arid, impoverished, and drought-stricken areas. When SEWA first started working there in 1987, the organizers found that degraded lands, lack of water, and the hot climate meant minimal livelihood opportunities. Many families, especially those who survived on livestock, migrated during the summer months.

SEWA started by creating employment through women's skills. First, skilled embroiderers were linked with markets. Their craft immediately became a significant source of income in the region. Dairy and livestock developed into new resources as SEWA reactivated defunct cooperatives and urged the dairy to resume processing milk and experimenting with fodder–security systems. Women initiated ecological regeneration of the land base with large-scale nurseries and plantations, with technical assistance provided by the agricultural extension services. Salt farming and gum collection from adjacent jungles created new income generating activities. These multiple sources of income have made out-migration unnecessary for most of the region's families. Regional development became a reality here in a few years through women's leadership, and 20 years of their collective experience in an organization. Regional planning supports SEWA's notions of integrated approaches to resources, of governments which deliver, and of people deciding their own priorities to strike a balance between traditional land-based and modern production-based economies.

Child care facilities for self-employed women likewise emerged from a balance of traditional and modern systems. Women are closely connected with children traditionally, yet combining work with child care can become an intolerable burden. The solution for SEWA has been provision of modern child care facilities at the work site or at home with hours suited to particular women's occupations.

Even while challenging oppressive structures, SEWA women have strived to build upon the positive social and cultural traditions to move towards something new. It has remained an all-women's organization because women feel open, united, and affectionate when they are together as a group without men being present. SEWA draws out this natural affinity, and encourages women to extend this inclusiveness to women of all trades, castes, and religions. These women often refer to SEWA as their *piyar* or mother's home, and to other members, irrespective of community, as sisters.

Also known as their 'village well', SEWA is the place women can get together and exchange news and views. While retaining the informality of the village well, SEWA orients its meetings to address work and social issues. Through these meetings, women no longer perceive themselves as simply wives and mothers, but rather as workers who make a significant contribution to the economy. At this village well, a woman learns to stand up, say her name out loud, address a group, and recognize her strength, both individually and collectively as a group.

SEWA leaders refer to their movement as a *sangam* (confluence) of the cooperative, labour and women's movements. They do seem to have succeeded in extracting the kernel of each movement and making it relevant to women's everyday lives.

WOMEN AS LEADERS

The real force behind the SEWA movement is the self-employed women. They work endlessly. They have strong hearts, and an ability to be inclusive. They bring a desire for change, for respect, and for economic prosperity for their families and communities. With these abilities and aspirations, women are finding ways to unite to overcome their inhibitions and oppressions. Their union testifies to women's ability to assume leadership and use it in various ways. They have highlighted the economic issues impacting them, asserted the values they want to advocate in the economy, and shaped far-reaching economic and social changes.

The home-based workers' campaign, for example, was originally taken up by SEWA members. They organized and highlighted the issue first locally, then nationally, and finally internationally. The International Confederation of Free Trade Unions took heed, and many of its member Federations are now engaged in organizing home-based workers. The International Labour Organization is moving, albeit slowly, towards a global convention on the issue. Groups and unions all over the world are organizing, researching and highlighting the issues of home-based workers. SEWA women who initiated this worldwide movement continue to lend direction to the actions.

Similarly, SEWA Bank is a forerunner of an emerging global movement of self-help groups. SEWA Bank's testimony to poor people's ability to save and be punctual repayers of loans has led to groups mushrooming across the country and in communities around the world, marking the importance of savings and credit for the poor. India's central banking institutions, like NABARD and the Reserve Bank of India, are sponsoring these groups to inform potentially far-reaching policy changes. That these institutions are drawing on SEWA's experience is a powerful testimony to the validity of policies shaped by poor women.

All of SEWA's strategies toward economic and social stability for women require extensive training. Training is an integral part of organizing women, formalizing their skills, and involving them in shaping their occupations, incomes, and social policies. SEWA conducts standard training sessions for a broad section of women, and also specific training programmes for specialized skills.

SEWA's training strategy focuses on 'cascading' empowerment to women at all levels of the organization: the initially trained women go out with new information and train their sisters, who in turn train their family members, and so on. Training is directly linked to action—there is an interrelationship between training and production, training and organizing, trainer and practitioner, reflection and practice. SEWA's training draws on the way women traditionally spread news and skills, and on the way their village organizations address problems. Women from labour and community organizations around the world come to SEWA to learn about their organizing and training methods, as organizing women has become an economic imperative worldwide.

In 1988, when Bhatt completed the *Shramshakti* Report, she laughed as she said, 'It is little ironic, asking the government to support women's organizations so that those organizations can pressure the government.' Yet SEWA has grown well into that irony—pressuring for many years, and now acting with the government as policy planners and developers.

Women at SEWA have a strong vision. Bhatt believes that 'when women lead the movement of the poor, the growth rate of economy will be as fast as the growth of social harmony and the growth of national integration.'

That is a tall order in the face of global economy shaped by policies and practices that do not value women's labour or the integrity of communities over profits.

Yet these women literally have learned to stand tall in their work with SEWA and in their commitment to change. They have evinced courage and overcome enormous obstacles in their movement from invisible sisters, mothers, and wives to outspoken proponents for economic change. If the past bears any reliable witness, we can continue to look to these women leaders for new, viable solutions to the economic turmoil that people of the world face. We can learn from their spirit and follow their lead in our respective work and places.

As Ela Bhatt said after her work on the National Commission on Self-Employed Women, 'I saw that women everywhere are ready to take leadership. In every group we met, there were women whose eyes were burning with an inner fire. If these women are reached and encouraged, it is they who will be our future leaders.'

Appendices

APPENDIX I: SEWA UNION MEMBERSHIP, 1989

Vendors
    Vegetable/fruit   3040
    Used-garments dealers   300
    Fish, kerosene, others   180

Tobacco Workers and Food Processors
    Bidi workers   7695
    Milk producers   3158
    Tobacco, agricultural workers and processors   3180
    Papad workers   60

Agricultural and Allied Workers
    Agricultural labourers   4590

Textile and Garment Workers
    Quilt-makers   680
    Garment stitchers   1480
    Weavers   140
    Block printers   100
    Handicrafts   1140
    Others   20

Other Labour and Service Providers
    Paper pickers   1400
    Headloaders   200
    Contract labourers   400
    Others   240

Appendix I (Continued)

Other Home-based Workers

Carpenters	20
Household workers	260
Child care workers	40
Agarbatti workers	180
Others	630
Total	**29,133**

APPENDIX II: COOPERATIVES: KIND,

MEMBERSHIP, PRODUCTION

Cooperative	Members	Active Members	Total Annual Income (Rs.)	Average Monthly Income/ Member (Rs.)
Crafts and Artisan				
Sabina patchwork	181	51	1,19,352	196
Block printing	77	44	85,219	194
Cane and bamboo	165	12*	30,263	222
Vijay handloom weavers	44	4	64,718	84
Utsah handloom weavers	51	17	2,97,015	318
Baldana weavers	17	17	44,709	219
Banascrafts				
Embroidery		274	3,00,725	91
Leatherwork		26	3,05,025	998
Beadwork		40	62,125	129
Applique work		45	20,000	37
Mirror work		30	24,000	67
Ornamental work		85	38,000	37
Kachcchi embroidery		22	14,680	55
Metaal beadwork		16	12,023	83
File making		16	6,760	123
Stitching		12	13,035	26
Khadi work		21	13,126	52
Ahmedabad weaving		6	5,169	99
Electronics assembly		4	11,894	248

Appendix II (Continued)

Cooperative	Members	Active Members	Total Annual Income (Rs.)	Average Monthly Income/ Member (Rs.)
Trading and Vending Cooperatives				
Haryali vegetable vendors	51	45	1,31,573	355
Matsyagandha fish vendors	61	15	43,050	400
Service Cooperatives				
Saundarya industrial cleaning	200	135	2,09,147	127†
Paper pickers group collecting		232	36,455	—

Cooperative	Members	Year Registered	Total Annual Income (Rs.)	Average Monthly Income/ Member (Rs.)
Dairy Cooperatives				
Ahmedabad District				
Devdholera	100	1979	4,44,579	335
Baldana	165	1979	5,19,854	288
Lagdand	35	1988	1,36,355	260
Dumali	72	1984	1,78,220	176
Ranesar	70	1988	77,599	202
Rupal	140	1986	2,79,933	249
Chikada	25	1989	24,418	183
Kathwada	72	1987	1,26,584	294
Pasunj	100	1987	4,61,986	223
Vanch	48	1989	64,881	179
Bilasiya	85	1988	1,61,092	285
Miroli	25	1989	43,873	241
Bahiyal	65	1987	45,455	107
Amarajinamuvade	26	1989	30,189	148
Nanimorali	25	1989	53,128	165
Waghpura	26	1989	38,884	262
Navapura	20	1989	7,398	155
Banaskantha District				
Gulabpura	52	1989		151
Latia	47	1989		144

Appendix II (Continued)

Cooperative	Members	Year Registered	Total Annual Income (Rs.)	Average Monthly Income/ Member (Rs.)
Sherganj	59	1989		190
Najupura	60	1989		168
Kalyanpura	62	1989		290
Gadh	48	1989		234

Land-based Cooperatives

Kind of Cooperative	Members	Land Developed	Water Resources	Saplings Raised/ Planted	Income/ Month
Ahmedabad District					
Baldana Wasteland Rehabilitation Agro-Forestry Cooperative	20	35 acres	3 ponds 1 check dam	10,800	282
Metaal Wasteland Rehabilitation Cooperative	20	10 acres		4,000	282
Dumali Wasteland Rehabilitation Cooperative	20	10 acres	boundary trenches	4,000	162
Mehsana District					
Sri Ganeshpura Wasteland Tree growers	44	10 acres	nursery tankpond, tubewell	27,000	143
Junagadh District					
Girnar Nursery	20		Nursery tank	1,25,000	400
Banaskantha District					
Sheregadh	5			20,000	240
Satun	4			20,000	300

Appendix II (Continued)

Kind of Cooperative	Members	Land Developed	Water Resources	Saplings Raised/ Planted	Income/ Month
Nanipipli	5			20,000	240
Gokhankar	5			20,000	240
Gadhakar	4			20,000	300
Kaliwada	5		tank	200,000	240

* Only 12 women sell their products actively through SEWA's shops and exhibitions. The majority of other members purchase bulk bamboo through the cooperative, but market on their own, and are therefore not counted as 'active' members.

† Members work only 2–4 hours per day.

APPENDIX III: OVERVIEW OF SEWA BANK 1974–1989

Table 1: *The Growth of SEWA Bank*

Year	Number of Share- holders	Share Capital (Rs.)	Number of Depositors	Deposits (Rs.)	Working Capital (Rs.)	Profit (Rs.)
1974–75	6287	71320	6188	243010	332231	−11802
1975–76	6634	74990	10459	936388	1060431	33016
1976–77	6945	78970	11038	1053480	1198872	21623
1977–78	7044	81100	11656	1448586	1267452	13729
1978–79	7131	81800	12366	2523722	2743564	35244
1979–80	7321	84080	13060	3024230	3324844	36953
1980–81	7507	88690	14022	2728876	3194930	54152
1981–82	7943	131350	16164	3503986	4119379	77632
1982–83	8398	195830	19057	5060240	5815669	116284
1983–84	8938	302610	20122	6830768	7981869	200085
1984–85	9457	427970	21656	6093587	7897007	161752
1985–86	9825	538130	22208	11278880	13537252	222767
1986–87	10339	707000	23834	10790000	13928000	334000
1987–88	10972	883730	23156	11232537	14930963	370054
1988–89	11742	1074000	23582	13890000	18301000	480000
*1989–	12089	1150000	25311	15600000	20000000	375000

Source: SEWA Bank.
* Provisional data for July through December 1989.

Table 2: *SEWA Bank Loans*

Year	† Number of Loans Extended	Total Funds Advanced
1974–75	0	0
1975–76	5	680
1976–77	70	37253
1977–78	73	39295
1978–79	113	79875
1979–80	145	150985
1980–81	163	248375
1981–82	301	618220
1982–83	413	1085750
1983–84	1297	2421315
1984–85	2801	3839234
1985–86	3366	4312237
1986–87	4030	6215000
1987–88	5058	7251000
1988–89	6354	8552000
*1989–	7017	9293228

Source: SEWA Bank.
* Provisional data for July through December 1989.
† These numbers represent cumulative number of loans disbursed.

Table 3: *Comparison of Public Sector Banks and SEWA Bank*

Particulars	Public Sector Banks		SEWA Bank	
	Dec. 86 Crores Rs.	Dec. 87 Crores Rs.	June 86–87 Lakhs Rs.	June 87–88 Lakhs Rs.
Deposits	111581	128389	108	112
Loans	64321	73114	62	72
Profit	192	261	3	4
Reserves and Reserve Fund	1095	1503	8	11
Ratios				
Profit/Deposits	0.17	0.20	2.77	3.57
Profit/Loans	0.29	0.35	4.83	5.55
Reserve/Deposits	0.98	0.35	4.83	5.55
Reserve/Loans	1.70	2.05	12.90	15.27

Source: SEWA Bank. Figures for 28 public sectors banks from *Indian Express*, 20 July 1988.

Glossary of Terms

aanganwadi nursery schools.
agarbatti incense.
Bharat India.
Bharwads shepherds.
bidi indigenous cigarette rolled in tendu leaves.
burkha head to toe veil worn by Muslim women outside of the home.
chindi waste cloth sold cheaply from the mills.
crore 10 million.
dharna sit-in protest.
godown warehouse.
Harijan the name Gandhi gave to people of the 'untouchable' castes. It means 'Children of God.'
ILO International Labour Organization.
kaccha temporary, salvaged, mud.
kilogram 2.2 pounds.
lakh 100 thousand.
laris handcarts mounted on four wheels.
masalas spices.
mohulla Muslim neighbourhood.
morcha protest march.
papad lentil wafers which women make on piece-rate for contractors.
paise one hundred paise make up one rupee in Indian currency.
purdah veiling or cloistering.
rupee Indian currency.
sammelan rally.
Sarpanch local elected leader.
satyagraha non-violent sit-in protest.

Index

agricultural extension, 217, 272
Agricultural Labour Association (ALA),
    59, 60
Anasuya, 84, 259, 262
Award, Ramon Magsaysay, 28, 56, 74,
    86

Banaskantha, 109, 210, 216, 226, 230,
    231, 234, 272
bank, credit, 19, 21, 25, 42, 45, 49–52,
    53, 60, 75, 101, 174–76, 181–85, 187,
    188, 190, 192, 193, 194, 199, 201,
    206, 208, 209, 211, 214, 215, 217,
    225, 262, 269, 271, 274; debt, 25, 43,
    44, 48, 53, 55, 176, 186, 188–90, 193,
    194, 203, 205, 210, 224, 230, 270;
    loans, 19, 21, 23, 25, 26, 42, 49–50,
    51, 52–55, 66, 102, 174, 176, 179,
    180, 181–88, 190, 192–95, 197, 198,
    199, 200, 210, 211, 212, 214, 225,
    227, 230, 250, 260, 271, 274; mobile
    bank, 176–80; savings, 52, 176, 177,
    178, 179, 180, 183, 184, 190–91, 262,
    271, 274; Women's World Banking,
    52, 78, 86, 198, 199
Bhatt, Ela, 14, 19, 22, 28, 31, 33, 36,
    39–44, 45, 50, 51–52, 55–56, 61, 62,
64, 67, 70–73, 74–80, 84–87, 89, 93,
    95, 96, 97, 99, 106, 107, 109, 110,
    111, 113, 132, 139, 172–74, 192, 198,
    199, 204, 226–27, 232, 251, 252, 262,
    263, 264, 267, 268, 269, 270, 274,
    275
block printing artisans, 20, 21, 66–67,
    91, 113, 137, 216, 260, 261
Buch, Arvind, 44, 71, 78, 79, 173

carpenters,   17, 19, 33, 37, 44, 53,
    110, 177, 184–85, 193
cartpullers, 17, 20, 41, 44, 110, 119, 141
Chatterjee, Mirai, 92, 246, 249, 251,
    256
child care, 102, 108, 125, 137, 209,
    238–39, 240, 249, 254, 266, 269, 272
communal violence, 32–33, 75, 77,
    111–12, 114–15, 133–34, 144, 179
cooperatives, 20, 21, 24, 29, 62–65, 67,
    68, 73, 87, 90, 91, 92, 93, 94, 106,
    109, 145, 146, 149, 158, 181, 184,
    204, 206–15, 216, 217, 218, 219, 220,
    221–22, 223, 224, 226–27, 228, 229,
    230, 231, 232, 233, 234, 235, 236,
    237, 238, 239, 240, 241, 242, 225,
    257, 259, 265, 272; block printing,

260, 261; dairy, 67–68, 73, 90, 109, 158, 204, 206, 208, 209–17, 218, 219, 223, 233, 234, 239, 241, 269, 272; embroidery, 41, 96, 226, 230, 234, 252, 258, 259–60, 261; paper pickers, 21, 119, 142–47, 177, 235, 236; pre-cooperative phase, 221, 224–26, 230, 234; wastelands, 220, 221–22, 223, 224, 234; weaving, 17, 20, 38, 60, 94, 108, 197, 206, 208, 209, 216, 227, 228–29, 230, 232, 233, 240, 258
credit, 19, 21, 25, 42, 45, 49–52, 53, 60, 75, 101, 174–76, 181–85, 187, 188, 190, 192, 193, 194, 199, 201, 206, 208, 209, 211, 214, 215, 217, 225, 262, 269, 271, 274

dairy producers, 67, 68, 73, 90, 109, 158, 204, 206, 208, 209–17, 218, 219, 223, 234, 239, 241, 269, 272
Datania, Lila, 158, 159, 246
debt, 25, 43, 44, 48, 53, 55, 176, 186, 188–90, 193, 194, 203, 205, 210, 224, 230, 270
Desai, Ranjan, 90, 91, 146–47, 251
Dholakia, Anila, 89–91, 203
drought relief, 203, 204, 221, 232, 234–35, 241–42

economic development, 263–64, 265, 268
Eighth Plan, 268, 269, 270
elections, 111, 146, 267
embroidery artisans, 17, 95, 96, 137, 157, 226, 230, 234, 252, 258, 259–61, 272
employment, 268, 269, 270, 272
environment, 270, 272

family planning, 103, 246, 247, 250–52, 255

Gandhi, Indira, 49, 79, 107
Gandhi, Mahatma, 28, 32, 33, 36, 39, 40, 62, 71, 73, 75, 76, 85, 89, 95, 106, 125
Gandhi, Rajiv, 98, 99, 138
garment stitchers, 17, 37, 61, 112, 130–35, 137

headloaders, 17, 19, 24, 28, 37, 41, 42, 44, 141, 177, 220, 228
health, family planning issues, 103, 246, 247, 250–52, 255; health care workers, 92, 158, 238–39, 241–42, 245, 246, 249, 252–55, 265–66
health issues, 20, 26, 27, 29, 55, 56, 70, 73, 76, 91, 92, 96, 99, 100, 101, 103, 121, 125, 137, 141, 143, 149, 150, 158, 194, 196, 209, 218, 238–39, 240, 241, 244–47, 248–56, 259, 265, 267
home-based workers, 30, 38, 47, 61, 64, 78, 96–99, 101, 106, 107, 116, 120, 121–38, 142, 153, 178, 195, 227, 265, 267, 270, 273, 274; International Labour Organization, 30, 34, 96, 97, 98, 107, 116, 133, 148, 253, 274
housing, 41, 52, 56, 120, 125, 128, 138, 185, 194–95, 201, 258, 265

interest, 25, 42, 43, 47, 48, 49, 55, 174, 175, 184, 187, 188–90, 200, 271
International Confederation of Free Trade Unions (ICFTU), 30, 68, 95, 97, 273
International Federation of Plantation, Agricultural and Allied Workers (IFPAAW), 89
International Labour Organization (ILO), 30, 34, 96, 97, 98, 107, 116, 133, 148, 253, 274

Jaisingh, Indira, 97, 139
jewellery, 55, 175, 184, 187, 188
Jhabvala, Renana, 64, 71, 89, 93, 95, 106, 107–8, 113, 134, 148–49, 150, 232–33, 237
joint action of union and cooperatives, 62, 206
Jumani, Jyoti, 158
Jumani, Usha, 89, 90, 200, 216–17, 222

Karima Ahmed Hussain Shaikh, 61–62, 63, 65, 66, 74, 96, 98–99, 112, 114, 115
Kishanrao, Godavaribehn, 118–19, 123, 125, 126, 127, 128–29, 153
Krishnaswami, Lalita, 90, 91, 216, 231, 236

loans, 19, 21, 25, 26, 42, 49, 50, 51, 52–55, 66, 102, 174, 176, 179, 180, 181–88, 189, 190, 192–95, 197, 198, 199, 200, 210, 211, 212, 214, 225, 227, 230, 250, 260, 271, 274

Magsaysay, Ramon Award, see *award*
Mahila Mandals, 106, 265
manufacturing, 269
maternity benefits, 19, 26–27, 55, 92, 103, 108, 121, 125, 127, 149, 240, 249, 250, 251, 254, 265
media, 104–5, 266
Mehta, Hansa, 90, 91
minimum wage issues, 16, 19, 33, 49, 58, 59, 60, 106, 112, 116, 119, 124–26, 130, 133, 134–35, 137, 149, 151, 152, 153, 207, 255, 260, 265
mobile bank, 176–80
mortgaged land recovery, 88, 189, 192–93, 203, 217, 224

Nanavati, Rima, 231–32
National Commission on Self-Employed Women, 31, 98, 99, 100, 101, 102, 103, 105–6, 198, 199, 264, 267, 268, 275
National Front Government, 31, 267, 268

occupational health, 27, 92, 96, 103, 236, 266

paper pickers, 21, 91, 112, 119, 142–47, 177, 235, 236
Papubhai, Chandabehn Jhagaria, 42, 43, 44, 46, 50, 51, 69, 73, 113–14, 200, 249
Patel, Meena, 140
Patel, Savita, 182–83, 214, 215, 241–42
Planning Commission, 31, 67, 85, 263, 267–69
policy issues, 23, 24, 27, 29, 30–31, 34, 45, 64–65, 67, 74, 94, 95, 96–98, 101, 102, 103, 105–6, 107, 108, 109, 120, 129, 131, 135, 137, 138, 140, 153, 188, 198, 209, 214, 225, 227, 231, 232–33, 250, 252, 255, 256, 262, 263, 264, 266–67, 268, 270, 274

prohibition, 267
Public Distribution System (PDS), 268, 269

Rahima Sheikh, 112, 131–35, 137–38
regional planning, 272
retrenchment, 20, 38, 61, 64, 142, 143, 266
rural development, 109, 271, 272

Sarabhai, Ansuyabehn, 40–41, 65–66, 84, 85
Saraswati Rameshchandran, 15, 16, 128
sati, 110, 130
Shankarbhavan, 244, 245, 246, 247, 248
Shramshakti, 31, 35, 99–100, 102, 103, 105, 106, 199, 201, 214, 264–66, 267, 274
social services, 269
Standing Committee, 89, 90, 92
Stuart Martha, 29, 156, 159
Supreme Court, 30, 98, 139, 140

technology transfer, 266
Textile Labour Association (TLA), 19, 40–45, 50, 55, 58, 61, 62, 71–72, 73, 74–80, 84, 85, 87, 89, 91, 92, 93, 111, 140, 143, 144, 173, 188, 257
tobacco workers, 118–19, 121–29, 149, 150–53
traditions, 271–72
training, 19, 21, 27, 29, 41, 45, 56, 64, 66–67, 68, 90, 91, 97, 101–2, 108, 109, 140, 143, 144, 156–59, 193, 201, 204, 206, 207, 210, 214–17, 219, 220, 221, 225, 226, 228, 229, 230, 231, 238, 246–48, 249, 251, 252, 253, 254, 256, 260, 261, 262, 264, 265, 269, 274
tripartite boards, 97, 107, 141, 153, 265

union, 16, 19, 20, 23, 25, 28, 29, 31, 40, 41, 44, 45, 47, 50, 52, 54, 57, 58–60, 61, 62, 64–66, 70, 74–76, 79–80, 84–85, 88, 90, 92, 93, 95, 97, 106, 112, 119, 120, 122, 123, 125–27, 128–30, 133, 134, 136, 137, 140, 144, 149, 153, 176, 179, 181, 183, 184, 186, 196, 203, 206, 208, 210, 219,

227, 230, 233, 236, 238, 249, 253, 255, 257, 259, 273, 274; carpenters, 17, 19, 33, 37, 44, 48, 53, 110, 119, 141, 177, 184–85, 193; cartpullers, 17, 20, 41, 44, 110, 119, 141; garment stitchers, 17, 37, 61, 112, 130–35, 137; headloaders, 17, 19, 24, 28, 37, 41, 42, 44, 141, 177, 220, 228; home-based workers, 30, 38, 47, 61, 64, 78, 96–99, 101, 106, 107, 116, 120, 121–38, 142, 153, 178, 195, 227, 265, 267, 270, 273, 274; ICFTU, 30, 68, 95, 97, 273; IFPAAW, 89; minimum wage issues, 16, 19, 33, 49, 58, 59, 60, 106, 112, 116, 119, 124–26 130, 133, 134–35, 137, 149, 151, 152, 153, 207, 255, 260, 265; paper pickers, 21, 91, 112, 119, 142–47, 177, 235, 236; Standing Committee, 89, 90, 92; tobacco workers, 118–19, 121–29, 149, 150–53

urban, 17, 24, 30, 32, 39, 41, 43, 56, 59, 61, 94, 104, 140, 147, 149, 159, 176, 190, 193, 194, 206, 209, 216, 219, 249, 250, 265

urban workers' issues, 17, 24, 30, 32, 39, 41, 43, 56, 59, 61, 94, 104, 140, 147, 149, 159, 176, 190, 193, 194, 206, 209, 216, 219, 249, 250, 265

vendors, 17, 19, 20, 22, 30, 32, 37, 39, 42–44, 46–48, 50, 51, 68–74, 98, 112, 113, 119, 121, 138–40, 153, 156, 157, 174, 177, 179, 193, 194, 209, 238, 240, 249, 265, 267, 271; kerosene, 68, 179, 209, 238, 240

video, 21, 29, 156–59

visibility, 24, 31, 45, 58, 67, 109, 263, 264

Vyas, Jayshree, 181–82, 190, 196–97, 201

Walsh, Michela, 52, 86, 198

wateland rehabilitation, 220, 221–22, 234, 265

weavers, 17, 20, 38, 60, 94, 108, 197, 206, 208, 209, 216, 227, 228–29, 230, 232, 233, 240, 258

Women's World Banking (WWB), 52, 78, 86, 198, 199